ESSAYS DEMYSTIFIED

for UPSC CSE *& Competitive Exams*

Nishant Jain, IAS
Abhishek Saraf, IAS
Snehil Tripathi

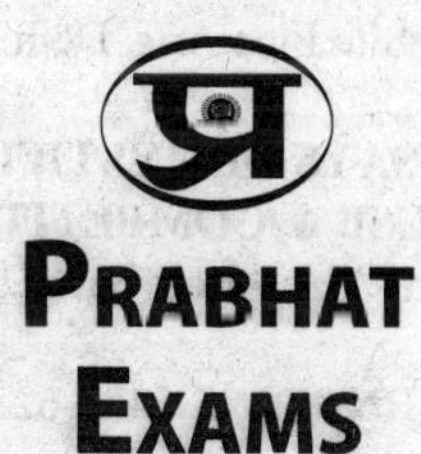

PRABHAT EXAMS

Publisher

PRABHAT EXAMS

Imprint of Prabhat Prakashan Pvt. Ltd.

4/19 Asaf Ali Road, New Delhi–110 002

Ph. 23289555 • 23289666 • 23289777 • Helpline/ 7827007777

e-mail: prabhatbooks@gmail.com • Website: www.prabhatexam.com

Price

Seven Hundred Twenty Five Rupees

ISBN 978-93-5488-622-5

Printed at

Sita Fine Arts, Delhi

ESSAYS DEMYSTIFIED

FOR UPSC CSE & COMPETITIVE EXAMS

***by* Nishant Jain, Abhishek Saraf, Snehil Tripathi**

ISBN 978-93-5488-622-5

₹ 725.00

PREFACE

Civil Services have always been one of the top choices as a career among youths in India. Essay paper in Civil Services Mains Exam has a very important role, both in terms of marks as well as the difference it can create in the overall score. So it's very clear that in order to get desired services one must score well in this paper and equally important to get into the list for that matter. For instance, in Essay Paper, an aspirant may score as high as 140-160 marks out of 250 which is considered good and can have a significant lead in the overall score. It is categorically highlighted by all toppers and civil services mentors about the pivotal role Essay paper along with Ethics (GS- IV) and optional paper plays a key role in deciding the final rank in the list.

It is beyond doubt that if one has conceptual understanding of how to build an essay along with regular practice; this paper in the Mains Exam can prove to be highly scoring with relatively lesser effort. So we wanted to come up with a book to facilitate aspirants to score considerably well in Essay Paper.

During our own preparation, we had kept some self-written essays with us. Meanwhile, after discussions with several young officers and successful aspirants, it was found that most of them had their unique way of building their essays. After knowing this, it occurred to us that why not publish a book that contains essays collected and compiled from selected candidates, a book which also contains various tips, strategies and style of essay writing along with axioms that form an essential part of the essay writing.

We wanted to include various essays from several young officers in this book so that readers get a glimpse of different styles of essay writing. Otherwise also, the essay has considerable scope of subjectivity. Here lies the peculiarity of this paper wherein any particular style of writing cannot always be the best. Therefore, various aspirants could score high in this paper despite having different approaches and methods of essay writing.

Although, all of us principally agreed with the thought of compiling and editing works of various officers, practically implementing the same was a real challenge. We all made contact with young officers known to us and got selected in UPSC in recent years. We persuaded them to share the essays they had written. While many friends searched their laptops, some of them even looked into their rooms for their self-written essay notes.

Some found their essays written in test series, while others took them from their friends and handed them to us.

Compilation of above works took almost six months. All our friends put in a lot of efforts. Some of them helped by giving single essays while some contributed with as much as 4-5 essays. This paved the way for this book. We had primarily targeted for compiling around 50 essays from various writers/toppers.

The book presented to you is special in many ways. Along with thoroughly depicting various techniques and styles of essay writing, this book also includes more than 50 model essays on various topics from across the spectrum along with the required fodder to build an essay.

All the essays have been written by IAS/IPS/IRS officers who have recently been selected in UPSC and thus are in accordance with the latest pattern of UPSC exams. Aspirants reading this book will immensely benefit from the essay writing style of young officers who excellently performed in their UPSC exams and have contributed towards this book. It also contains useful tables which will not only enrich the content of your essays but also make it exhaustively comprehensive. In addition to this, several axioms/anecdotes that are very useful in essay writing have also been given.

In all sense, this book serves as the complete package for the essay paper of the Civil Services Mains Exam. After reading this book, more or less, no other book will be required to prepare for the essay paper. All you need is to practice essay writing on your own, after having gone through this book.

This book is equally relevant and useful for PCS Exams of Hindi speaking states apart from UPSC Exams since essay paper is a compulsory paper in almost all state PCS Exams. This book will also benefit aspirants with Hindi background who are preparing to appear in UPSC Exams in English medium.

Special thanks to Prabhat Exams for giving platform to come up with the book. We expect aspirants to understand that there cannot be a single pill to tackle ever changing and evolving essay paper in the UPSC Exams but with the right guidance provided in the book and constant practice one can master the art of essay writing. This book can only act as a compass to give right direction in order to build the concept of essay writing.

Best Wishes!

Nishant Jain
Abhishek Saraf
Snehil Tripathi

CONTENTS

Preface *iii*

1. **Essay Strategy by *Abhishek Saraf, IAS*** **1-27**

2. **Essay Writing in UPSC Mains Exam: A Holistic View** **29-37**
   by *Nishant Jain, IAS*

3. **Do's and Don'ts by *Abhishek Jain, IAS*** **39-42**

4. **Quotes and Dimensions for Essay Writing** **43-78**

5. **Examples for Essay Writing** **79-136**

6. **55 Model Essays** **137-310**
   1 Artificial Intelligence: An End to Human Miseries or An End to Humanity Itself 139
   Akshat Jain, IAS
   2 Beware the Barrenness of Busy Life 142
   Akshat Jain, IAS
   3 Industry 4.0 is the Biggest Game Changer of Present and Future 145
   Jayant Nahata, IAS
   4 Life Happens to All, Only Few Make it Happen 149
   Jayant Nahata, IAS
   5 Nothing is Absolute, Subjectivity Applies Everywhere 152
   Jayant Nahata, IAS
   6 People Decide Their Own Destiny, Fortunes are Made or Unmade by Humans 156
   Jayant Nahata, IAS
   7 Science is a Beautiful Gift To Humanity, We should not Distort it 159
   Jayant Nahata, IAS

8 "To Be Beautiful, Life Doesn't Require To Be Big" 162

Jayant Nahata, IAS

9 "In Today's World A Culture of Death is Gaining Supremacy Over a Culture of Life" 165

Abhishek Bharti, IPS

10 "Raise Your Voice, Not The Sea Level" 168

Abhishek Bharti, IPS

11 Health is a Fundamental Right in India – Prospect and Challenges 171

Abhishek Jain, IAS

12 Is Our Higher Education System Future Ready? 174

Abhishek Jain, IAS

13 Privacy in the Digital Era: Myths and Realities 177

Abhishek Jain, IAS

14 The End of Law is Not to Abolish or Restrain but to Preserve and Enlarge Freedom 180

Abhishek Jain, IAS

15 What Will it Take to Make Gender Equality the Norm, Not the Exception 182

Abhishek Jain, IAS

16 Artificial Intelligence Has the Power to Make Human Intelligence Obsolete 186

Abhishek Saraf, IAS

17 Is Data The New Oil? 189

Abhishek Saraf, IAS

18 Strengthening Healthcare System in India – Is Privatisation the Only Answer? 192

Abhishek Saraf, IAS

19 Diversity in India, Does it Better or Fetter the Economic Growth 196

Ankush Kothari, AIR 429 CSE 2019

20 Evolution of India's Foreign Policy: Continuity and Changes 199

Ankush Kothari, AIR 429 CSE 2019

21 Gender Equality: Myth or Reality 203

Ashutosh Dwivedi, IAS

22 Cashless Economy – Challenges and Opportunities 206

Lavish Ordiya, IAS

23 Daughters of India – Their Strength, Their Plights and Their Achievements! 209
Nikhil Rakhecha, IAS

24 Diversity in India: Does it Better or Fetter the Economic Growth? 212
Nikhil Rakhecha, IAS

25 Ecological Consideration Need Not Hamper Development 216
Abhisek Oswal, IRS (IT)

26 Education is the Antidote to Poverty 220
Amrit Jain, IPS

27 The Higher We Are Placed, The More Humbly We Should Walk 223
Himanshu Kaushik, IAS

28 Poverty Anywhere is a Threat to Prosperity Everywhere 226
Himanshu Jain, IAS

29 Consumerism Kills Culture with Overproduction and Heightened Sense of Need Established by the Marketing 229
Himanshu Kaushik, IAS

30 Fighting Corruption is Not Just Good Governance But Also Self-Defence and Patriotism 232
Himanshu Kaushik, IAS

31 Yesterday's Score Does Not Win You Game Today 235
Himanshu Kaushik, IAS

32 In An Age of Digitalisation, Data is the New Oil 237
Nikhil Rakhecha, IAS

33 India is Yet to Celebrate its Diversities 240
Abhisek Oswal, IRS (IT)

34 India's Focus Shift from SAARC to BIMSTEC is Strategic but Underused 245
Abhisek Oswal, IRS (IT)

35 New India in the Pursuit of Excellence 248
Mudit Jain, IRS

36 Women Empowerment: The Need of the Hour is to Move Beyond Emotive Posturing 251
Mudit Jain, IRS

37 Courage to Accept and Dedication to Improve Are Two Keys to Success 255
Namrata Jain, IAS

38 Economy is Losing Out on the Potential of Women 258
Namrata Jain, IAS

39 The Greater the Difficulty, the More Glory in Surmounting it 261
Namrata Jain, IAS

40 Expect the Best, Prepare for the Worst, Capitalise on What Comes 263
Pradeep Kumar Dwivedi, IAS

41 Role of Media in Elections 266
Pradeep Kumar Dwivedi, IAS

42 Cooperative Federalism in the Era of Developmentalism 269
Rajarshi Shah, IAS

43 Globalization is Making our Societies More Creative and Prosperous, but also More Vulnerable 272
Ravi Mittal, IAS

44 Vision of a Clean India: Prospects and Challenges 275
Ravi Mittal, IAS

45 Management of Indian Border Disputes – A Complex Task 278
Rishab Jain, IAS

46 Risk of Artificial Intelligence Outweigh Benefit 281
Abhisek Oswal, IRS (IT)

47 Start by Doing What is Necessary, Then Do What's Possible and Suddenly You will be Doing What's Impossible 284
Shreyans Kumat, IAS

48 The Greatest Threat to Our Planet is the Belief That Someone Else Will Save it 286
Shreyans Kumat, IAS

49 Consumption, Consumerism & Environment 289
Somesh Upadhyay, IAS

50 Information is the Ultimate Power in the Digital Universe of 21st Century 292
Swapnil Hanmane, IAS

51 There is No Education Like Adversity 295
Swapnil Hanmane, IAS

52 Democracy and Socialism are Means to an End, Not the End in Itself 298
Vaibhav Jain, IRS (IT)

53 A Good Life is One Inspired By Love and Guided By Knowledge 301
Vaibhav Jain, IRS (IT)

54 Water Water Everywhere, Not A Drop To Drink 304
Swapnil Hanmane, IAS
55 Tourism: Can This be the Next Big Thing For India? 307
Nav Goel, IRAS

7. 15 Model Practice Sets 311-327

Practice Set-1 313
Practice Set-2 314
Practice Set-3 315
Practice Set-4 316
Practice Set-5 317
Practice Set-6 318
Practice Set-7 319
Practice Set-8 320
Practice Set-9 321
Practice Set-10 322
Practice Set-11 323
Practice Set-12 324
Practice Set-13 325
Practice Set-14 326
Practice Set-15 327

8. Previous 7 Years Essay Papers 329-337

Essay Question Paper – UPSC Civil Services IAS Mains – 2018 331
Essay Question Paper – UPSC Civil Services IAS Mains – 2019 332
Essay Question Paper – UPSC Civil Services IAS Mains – 2020 333
Essay Question Paper – UPSC Civil Services IAS Mains – 2021 334
Essay Question Paper – UPSC Civil Services IAS Mains – 2022 335
Essay Question Paper – UPSC Civil Services IAS Mains – 2023 336
Essay Question Paper – UPSC Civil Services IAS Mains – 2024 337

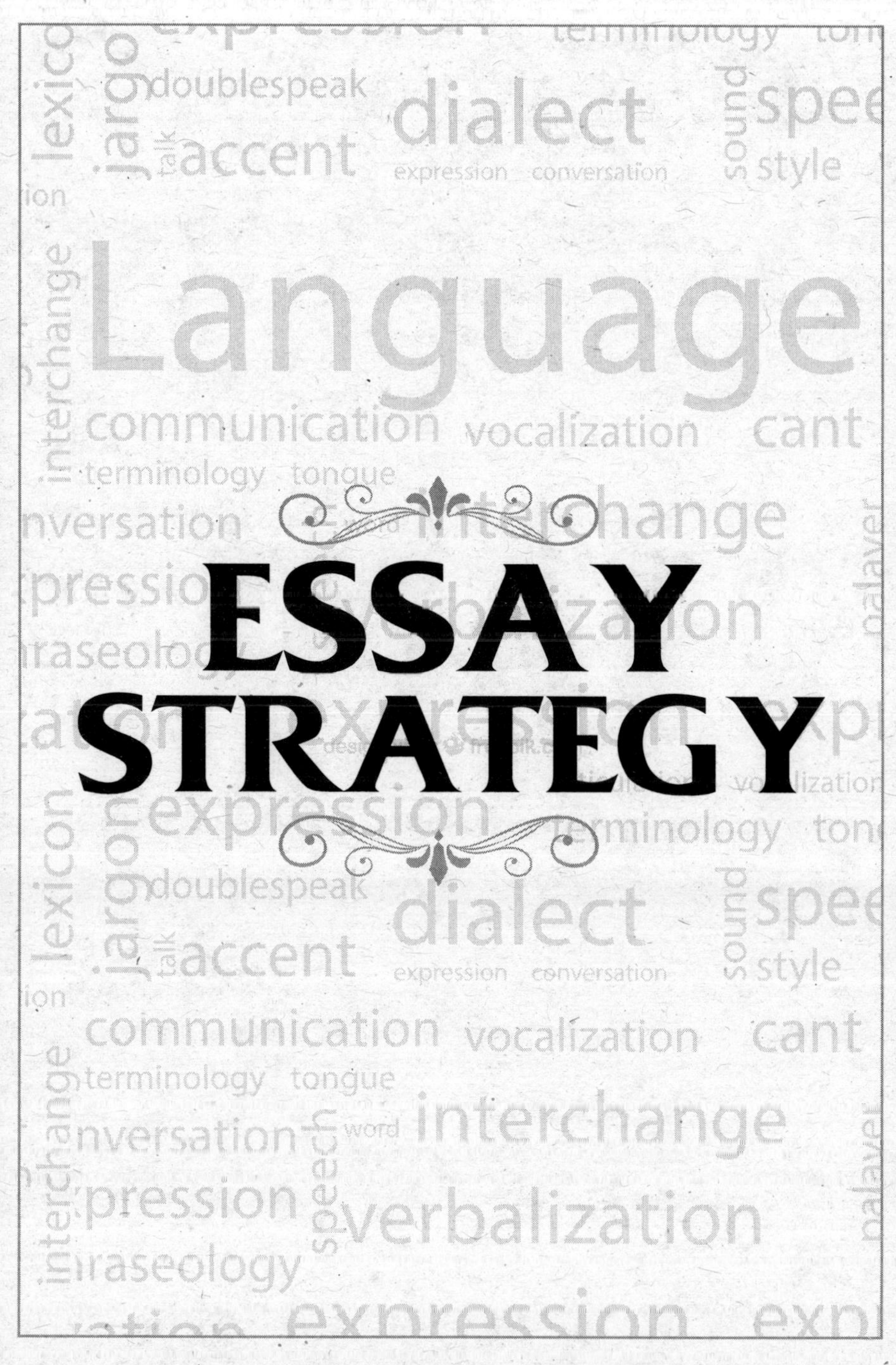

ESSAY STRATEGY

1 Essay Strategy

Abhishek Saraf, IAS

It was 27th April 2018 when the results of CSE 2017 were declared and I had secured AIR-402. While it was satisfactory for my first Mains, it was not until the second week of May that I realised while personality test single-handedly got me into the list, essay paper single-handedly kept me from becoming an IAS. When the highest marks secured were above 170, average score for a selected candidate was above 135, I had secured only 105 marks. Every once in a while history repeats itself and it sure did for me too. On 5th April 2019, when results of CSE 2018 were declared, while I had secured AIR 248, a known Achilles heel of mine became my undoing. I got 79 marks in the essay paper. Single-handedly it had kept me from securing a rank in top 20. In an exam where fresher candidates score 130 without any special preparation, why was I not able to get even an average score??? What am I doing wrong? The answer lay not in the content but something else entirely!

Here based upon my experiences I will elaborate on how to write a good essay for UPSC CSE. I will elaborate on:

- What the essay paper is about?
- How to strategise our preparation?
- How do we go about attempting the essay paper?
- Some useful tips for the essay.

That's why I think before we strategize to attempt the essay paper let's understand what the essay paper is about. Also, what it isn't about.

1. It's not about your knowledge – that gets tested in GS papers, also many candidates performing average to below average in GS papers have done consistently outstandingly in essay paper.
2. It's not about your linguistic skills – that how flowery language you can write ... or how good your vocabulary is.
3. It's not about your literary skills – how many quotations/poems can you write about a subject or can you compose couplets about the subject.
4. It's definitely not about your handwriting (legible handwriting written neatly is enough).

M.H. Abrams, the American literary critic, notes that the essay is "Any short composition in prose that undertakes to discuss a matter, express a point of view, or persuade us to accept a thesis on any subject."

1. How accurately we understand an issue – from historical (why) to present (what) to future (how) aspects of it.
2. Ability to think holisitically covering various perspectives of an issue like social, economic, political, cultural, technical, environmental, international, ethic, sports, etc.
3. Ability to break the issue down to few thematic and pertinent questions – who (stakeholders), when, what, where, why, how.
4. Ability to provide creative solutions to the problem at hand.
5. Ability to document your thoughts into a coherent and concise text.
6. Orientation as to whether you are broadly an optimistic or a pessimistic person.

During the course of our preparation it is better to have overall knowledge about a vast number of things, thus its not very difficult for an average candidate to summon knowledge. However, in my three Mains and two debacles in the essay paper I have come to know that it's not the lack of knowledge but improper selection of content from our knowledge base, lack of proper organisation and incoherent presentation that holds us back.

All in all it can be thought of as a written form of personality test - as it judges your entire thought and execution process as well as the practicality of the same.

Having seen what the essay paper is about and what it's not, we should proceed to preparing for the essay paper.

STRATEGISING THE PREPARATION

The strategy to prepare for the essay paper begins with understanding the kinds of questions one can expect to face in the essay paper. Once we know the types of questions we can face, we can start preparing accordingly. The essay types can broadly be sub-categorised into the following heads shown with examples from previous year questions (PYQs)-

Essay Type	Essay Topic
Social Issues	• The Indian society at the crossroads. (1994) • The new emerging women power: the ground realities. (1995) • New cults and godmen: a threat to traditional religion. (1996) • Greater political power alone will not improve women's plight. (1997) • The composite culture of India. (1998) • Woman is God's best creation. (1998) • Youth culture today. (1999)

	• Women empowerment: challenges and prospects. (1999) • Modernism and our traditional socio-ethical values. (2000) • Indian culture today: a myth or a reality? (2000) • Empowerment alone cannot help our women. (2001) • As civilization advances culture declines. (2003) • Whither women's emancipation? (2004) • If women ruled the world. (2005) • The hand that rocks the cradle. (2005) • Women's reservation bill would usher in empowerment for women in India. (2006) • From traditional Indian philanthropy to the Gates-Buffet model – a natural progression or a paradigm shift? (2010) • Managing work and home – is the Indian working woman getting a fair deal? (2012) • If development is not engendered, it is endangered. (2016) • Fulfillment of 'new woman' in India is a myth. (2017) • South Asian societies are woven not around the state, but around their plural cultures and plural identities. (2019) • Best for an individual is not necessarily best for the society. (2019) • Neglect of primary health care and education in India are reasons for its backwardness - A socio-economic topic. (2019) • There can be no social justice without economic prosperity but economic prosperity without social justice is meaningless - A socio-economic topic. (2020) • Patriarchy is the least noticed yet the most significant structure of social inequality. (2020)
Economic Issues	• Multinational corporations – saviours or saboteurs. (1994) • Resource management in the Indian context. (1999) • Globalization would finish small-scale industries in India. (2006) • BPO boom in India. (2007) • Special Economic Zone: boon or bane? (2008) • Are our traditional handicrafts doomed to a slow death? (2009) • Is the criticism that the Public-Private-Partnership (PPP) model for development is more of a bane than a boon in the Indian context, justified? (2012) • GDP (Gross Domestic Product) along with GDH (Gross Domestic Happiness) would be the right indices for judging the well-being of a country. (2013) • Was it the policy paralysis or the paralysis of implementation which slowed the growth of our country? (2014)

	• Tourism: Can this be the next big thing for India? (2014) • Can Capitalism bring inclusive growth? (2015) • Crisis faced in India – moral or economic. (2015) • Near jobless growth in India: An anomaly or an outcome of economic reforms. (2016) • Digital economy: A leveller or a source of economic inequality. (2016). • Innovation is the key determinant of economic growth and social welfare. (2016) • Farming has lost the ability to be a source of subsistence for majority of farmers in India. • Impact of the new economic measures on fiscal ties between the Union and States in India. (2017) • Poverty anywhere is a threat to prosperity everywhere. (2018)
Polity, Governance and Administration	• Politics, bureaucracy and business – fatal triangle. (1994) • Whither Indian democracy? (1995) • Politics without ethics is a disaster. (1995) • The VIP cult is a bane of Indian democracy. (1996) • Need for transparency in public administration. (1996) • What we have not learnt during fifty years of independence. (1997) • The language problem in India: its past, present and prospects. (1998) • Why should we be proud of being Indians? (2000) • What have we gained from our democratic set-up? (2001) • How should a civil servant conduct himself? (2003) • How far has democracy in India delivered the goods? (2003) • Water resources should be under the control of the central government. (2004) • Evaluation of Panchayati Raj System in India from the point of view of eradication of power to people. (2007) • Is autonomy the best answer to combat balkanization? (2007) • National identity and patriotism. (2008) • Creation of smaller states and the consequent administrative, economic and developmental implication. (2011) • In the context of Gandhiji's views on the matter, explore, on an evolutionary scale, the terms 'Swadhinata', 'Swaraj' and 'Dharmarajya'. Critically comment on their contemporary relevance to Indian democracy. (2012) • Is the colonial mentality hindering India's success? (2013) • Is sting operation an invasion on privacy? (2014) • Cooperative federalism: Myth or Reality. (2016) • Water disputes between States in federal India. (2016) • Biased media is a real threat to Indian democracy. (2019)

International Relations	• Has the Non-Alignment Movement (NAM) lost its relevance in a multipolar world? (2017)
Technology	• The modern doctor and his patients. (1997) • Value-based science and education. (1999) • The march of science and the erosion of human values. (2001) • Spirituality and scientific temper. (2003) • The lure of space. (2004) • Science and Mysticism: Are they compatible? (2012). • Science and technology is the panacea for the growth and security of the nation. (2013) • Technology cannot replace manpower. (2015) • Digital economy: A leveller or a source of economic inequality (2016) • Cyberspace and internet: Blessing or curse to the human civilization in the long run (2016) • Social media is inherently a selfish medium. (2017) • Alternative technologies for a climate change resilient India. (2018) • Rise of Artificial Intelligence: the threat of jobless future or better job opportunities through reskilling and upskilling. (2019) • Technology as the silent factor in international relations. (2020)
Education	• Restructuring of Indian education system. (1995) • Literacy is growing very fast, but there is no corresponding growth in education. (1996) • Irrelevance of the classroom. (2001) • Privatization of higher education in India. (2002) • Modern technological education and human values. (2002) • What is real education? (2005) • "Education for all" campaign in India: myth or reality. (2006) • Independent thinking should be encouraged right from the childhood. (2007) • Is an egalitarian society possible by educating the masses? (2008) • Credit-based higher education system – status, opportunities and challenges. (2011) • Is the growing level of competition good for the youth? (2014) • Are the standardized tests good measure of academic ability or progress? (2014) • Education without values, as useful as it is, seems rather to make a man more clever devil. (2015) • Destiny of a nation is shaped in its classrooms. (2017) • Youth is a blunder, manhood a struggle, old age a regret. (1994)

- Useless life is an early death. (1994)
- Disinterested intellectual curiosity is the lifeblood of civilisation. (1995)
- When money speaks, the truth is silent. (1995)
- Our deeds determine us, as much as we determine our deeds. (1995)
- Truth is lived, not taught. (1996)
- True religion cannot be misused. (1997)
- Search for truth can only be a spiritual problem. (2002)
- The paths of glory lead but to the grave. (2002)
- If youth knew, if age could. (2002)
- There is nothing either good or bad but thinking makes it so. (2003)
- Discipline means success, anarchy means ruin. (2008)
- Be the change you want to see in others. (2013)
- With greater power comes greater responsibility. (2014)
- Words are sharper than the two-edged sword. (2014)
- Character of an institution is reflected in its leader. (2015)
- Quick but steady wins the race. (2015)
- Lending hands to someone is better than giving a dole. (2015)
- Need brings greed, if greed increases it spoils breed. (2016)
- "The past' is a permanent dimension of human consciousness and values. (2018)
- Reality does not conform to the ideal, but confirms it. (2018)
- Attitude makes habit, habit makes character and character makes a man. (2007)
- Joy is the simplest form of gratitude. (2017)
- A good life is one inspired by love and guided by knowledge. (2018)
- A people that values its privileges above its principles loses both. (2018)
- Customary morality cannot be a guide to modern life. (2018)
- The past' is a permanent dimension of human consciousness and values. (2018)
- A people that values its privileges above its principles loses both. (2018)
- Reality does not conform to the ideal, but confirms it. (2018)
- A good life is one inspired by love and guided by knowledge.(2019)
- Wisdom finds truth. (2019)

	• Values are not what humanity is, but what humanity ought to be. (2019) • Courage to accept and dedication to improve are two keys to success. (2019) • Life is long journey between human being and being humane. (2020) • Mindful manifesto is the catalyst to a tranquil self. (2020) • Ships do not sink because of water around them, ships sink because of water that gets into them. (2020) • Simplicity is the ultimate sophistication. (2020)
Environ-mental	• We may brave human laws but cannot resist natural laws. (2017)
Sports	• Fifty Golds in Olympics: Can this be a reality for India?
Culture	• Culture is what we are, civilization is what we have. (2020)
Internal Security	• Management of Indian border disputes – a complex task.. (2018)

Once we know the types of essays preparation entails collecting **quotations, anecdotes, case studies,** data from sources like reports by **global, national** and **state level organisations, census,** etc., and designing diagrams. After having collected appropriate content, we should look at how to use it when we write an essay.

Attempting the Essay Paper

Topic Selection

To select a topic for the essay it's important to choose a stong and engaging topic so that the audience will more easily understand. For that, from the topic of the essay we should differentiate the base and the argument. The base indicates the broad topic of the essay. The base is something that should help us figure out which of the 7 types (mentioned at page no. 13 in bold) is the essay about. On the other hand an argument indicates the specific issue the essay deals with in the broad field defined by base. Things will become clearer with the following examples from PYQs.

1. Truth is lived, not taught. (1996) - Base - Truth; Argument - Lived, not taught
2. Privatization of higher education in India. (2002)- Base - Higher Education; Argument - Privatization
3. Discipline means success, anarchy means ruin. (2008) - Base - Discipline, anarchy; Argument- success; ruin

4. Are the standardized tests good measure of academic ability or progress? (2014) - Base - standardized tests; Argument - academic ability or progress
5. Digital economy: A leveller or a source of economic inequality (2016) - Base - Digital economy; Argument - economic inequality
6. Destiny of a nation is shaped in its classrooms. (2017)- Base - shaped in its classrooms; Argument- Destiny of a nation
7. A people that values its privileges above its principles loses both. (2018) - Base - people that values its privileges above its principles; Argument - loses both
8. Alternative technologies for a climate change in resilient India. (2018) - Base in Alternative technologies; Argument-climate change resilient India
9. Biased media is a real threat to Indian democracy. (2019) – Base-Biased media; Argument threat to Indian democracy
10. Technology as the silent factor in international relations. (2020) – Base – Technology; Argument – international relations

We should pick up the topic with whose base we are comfortable. It has been found that if we are comfortable with the broad topic of the essay we are likely to develop the content relatively comfortably.

Defining Broad Framework of The Essay

The second step after topic selection is to frame thematic questions (i.e. 5Ws and 1H – Who, When, What, Where, Why and How) each of which should address a perspective of the essay topic. These questions should be designed in such a way that incorporates as many perspectives of the essay as possible. These questions help us define the broad outline of the essay and answering these questions should help us produce a holistic text on the topic. One need not necessarily frame questions for each of the 5Ws and 1H. Also the questions we frame need not necessarily be restricted to 5Ws and 1H. The idea of framing questions based on 5Ws and 1H is only indicative - its neither mandatory nor exclusive. We can frame as many questions as we think are relevant to the essay topic. We can frame questions in any wording that we think is relevant to the essay topic. Following examples may help clarify the idea:

Topic: Destiny of a nation is shaped in its classrooms. (2017)

Questions:

1. Why is the destiny of a nation shaped in its classrooms?
2. How are is humanity doing in the classrooms?
3. What are the challenges we are facing in classrooms?
4. Why are we facing those challenges?
5. What can we do to overcome those challenges?

Topic: Customary morality cannot be a guide to modern life. (2018)

Questions:

1. How does customary morality hinder the march to modernity?
2. Why does customary morality exercise so much dominance?
3. Is customary morality all bad?
4. How can we ensure that customary morality does not restrict the march to modernity?

Topic: Best for an individual is not necessarily best for the society (2019)

Questions:

1. What is best for individual may or may not be best for the society ?
2. Why does it happen that best for the individual may or may not be best for the society?
3. Can it happen that worst for the individual is the best for society?
4. How can we make sure that best for the individual is best for the society too?

While framing the questions one must think about various possible interrelated ideas of the essay topic and try to cover all the fields relevant. The examiner must not be left with any unanswered questions in their mind after having read our essay.

As we saw above the historical aspect deals with the evolution of the problem at hand. Social, political, economic, cultural, environmental, international, geographical, humanitarian, ethical, sports, technological, etc., aspects of the essay are one of the many perspectives of the essay. We are free to choose to end our essay with a discussion of these aspects (which broadly cover the what perspective) or we could cover other perspectives as well.

Coverage of other perspectives (5Ws and 1H) help us delve deeper and wider into the topic. Successful candidates have been known to use both the strategies. However, it may be observed that covering other perspectives as well leads the reader to be naturally curious about the solution of the problem at hand. This not only provides for a holistic read but also enables the reader to associate more intuitively with the essay, thereby translating into score. So in our opinion it is advisable to frame questions covering many more perspectives rather than just the what perspective as explained above.

Having framed thematic questions we need to develop answers to the said questions. Along with answers to the thematic questions, we need to ensure we devote equitable space to these answers. Amount of space will depend on the context of the essay topic. However, broadly we can divide the entire 10 to 11 pages as follows:

1. 1.5 to 2 pages for opening discussion aka introduction (explained later).
2. 5 pages for the aspects aka body (explained later).
3. 0.5 to 1 pages for the counter-thesis aka body (explained later).
4. 1 page for exploring the underlying reasons aka pre-conclusion (explained later).
5. 2 pages for solutions/closure aka conclusion (explained later).

Iteratively with allocating space, answers need to be brainstormed for each of the questions framed/ perspectives. One can and does impact the other and a balance between both develops a holistic body of text. This entire exercise is supposed to be a part of the brainstorming session.

Brainstorming Session

This session usually entails about 20-25 minutes of the 1.5 hours devoted to each essay. This session has two purposes – introspecting content and structuring it in the broad- heads as explained above.

Introspecting usually works on two lines – free run and predefined coverage.

1. **Free run:** During the free run we should cover and note down anything and everything relevant to the essay that comes to our mind. One should not let the mind be restricted by the questions framed (as per 5Ws and 1H) or which aspect does the idea relate to. It is at this point one can think of quotes, diagrams, case studies, data, anecdotes, etc.
2. **Predefined coverage:** This should always follow the free run. More often than not we miss some perspectives during the free run. During the predefined run we are supposed to pick up the questions framed above and find answers to all of these. Following can be the pointers to develop answers to various perspectives.
    - **Historical:** ancient, medieval and modern.
    - **Social:** casteism, religion – secularism and communalism, marginalised sections – ST, SC, OBCs, minorities, women, differently-abled people, senior citizens, children, classes – rich and poor, institutions – marriage, family, etc., crime
    - **Polity:** preamble (justice liberty equality and fraternity, sovereignty, socialism, secularism, democracy, republic), natural justice, basic structure of constitution, fundamental rights, directive principles of state policy, fundamental duties, good governance-participatory, consensus-oriented, accountable, transparent, responsive, effective and efficient, equitable and inclusive and follows the rule of law, citizen centricity, social audit, judiciary and cases, political parties, e-governance, elections and electoral politics and associated reforms, institutions – constitutional, statutory, executive, NGOs etc., local self governance.

- **Economic:** agriculture and allied sector, manufacturing and industry, services- traditional corporates and advanced (IT and ITES), equality and inclusion, finances, employment, skill development, resource mobilisation and investment, PPP.
- **Cultural:** food, dance, music, theatre and movies, linguistic, literature, architecture, paintings.
- **International:** neighbour, regional, global, unconventions, treaties, pacts, international bodies – WB, IMF, WTO, UN etc., geopolitics, geo-economics and geo-strategic aspects.
- **Ethical:** values, virtues, ethics and morality, categorical imperative etc., attitude, aptitude, emotional intelligence, work ethic.
- **Humanitarian dimensions:** compassion, rights and empathy.
- **Geographic:** human and physical geography, economics aspects.
- **Environmental:** global warming and climate change, man-animal conflict, disasters, flora and fauna, ecological footprint, land, air, water, wildlife, sustainable development.
- **Sports:** sports in India and abroad, values associated, technological and administrative developments.
- **Scientific and Technological:** media – print, electronic and social media, AI, big data, augmented reality, virtual reality, 3D printing, robotics and automation, internet of things.

These are just illustrative sub-heads for the what and why perspectives. The brainstorming may include these but does not have to be limited to these. Furthermore, brainstorming should cover other perspectives as well.

Structuring the Essay

Having seen what needs to be incorporated in the essay, we need to focus on how it needs to be presented. This leads us to categorising the brainstormed content into in the order of introduction, body, pre-conclusion and conclusion. So that we are able to align our content properly we should understand what each of the above entails.

Introduction

As indicated above introduction is supposed to be presented in the first two pages of the essay. The main goal of an introduction is:

1. To show the examiner that we have understood the essay topic – both base and argument.
2. To give the broad outline of the essay.
3. Interpretation of the keywords of the topic.

The first goal can be fulfilled by

1. **Stories**
   - From the life of eminent personalities (dead or alive).
   - Excerpts from Mythology.
   - Fiction.
   - Anecdotes from real life.
2. **Dramatic start**
   - Sensational fact or data (before 2100 Maldives, Tuvalu and many more islands will be submerged due to sea-level rise consequent to global warming).
   - Paradox (like India is a food surplus country yet more than 7,000 people die of hunger everyday in India).
3. **Current Affairs related to the essay topic**
   - Recent news.
   - Excerpts from reports by well-renowned national or global organisations (eg. Global Risks Report by World Economic Forum on climate change, OXFAM reports on poverty).
4. Statement by eminent personalities (concerns expressed by Mr. Elon Musk and The Late Dr. Stephen Hawking on artificial intelligence).
5. Description or definition based start (least recommended) like the kind we see in most editorial, op-ed. article in mainstream newspapers.

While the description is the easiest and the most way to explain our understanding of the essay, it is least recommended for the fact that it tends to be very bland and monotonous. However, short of other options we can always rely on description. Personally, I believe that introduction should have a humanitarian touch so that the examiner is hooked to the essay on a personal level right from the introduction.

Once we have used one of the above techniques we need to link the story/data/current affairs/statements by eminent personalities mentioned to the topic of the essay. This is done by picking up the crux of the story/drawing a lesson from it that explains the topic. Using the fact/data/paradox/statement by eminent personalities to explain the essay topic (like in the above example the sensational data explains the real impact of climate change, the paradox explains the urgent need to work on food security and distributive justice).

The second purpose can be achieved by giving hint of the perspectives that we are going to be covering in the essay. It is here that we should set out the primary idea of the essay clearly so that the examiner knows exactly what they are going to find in the essay. This saves them from the exercise of picking up ideas while reading the essay on their own. Thus it enhances the ease through which they can go through and understand our essay. On the very first reading they are able to appreciate the point being made and connect it with the essay topic because they had a clear cut idea of what was coming in the essay.

1. This can be done by using:
   - Language that excites curiosity either by being argumentative. For example the essay explains need to prepare for the second cold war which might not be as far as some of us might think ... in fact it might be underway already.
   - Example of question: In this essay we will see why public healthcare system needs to focus on primary healthcare as a top priority?
2. If needed state your opinion outright. This needs to be done only in 'or' kind of essays where the topic specifically gives us this leeway.

The third purpose of the introduction is to provide a description of the keywords that are going to be interpreted and discussed in a broad manner. For instance in the topic "Best for an individual is not necessarily best for the society" the word individual need not necessarily mean a person, it can mean a religious community, a gender, a class of persons, a market player - be it buyer or seller, an age group, a species, a state in the country, a nation in the world, a business entity, a political party. The idea here is that to cover the various perspectives we take a much broader than literal interpretation of a particular keyword. This is not naturally intuitive to the examiner. Hence, the in the absence of the description in introduction the burden to understand the interpretation made falls on the examiner (when we eventually use this interpretation in the body of the essay). Examiner has to go through few lines to understand the interpretation and then read them again to understand the argument made. This creates a lag and an abruptness in the reading of the essay which translates to lesser marks.

An alternative to this abruptness is to explain the relevant beyond-literal interpretations at the start of each paragraph. This leads to clear linkage of the interpretation and the essay topic in the mind of the examiner. However, this causes entails for a monotonous structure of essay and also has an opportunity cost of one line at the start of every paragraph. Hence, it is advisable to do that in the introduction itself.

Having completed the introduction, we shift to the body of the essay.

Body

The body of the essay entails a discuss on various perspectives of the essay. Overall the direction of the essay has to be from past to present to future. This makes for a very chronological and intuitive read. Hence, it is advisable that we pick up the perspective or the question (framed during brainstorming) that explains the historical origin and evolution of the said problem. Here, the key question to be answered can be 'when' did the issue at hand takes root? 'How' did we get to the current situation? After having covered the historical perspective one may choose to cover one of the social, political, economic, cultural, ethical, technological, environmental, international, geographic, sports, etc., perspectives of the essay. These perspectives explain the present situation of the issue, thus covering the present part of the chronology.

It is advisable to devote one page each to the social and economic aspects. It has been seen that designing the paragraphs such that there are three paragraphs per page enhances the readability of the essay. Other than connector paragraphs (explained in "concept of flow") average length of the paragraph should be about 30–35 words. This means a paragraph should have about 3–4 sentences.

The first sentence is supposed to put for the argument pertaining to a social and political aspect. This is a simple and straight-forward assertion that we make. It can discuss the impact of a phenomenon to make a point. The second sentence should be an explanation of the assertion made in the first sentence. The third sentence has to be an example, fact, case study, etc., to substantiate our argument in real life and draw the point home. Data, examples, expert opinions and constitutional provisions can be used to provide substantiation to our argument. For instance, for a topic like "Social media is a pillar of democracy" this can be a paragraph in the essay.

Social media has deepened social democracy globally. Today, even the powerless can present their opinions and share information globally in real time. The 'MeToo' movement exemplifies how the victims joined forces globally to fight systemic injustices.

Generally, it is advisable to cover 3 points in each of the social, economic and political aspect. It gives a sense of logical flow and agreeability if we follow a bottom-up strategy in social, economic, etc., aspects. This can be executed by focusing the discussion on the following units in the mentioned order – Individual, Family, Professional Workplace, Society, Community, National, Global.

This way we can cover various aspects while maintaining a proper balance between the content and the presentation of the content (thereby enhancing the readability of the essay).

Having covered the various aspects we can move to the anti-thesis. By anti-thesis we mean the other side of the coin. It must be borne in mind that nothing is entirely black and white and that there is always a grey aspect to things. This means that even though the essay topic commands us to stick to a certain aspect of an issue, there is a shade of opinion which disagrees with the essay topic and which can be substantiated with logical arguments and fact.

For instance, for the essay topic "Customary morality can never lead to modernity" the anti-thesis can be the timeless ideas of "atithi devo bhava" or 'vasudhaiva kutumbakam" espoused by Indian culture and lifestyle. The topic 'Best for an individual is not necessarily best for the society" asks us to show best for the individual may or may not be best for society. Here the anti-thesis can be even worst for the individual can also be the best for society. An example can be a soldier who lays down his or her life for the security of the nation. The line of thought here is while on the one hand death is worst for the individual, but on the other hand safety and security is best for the society as a whole.

Now the question arises that on the one hand we are advised to stick with the essay topic and on the other hand we are being advised to cover the anti-thesis. While it may sound contradictory at first the answer lies in the space devoted to the anti-thesis. The anti-thesis must never be larger than a page. Usually one or two paragraphs are good enough to cover it. The idea of the anti-thesis is that

1. It has to be included to show the examiner that we as candidates are capable of thinking about the issue from every perspective even if UPSC has chosen itself to restrict it to one.
2. Since, UPSC has chosen to restrict itself to one perspective we will devote most of our time and energy to the same, hence the anti-thesis should not be so long that itself becomes a digression from the topic.

So in nutshell the anti-thesis will show the diversity of our thought while respecting the directions of UPSC. This is a part where you can make your essay stand out from everyone else who may just cover social, political, economic, etc., aspects.

Having covered the various aspects and having given the anti-thesis we need to move towards the conclusion. The transition from body to conclusion is done through the pre-conclusion. Let's see what that entails.

Pre-conclusion

While the pre-conclusion sets the tone for the conclusion, it can be used to cover another perspective that we developed during brain-storming. One of the perspectives to be covered here can be 'why' does the particular challenge exist? Here we can delve into the moral as well as the ethical issues at the base of the problem. We can discuss systemic/ institutional causes of the problem as well. We can discuss the causes at the individual, group/ community/ collective/ organisational level, national, regional or international level. This discussion of causes will be automatically link the pre-conclusion with the body of the essay. While the problem was discussed in various aspects in the body, the causes of the problem (in its various aspects) being discussed here will develop an organic linkage between the body and the pre-conclusion.

Not only does it have academic utility but let's appreciate the exam-oriented utility of the pre-conclusion. This part is where we can display our analytical skills to the fullest. We have displayed our knowledge of the present situation (in the various aspects). Now, this is where we can display our understanding of the evolution and causes of an issue. This can be the defining thesis statement of our essay and can set our essay class apart from others. This is where we explore the topic deeper than what we do in the GS paper which mostly deals with a 'show of knowledge and less of understanding'.

A discussion of the causes of the problem logically leads to the quest for solutions which is what the conclusion is all about! The deeper we analyse the problems the more targeted will be our solutions.

Conclusion

The conclusion is supposed to be the last part of the essay. It's where we bring out the futuristic aspect of an essay thus completing the chronological coverage of history to present to future. We have already explained that one of the qualities that the essay paper intends to check is how optimistic the candidate is. Optimism here does not mean being unrealistic. Optimism means being able to look on the positive futuristic side of things while being grounded in reality. It means being imaginative but at the same time the imagination should produce ideas that can produce results that can work within the constraints of reality. Being optimistically imaginative while keeping our bearings aligned with reality would translate to solutions that can solve the problems we discussed in the body of the essay. That would be best achieved if we target our solutions to the root causes of the problems we discussed in the pre-conclusion.

Having understood the idea of the conclusion, let's see how do we actually go about writing it. The conclusion for an essay usually covers about 2 pages. The conclusion, as opposed to the body, can follow a top- down approach. While giving solutions, one can mention what the government (India, foreign and global governance institutions) has been doing to address the problems enumerated in the essay. Similarly, one can give their suggestions regarding the solutions government(s) could implement. Following the top-down model the next step can be what NGOs have been doing or can do as a solution to the issues mentioned. The last level can be what we as individuals have been doing/ can do. This kind of structuring generally works well for non-philosophical essays.

For philosophical essays, a slightly different approach is needed. In a philosophical essay, along with the above we need to mention learnings from this 1.5 hours of intellectual exercise. How those learnings are being implemented at the government, civil society and individual level. In addition, to this we can also explain how those learnings can be implemented at the aforementioned levels.

Another purpose of the conclusion is to give the feeling of completeness to the essay. This can be done by clearly deciding what exactly will be the thesis statement of the essay, what problems will be raised in the essay that can be solved in the conclusion. The entire essay, from aspects to perspectives to pre-conclusion to conclusion, can be designed around this thesis statement. Building on this statement will be the final conclusion which will automatically give a sense of completeness to the essay. This is a sort of a conclusion to introduction kind of approach which is opposite of the introduction - body - conclusion approach discussed so far.

The last paragraph of the essay can be designed on a more personal/ individual/ humanitarian note. It is always a good idea to show compassion in the last part of the essay (conclusion) and last part of the conclusion. This approach has an exam related value. The conclusion is the last thing what the examiner will read just before they award you marks. It is your last chance to persuade the examiner to your point of view and to impress yourself regarding your essay and clarity your feelings abour the issue. The cumulative connect you have developed with the examiner either through the diversity of your coverage or through insightfulness of your ideas or through the creativity and freshness of your ideas will culminate here. Hence, its very important to end the essay on a note that touches the examiner and to which the examiner can connect on humanitarian and personal grounds.

This can be done by giving a very optimistic vision of future which can be achieved by implementing our suggestions. We can do that by connecting the conclusion back with the introduction. By giving a happy ending to the anecdote we might have started in the introduction or by giving a solution to the problem or a paradox we might have mentioned in the introduction.

Alternatively, we can implore the examiner 'take a vow' to address the problems discussed. We can also achieve the same effect by using rhetoric, high sounding lofty expressions, constitutional ideals, slokas and quotes to bind the essay in one line. These can be used to substantiate the central thesis or the learning we have drawn in the essay thereby give it a sense of closure.

Furthermore, we can keep the examiner hooked to your essay even after it has ended. That can be done by leaving an optimistically framed question at the end of your essay (for instance, with a workforce trained in state-of-art technology, a compassionate society rich in social capital, a polity fuelled by the ideas of youth and wisdom of elders, infrastructure designed to serve the needs to present as well as future generations can the dream of the Vishwaguru Bharat be far away? Will it not achieve Gandhiji's vision of Sarvodaya and wipe tears from every eye?).

Back To Structuring Again

Having seen what introduction, body, pre-conclusion and conclusion entail, we need to understand how to structure the essay. We understand the procession from intro body conclusion (including pre-conclusion) and the general flow from history to present to future. But now we need to understand how to achieve this structuring when we are about to start writing.

For that we need to go back to the brainstorming session again. Reason being after having completed the brainstorming session we need to decide the content that will go into the essay and in which part it will go. For every aspect of social, economic political, etc.,, it is enough to present three points. Right after brainstorming is when we decide and mark which of the points are to presented. I used to mark the points as S1, S2, S3 or P1, P2, P3 for social and political points respectively. C1, C2 and C3 was used for conclusion.

This was done in the very same page where I have noted down the points from the brainstorming. This helps us to execute the bottom-up or top-down perfectly. Any other system can be chosen as per convenience.

But its important to ensure that the entire content and order of what is to be presented in the text of the essay is decided before we commit pen to paper. This is important because we have limited words to present our ideas and any digression will cost us at least a paragraph to come back to track. Besides, it will be very undesirable if we come up with an impactful point during brainstorming and miss it solely because we did not sort and earmark our content properly before writing.

After structuring to present the content in a logically agreeable and intuitively connectable manner one last step is needed so that the entire essay becomes one coherent body. This is needed so that each section draws from the preceding one and leads to the following one. The way to do is to develop the ever-talked about and never clearly explained mythical concept of flow.

Concept of Flow

The whole essay really becomes one coherent text when one paragraph is organically linked to the next. Flow is said to have been achieved when the examiner cannot perceive the 'shift' from one paragraph to other while reading our essay. This happens when after having read one paragraph (clearly demarcated or not – both ways work fine), the reader should logically and naturally feel curious about the next paragraph that has been presented. Answer to one thematic question should logically make the reader inquisitive about the next question.

Personally, I struggled a lot with flow. Being an engineer, writing long pieces of text was not in my comfort zone. On top of that, my peers would review my essay and say flow is missing ... but no one could clearly tell how to develop it. Over the years, I came across some and developed some techniques to achieve this flow.

1. **Use of connector sentences**: A connector sentence states what has been explained/discussed and based on that makes a logical assertion announcing what is coming next. That way it not only refreshes what has been covered but also gives the examiner a couple of seconds to think about what should be next. When what the examiner thinks should follow and what we have actually written in the next paragraph are the same, it's then when the examiner feels most connected to our essay. Obviously, it will help our score. There are many ways to develop connector sentences. We can even find examples of these in this very strategy that has been presented. Few ways to do so are:
   - Statement connector to move from body to pre-conclusion. For example "Having dwelled upon the social, economic, political, etc., aspects we should delve in to the causes of the aforementioned issues". Here, its natural for

the examiner to ask why after having seen what ... and when we do that it instantly hooks the examiner to our essay.

- Statement connector to shift from one aspect like social to economic – For e.g. "patriarchy not only works in social settings like purdah system but also has an economic aspect to it like gender wage gaps". Then we can delve into economic aspects. Here keywords social refreshed the examiner that social aspect has been covered and tells the examiner that economic aspect will follow.
- Question connector - Presenting anti-thesis. For instance "From the above discussion, it is apparent that customary morality cannot lead to modernity, one needs to wonder is it always the case?" This is more a engaging way as it implores the examiner to think thus hooking them into our essay.

2. **Connecting following paragraph using content:** For instance, we are moving from one aspect (social) to another (political). That can be done by aligning our content to present purely social aspects, then presenting socio-political aspects and then moving to political aspects. For instance in an essay on casteism after discussing how it has stratified the society into groups which follow endogamy, socialise only within themselves and even cause social evils like untouchability and crimes like honour killings we can discuss issues like how in rural hinterland today so-called lower castes are forced to vote in a ceration way, thus presenting a socio-political aspect. Then we can move even more strictly political aspects like caste based vote-bank politics.
3. **Indicatives:** This can be done by explicitly using terms like social, socio-political, political, economic, etc., in the start of the next paragraph. Here no separate connector sentence is used. For instance "Not just social, but patriarchy also manifests in economic domain". This clearly states the economic aspect is to follow.
4. **Using keywords from the essay topic:** It is always advisable to use keywords of the essay topic in our essay. That not only helps us keep our essay focused on the topic but also helps the examiner understand our point and connect it with the essay topic quickly. This improves readability. We can also use it for building flow. For instance in the essay "Rise of Artificial Intelligence: the threat of jobless future or better job opportunities through reskilling and upskilling" the keywords are Artificial intelligence, jobless, reskilling, upskilling. A good essay would discuss them all. A better essay would not only discuss them all but also move from rise of AI to explain joblessness to reskilling those let off in other skills, and then to upskilling, while using these same keywords in the paragraphs so the examiner connects them to the topic easily.

5. **Connector words:** Last but not the least is the use of connector words like furthermore, moreover, also to move from one aspect to another (for instance, social to international). Words like however can be used to shift to the anti-thesis. Words like nevertheless can be used to signal the shift to solutions. This is the easiest way to execute a shift while avoiding disruptions.

SOME USEFUL TIPS

Having covered broadly what essay is about, we should look at some tricks that need to be kept in mind while attempting the essay:

1. Understanding command directives in the essay: there can be several command directives like 'and', 'or', '?'.
   - Often we are confused about the difference between the 'and' and 'or' directive. The difference is simple in the 'and' directive we are required to cover both aspects and our opinion is not needed. Please note that in 'and' kind of topics we do not have any such leeway of making choices and stating opinions. In such topics we are required to cover both the opinions to justify both.
   - However, in the 'or' directives we are still required to cover both aspects in the discussion but we need to clearly state and justify our opinion (one of the two options) as well.
   - Same goes for the'?' directive. We need to discuss both aspects. This like in the 'or' directive shows the width of our thinking. However, as in the 'or' directive from the given alternatives we need to make a decision and substantiate it with logical arguments.

   Let us realise that we should avoid taking extreme views. Our essay should reflect our balance of judgement. This might seem contradictory with what we just saw about handling the 'or' directive. But it's not. It needs to be borne in mind that to avoid extreme views does not mean not taking a decision at all. We must realise that we are aspiring bureaucrats. The way to be a bureaucrats is not to be indecisive. We need to take decisions at the end of the day. However, balance in the decisions is brought by being able to analyse the cons of our choice and pros of the choice not made. That way when we do make a decision it is well thought out and conscious and not just a casual one. When we do make a choice in the essay with the 'or' directive we come across as an aware, analytical, rational and conscientious individual. These are few of the qualities being tested in the essay paper.

   Another thing to keep in mind is that while we are allowed to have an opinion and present it, we must make sure it is well thought out by weighing all the alternatives with each other and at the same time it must be respectful to all other views as well. In other words, we are allowed to have an opinion but we must not look down upon the other shade.

Also, when we do give a final opinion on an issue, it's advisable to avoid extreme or highly unpopular opinions. We can do so in the privacy of our minds but we should not take that risk with UPSC CSE.

2. Keeping the examiner engaged - That can be achieved through a number of ways.
   - One way can be through use of diagrams like flow charts, pie charts, bar charts, tables, bubble diagrams, etc.
   - Another way is by using questions. We have understood that we need to present logical arguments in the essay to support our opinions. One way to present our arguments can be stating it in the form of a sentence. Another way can be framing the same argument in the form of a question. For instance in an essay on capitalism while discussing its ill-effects one can deal with social and environment aspects as follows.

   "Capitalism leads to exploitation of labour to cut costs and maximise profits. This leads to widen inequality. Poor standard of living for the masses, sanitation facilities and unhygienic living conditions for working class in London in 18th and 19th centuries show this.

   Capitalism also leads to environmental degradation. Industries have no incentive to spend on environmentally friendly expensive technology, but a disincentive of reducing profits. This can be seen in both London smog of 19th and 20th centuries as well as Volkswagen car scandal."

   Another way to say the same thing can be:

   "Exploitation of labour to maximise profits is a well known issue with capitalism. But can it lead to lowering standard of living for the masses? Does the unhygienic living conditions for working class in London in 18th and 19th centuries not show this.

   No only economic inequality but capitalism lead to environmental degradation as well? The Volkswagen scandal and the London smog of 19th and 20th centuries clearly show that capitalism disincentivizes environmentally friendly expensive technology due to reducing profits."

   Of the above two which one did you find more engaging? Of course asking questions can only be one arrow in our quiver. In other words, not every argument can be posed as a question. Otherwise our essay will read more like a question paper rather than an essay".

3. It has been emphasised elsewhere too that we need to show our humanitarian and compassionate aspect at at least two to three places in the essay. This can be done by showing compassion for the marginalised sections of the society like women, children, SC, ST, OBC, senior citizens, etc., This can be done in

introduction to make a sensational start or in the body while framing and argument. This can also be done in the conclusion while giving a solution or by linking the conclusion in the introduction. The last paragraph where we give an optimistic and futuristic end is also a good place to show our compassionate aspect. All these techniques have been discussed already. An example would help. While talking about food security we can say:

"While we are a self-sufficient nation in terms of food production, it is a matter of great agony that even today 7,000 people die of hunger daily in India. Due to mismanagement of the produce children suffer from stunting, wasting and underweight. We call them future of our nation while in reality we are threatening their future and ours due to this mismanagement of food."

4. While essay is about presenting our analysis of a situation, its causes and giving solutions so it would be more desirable if we don't reproduce the solutions by committees and eminent personalities. It's great if we are able to give innovative ideas in our solutions, but it might not always be possible. In that situation, I used suggestions given by committees and eminent personalities liberally (without quoting them). This is advisable if you understand their solution, if you agree with it and if it has not been implemented yet.

5. In comparative essays one needs to show the pros and cons of the available choices and then make a choice. However, we can earn extra score if we are able to solve the cons of the less preferred alternative through our chosen alternative. In addition to this, it would be great if we are able to analyses the cause of the cons of our alternative and give solutions for them as well. For instance in the essay "is democracy the best setting for economic growth?" We need to show pros and cons of both democratic and authoritarian regimes as far as economic growth is concerned. Suppose we prefer democracy, we need to show that it solves the cons of authoritarian setting. Moreover, we should also delve into the cause of cons of democracy and try to give solutions for them as well.

6. For us to be able to score better, not only our content but also our language has to be impactful. That comes with practice. But a shortcut to achieve that is to note down powerful sentences, paragraphs, and quotations whenever we find them and start using them in our essays.

7. While selecting a topic our knowledge is the first priority.
   - We must not select an obscure topic thinking less candidates will attempt and thus we may score well. If we are not comfortable with the obscure topic we are bound to write a mediocre essay and end up with less marks. Instead, we should select a topic we are comfortable with regardless of how many people are likely to attempt it. Its true that mind of the examiner tends to compare one essay on a topic with the other on the same topic. But, its also true that everyone of us has unique way of thinking and when we apply ourselves

we will produce a unique learning which is bound to be appreciated and rewarded.

- Selecting a topic about which we are too passionate or feel strongly about may get us too excited. This might lead to a failure in writing a balanced essay. Hence, one should be calm and patient while selecting the topic. Similarly, we must cover both sides of the coin and select a topic which we can do such justice. Topic selected should be such that we do not go ranting about one shade of opinion because we subscribe to it and feel very strongly about. It should be such that we have enough content to provide a proper discussion of pros and cons of each shade of opinion in a fair and objective manner.
- Some very superficial level of brainstorming has to be done while selecting the topic. We may or may not note down the points that come to our mind just yet.
- If there is a technical term in the topic, before selecting it we must be absolutely sure that we understand it correctly. Otherwise the entire essay can literally gets derailed.

8. We must highlight/underline the core point or keyword in every paragraph. Thus in every page about 4 to 5 words or phrases must be underlined. Over underlining reduces the impact and thus the utility of underlining. Using this optimally enables the reader to grasp the essence of each paragraph in a glance, thus improving their readability and our score.
9. We must avoid making political/controversial statements. Everything we say must be consistent with Constitutional values and existing laws at all times. We should be democratic while addressing issues. We must avoid taking absolutist/extreme positions. We should try not to make sweeping generalisations on any given issue. Instead, we must exercise patience, justice and understanding in addressing or discussing any given topic.
10. Be on the look out for quotes, real life stories and anecdotes that you can use in the essay paper whenever you read books or newspapers. Collect statements by eminent personalities to support your arguments.
11. It is desirable to place the critical paragraphs at the last, however there is no hard and fast rules. For some topics they may even be used as an opening paragraph.
12. We must not question/contradict the topic itself. If we do not agree with the topic or have difficulty finding arguments to explore various aspects of the topic, then it's better to pick another topic.
13. Finally, some tips on the language that should be used in the essay:
    - Write in a clean and organised manner. Handwriting does not need to be beautiful but it should be very clear enough to be read easily. Presentation

should be systematic. Paragraphs should be well organised and presented. They should be clearly distinguishable from each other. This can be done by leaving a line blank between consecutive paragraphs. Words should be neatly spaced. While all this is not contingent on knowledge still it enhances the readability of our essay, thus translates to 1 to 2 extra marks towards the end when the examiner is able to move through our essay very smoothly. Let's not undervalue the one mark. It can literally change our service(s).

- As already mentioned a paragraph should be about 35 words. This can vary depending on the argument but should not go beyond 50 words. There should be 3 or at least 2 paragraphs per page.
- We should use simple and coherent words and sentences. Using difficult/ unusual words or irrelevant sentences doesn't look impressive. It makes our text answers look forced. We should avoid that. It has been told essay is not the test of our prowess in language and literature. Difficult words reduce the readability of our essay by making it difficult for the examiner to understand and connect with the essay. Having said that, occasional use of a powerful word, or a good phrase definitely gives your write-up an edge. But then, if we do use complex terms like 'constitutional morality' we should define it just before we use it. That way the examiner can clearly understand our point.
- We should avoid verbosity. Rather it should be crisp and concise. We should not use 4 sentences to tell what can be told in 1.
- Value addition: If necessary or if there is a scope, we should not hesitate from using examples, quotations, data or anecdotes. It makes our answers more interesting and authentic. But we need to make sure that what we are presenting is relevant and in sync with the topic we are discussing. Also, we must never misquote great personalities. It's better to paraphrase if we are not sure of the exact words rather than misquoting.
- We need to understand that even though its not a test of our prowess in the language yet a certain minimum level of command is needed to attempt the essay paper. This includes grammar. This will help us avoid verbosity and present content in a more impactful manner (for instance, by framing grammatically correct and impactful questions). Please understand that our command over language, the lucidity in our writing would not develop overnight. It needs practice and time.
- We must try and keep our sentences short. Short sentences are faster to read and easier to comprehend. Thus, they are more examiner-friendly hence useful in increasing our score. A simple rule of thumb can be - If we run out of breath while reading a sentence, then it is a good idea to break the sentence into two.

14. We must develop habit of reading, writing, discussing and most importantly thinking.
    - Participating in group discussion will improve our understanding of the topic and give new points to ponder over.
    - We should utilise the time of the day spent doing mundane activities to brainstorm on possible essay topics. One day can be spent to ponder over one essay topic. That way we will develop the habit of interlinking ideas which will help us in both essay and GS papers. We will also have a huge repository of points as well as innovative ideas even before we enter the exam room.
15. Practice time-management. Both essays carry equal marks. We must devote equal time to them. 20 minutes spent extra on the first essay will probably give us less reward than spending them for brainstorming properly for the second essay.
16. Do not exceed the word limit, as you will not get any credit for it. In case you do so, make sure you have relevant and riveting content because you are basically asking to extra-work (than reading the 1,200 words that they are expected to according to the word limit).

It is sincerely believed that the above discussion must have been helpful as a starting guideline for us to go about preparing for the essay paper. I would like to emphasise that these guidelines are based out of my own personal experience. These have worked for me hence, I have taken the liberty of sharing them with you. However, each one of us is different. Each one of us has a unique way of thing. We need to realise our own skill set and use it to our advantage. I am fond of saying UPSC CSE is like martial arts and every master has to develop his/her own style. But for that we need consistent practice. So let's be patient. Let's start practicing today. We shouldn't push it to tomorrow. Tomorrow never comes.

❑❑

ESSAY WRITING

IN UPSC MAINS EXAM

A Holistic View

2 Essay Writing in UPSC Mains Exam: A Holistic View

Nishant Jain, IAS

Essay Paper is a game changer in your UPSC Mains Exam. I would try to discuss about the right preparation strategy for Essay Paper.

First of all, let us understand the expectations of the Union Public Service Commission from the aspirants appearing in this paper. The UPSC syllabus states:-

"Candidates may be required to write essays on multiple topics. They will be expected to keep closely to the subject of the essay to arrange their ideas in orderly fashion and to write concisely. Credit will be given to effective and exact expression".

We find in it that the emphasis is on the following four points:

1. To remain completely focused on the topic:

The best mantra for the essay writing is to remain connected to the basic idea or theme of the topic. The inclination of the whole essay should be towards the topic. If you cover the positive as well as the negative aspects of that topic, and present your ideas in an organised manner, then it will not be difficult to fetch good marks.

2. To express your views in an organised manner:

In fact, an essay reflects not only the writing style of the writer, but it also reflects the writer's knowledge, experience and thought process as well. Many aspirants, though they are rich in their ideas, but while writing an essay they fail to express their ideas in an orderly, organised and well planned manner.

It is better to make a brief framework to express your ideas in a well planned manner and include the various aspects of the topic in this framework, substantiating each aspect with the relevant examples, data and quotes, etc., if any.

3. To write briefly but comprehensively:

We must write to the point, but comprehensively and effectively. Remember, you are supposed to write two essays within the limited time frame of three hours, therefore avoid crossing the word limit. Write in paragraphs, but avoid writing long paragraphs. 'Expressing more ideas in less words' is a skill, and we should develop this skill.

4. To present an error-free and effective expression:

This is the most important aspect of Essay writing. We will discuss it in detail. However, if you keep the above points in your mind and follow them while writing your essay, then your essay will definitely become more accurate and effective.

To meet the above four-point criteria for writing the Essay paper, you must keep in mind the following 10 points:

(a) **Flow:** The most attractive feature of the essay writing is its 'flow'. If there is a spontaneous flow in the essay, the examiner will not loose his/her interest while reading your essay. This will definitely help you in getting good marks. Remember, essay is an organised, well planned and sequential presentation of ideas. Therefore, while presenting your ideas, identify the interrelated ideas, and present these interrelated ideas sequentially in your essay. When you complete one paragraph and start writing another paragraph, link the beginning of the second paragraph with the end of the first paragraph. There must be a connection between the two paragraphs. In an essay, such flow can be developed with regular practice.

(b) **Balanced view:** Instead of choosing the extreme Path, it is better to take a middle path while writing an essay. Buddha's philosophy of 'Middle Path' can be very beneficial while writing an essay. So try to maintain a balanced view as much as possible while expressing your ideas.

(c) **Comprehensive views covering all the aspects:** If your narrative is broad, your expression can be more effective. Avoid the narrow ideas and use a balanced view, viewing everything in its totality.

For this, it is necessary to identify the various interrelated aspects inherent in the topic, and discuss them in a well-organized manner.

We all know, this is an age of the inter-disciplinary studies, where the various subjects/disciplines of learning are considered to be interrelated. It is similar to the syllabus of General Studies in which all the segments are interrelated.

An essay is 'the well planned and organised development of a specific topic which covers all its relevant aspects'.

To understand the various aspects of the essay topic and to develop it in an organised manner, the dimensions of essay's topic need to be explored. Some of the probable aspects can be as follows:

1. Social
2. Cultural/literary
3. Economic
4. Political/Administrative
5. Philosophical

6. Religious/Spiritual
7. Scientific/Technical
8. Historical
9. Geographical
10. Diplomatic
11. Demographic
12. Environmental/Ecological

By keeping the above list in your mind, you can develop the various aspects of the topic in an organised manner.

In addition, you must keep in mind the following points also:-

(i) Try to understand all the possible aspects of various problems/issues.

(ii) Welfare activities for the deprived classes is the main responsibility of 'a welfare state'. As an alert and responsible citizen, it is our moral duty to be sensitive towards them.

The list of marginalised or deprived classes can be as follows:

1. Scheduled Caste/Tribe (SC/ST);
2. Other Backward Classes (OBC);
3. Minorities;
4. Differently-abled Persons;
5. Women and Children;
6. Senior Citizens;
7. Marginal Farmers and Labourers of the Unorganised Sector;
8. Third Gender.

(iii) Further, there may be various aspects of development including:-

1. Education
2. Health
3. Employment
4. Agriculture
5. Rural development
6. Poverty eradication
7. Sanitation
8. Justice
9. Energy
10. Environment and bio-diversity conservation
11. Communication and transportation etc.

These tables may help you developing the content of your Essay and covering most of the aspects.

(d) Totality and respecting other's view: Try to look at the things in totality. The learning is multi-dimensional. Just focusing on one aspect of anything, and ignoring its other aspects, is not logical.

Respecting others' views ('Anekantavada' of Jainism) and perceiving the subject in its totality can make your essay extensive, balanced and multi-dimensional.

(e) Introduction and conclusion: There is no fixed formula for writing the introduction and conclusion. There are different ways and techniques for it, e.g., some aspirants begin the Essay with a saying/quotation, some begin with a story, some with the topic's background, while some begin with the basic facts of the topic. You can select from any of these techniques, or you can use some other technique.

After writing the introduction, develop the essay's topic and try to maintain a flow. Do not forget to write the conclusion in the end. There can be many ways of writing a conclusion. Mostly, we should try to present a very brief summary of the whole topic. Meanwhile, one should avoid taking an extreme view or a pessimistic conclusion. Try to write a balanced, positive and optimistic conclusion. A good conclusion should also be futuristic.

(f) Writing style and presentation: We observe that the 'taste of the food' and 'the way it has been served' are two completely different things. If the food is tasty and it is served in a nice way also, it looks like an icing on the cake. In the same way, if your ideas, facts and logics are good and effective, and you have also presented those ideas in an effective manner, it will impress the examiner for sure.

The Commission's guidelines do not clarify the presentation style much, though, it emphasises on a 'legible hand-writing'. In my view, if you keep the following points in mind, you can improve your style of presenting the ideas:

(i) Write in small paragraphs. Generally, writing two to three paragraphs on a page of your answer sheet leaves a good impression on the examiner.

(ii) grammatical errors leave a negative impact on the examiner. Therefore, try to avoid these language errors.

(iii) Grammatical correctness does not mean 'use of a pure language'. It means that you should use simple vocabulary. You may use the technical terms/terminology also, only if it is required in the context. You must always keep in mind that the language used by you should not be mechanical or artificial, instead it should be simple and spontaneous.

(iv) Many aspirants worry about their hand-writing. No doubt, a good hand writing beautifies your presentation, and leaves a positive impact on the examiner's mind. Thus, better write neatly and clearly. Readability should be maintained, so that the examiner does not face any difficulty while reading your essay.

(v) You can underline the important points which you want to highlight.

(g) Use of quotations: Sometimes, the aspirants ask questions, like 'Whether one should use the dictums/statements/quotations or not, and 'which kind of quotations should be used'.

I feel, if the sayings or quotes of the learned persons/thinkers/philosophers are relevant to the topic, they can be used without hesitation. Quotes should be used according to the context and in a natural manner. It should not appear as if it is being imposed; rather it should suit the essay's topic. Try to maintain a flow. Avoid quoting the controversial statements and also avoid using too much of quotations.

(h) Use of qualitative content: Good and qualitative material always helps in improving the quality of your essay. Remember, never let the ideological narrowness or superficiality be reflected in your essay. For instance:

(i) The ideas expressed in your writing should not reflect casteism, regionalism, communalism or any other kind of bias/discrimination.

(ii) The philosophy of life and statements of many thinkers/personalities, like Aristotle, Socrates, Plato, Buddha, Mahavira, Guru Nanak, Kabir, Tulsi, Gandhi, Nehru, Tagore, Ambedkar, Vivekananda, Aurobindo, etc., may be quoted without any hesitation.

You may use the quotations of renowned Indian and Western scholars of history, language, literature, psychology, political science, sociology, science, technology, management, law, administration, etc., as per the need of the context.

The values and ideals of Indian Freedom Movement and the philosophy of Indian Constitution is our guide and inspiration. According to the context in your essay, you can take the references from the preamble of the Constitution of India, the fundamental duties, directive principles of the state-policy and the fundamental rights.

(iii) It is better to take help of the facts and figures, wherever they are required for validating your views; but it should be done without affecting the flow of your essay.

(iv) Merely criticising the government's policies can not be the solution of any problem. Actually, it is easy to pose a problem, but it is very difficult to offer a solution to that problem.

There is a famous statement by Shiv Khera "If we are not a part of the solution, then we are the problem in ourselves".

Hence, avoid the tendency of complaining about everything. Lapses and mistakes will always exist and there cannot be any perfection.

(i) Choosing the topic: You can win half of the battle, if you select the right topic for the essay. If you select a right topic, then the probability of writing a good essay enhances. Therefore, while selecting the topic of an essay, try to keep the following points in mind:

(i) Select a topic, you are most familiar with. For example in my exam, I selected the topic, 'Is sting operation an invasion on privacy', because I had a decent understanding of this topic.

In the same way, you can select your topic from any field like; literature/ philosophy/geography/science/culture, in which you feel more comfortable.

(ii) Give first preference to those topics in which you possess enough information and understanding and you have logics to validate your statements. Not only this, you should be confident also that you can write a good essay on this topic.

You are definitely lucky, if some topics in the exam paper are similar to the topics you have already prepared during the essay writing practice. I would suggest that you should prefer such topics.

(j) What to do and what not: In addition to all the above points, you should understand the following things also which can assure a better performance in the essay paper:

(i) The habit of studying and then thinking over it, makes your ideas more mature. It also increases your power of rational thinking.

Do develop and maintain the habit of reading, writing, discussing and thinking over. Do not limit the sources of knowledge; keep reading good books and magazines and learning new things.

(ii) There is no other substitute for writing practice. If you want to develop good writing skill, better practice writing essays weekly or fortnightly and get them evaluated by some senior so that you can improve your writing skill.

(iii) Group Discussion is a dynamic and participatory way of doing the preparations which makes our ideas rich and long lasting.

(iv) Knowledge is infinite like an ocean. Remember, we have tasted only a few drops of this ocean. Therefore, never behave like an 'empty vessel' which 'makes much noise', and never let your ego come in the process of learning. Socrates, the great philosopher, says, "The only true wisdom lies is in knowing you know nothing".

(v) Have full faith in yourself and your preparations and thoughts, instead of having overconfidence. If you practice Essay writing regularly, the quality of your essays will improve gradually. Then, you will be able to write a better essay in the examination.

(vi) Give special attention to proper division of time. It is compulsory to write both the essays in the paper. So, devote equal time to them. It does not matter, if you give more 5 to 10 minutes more to the first essay. Try to write the essays in the same sequence in which they have been asked in the paper.

(vii) Do not cross the word limit, as you will not get any credit for it.

(viii) Lastly, try to maintain the positive energy. You should not lose your hope at any cost, neither during the preparations nor in the examination hall.

Always remember the following lines of Robert Frost,

The woods are lovely, dark and deep.
But I have promises to keep.
And miles to go before I sleep.

❑❑

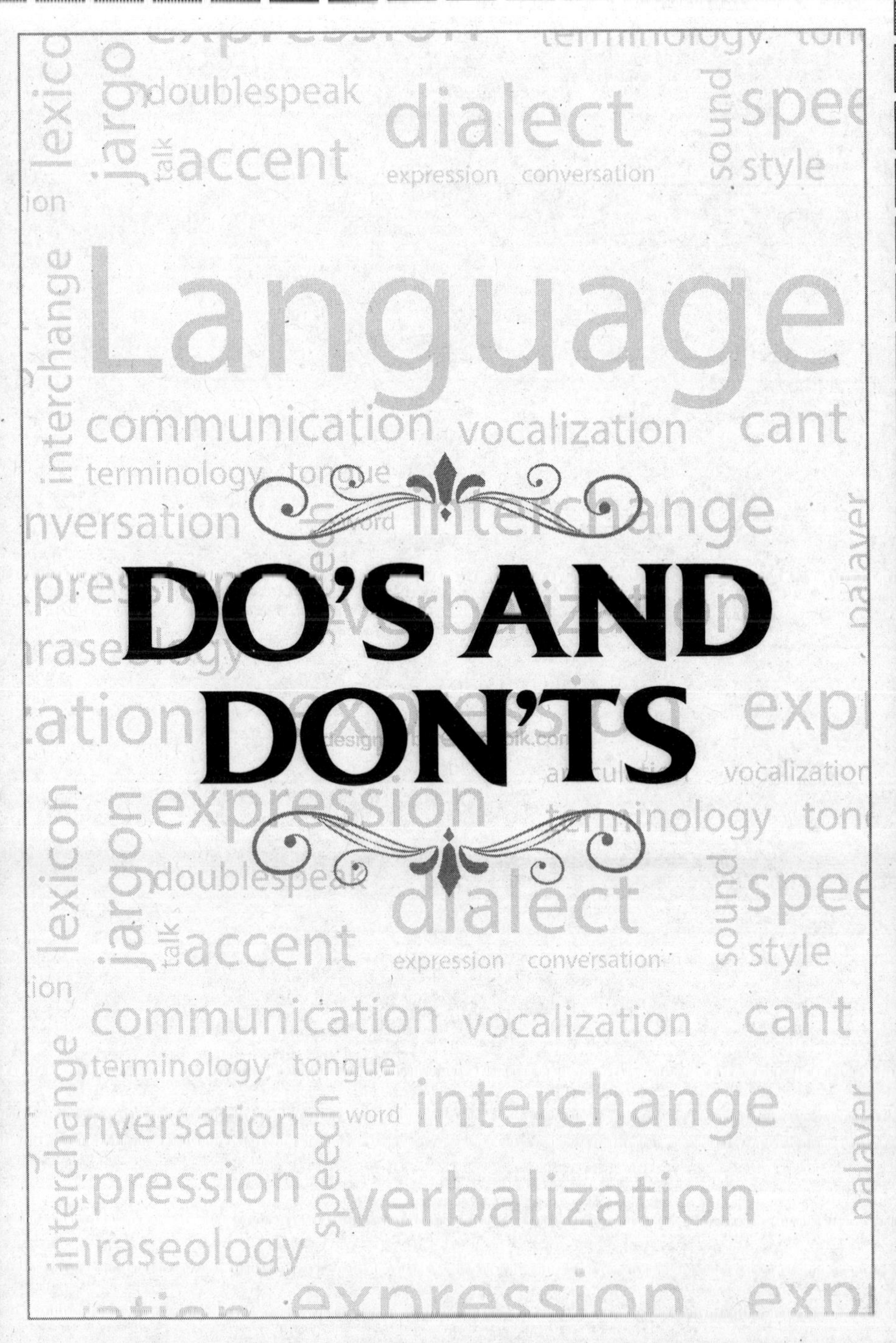
Language
DO'S AND DON'TS

3 Do's and Don'ts

Abhishek Jain, IAS

I have always felt that I am not very good at expressing myself when I write. Naturally, the thought of writing two essays in UPSC exam scared the hell out of me! However, I also knew that essay paper is crucial because of three reasons. First, it carries 250 marks! Second, the variation in marks among candidates in this paper is shockingly high and thus, this can become the reason for one being in or out of the holy list. Third, I believed that if I am able to improve my essay writing skills, then it will also make it easier for me to write General Studies answers. But, the question was what did I do? So let me summarize my strategy in the form of some Do's and Don'ts for your ease –

Do's

1. Firstly, you have to prepare for essay in a dedicated manner. It is often said that essay paper does not need any separate preparation. However, I feel that this is too big a risk to take! So, you need to keep out some time to prepare for essay writing.
2. Make notes! Yes I am right! I personally did not make lengthy notes for anything except essay. How did I do it? I scanned the UPSC essay question papers of last 20 years. If you do this, you will find out that there are certain key areas from which UPSC gives essay topics regularly. For e.g. – Women Related Issues, Education, Health, Climate Change, Fundamental Principles of Indian Philosophy, Corruption, etc. I noted down these topics and prepared detailed notes on each.
3. In my notes, I included every dimension of the topic – Economic, Political, Social, International, Security, Environmental, etc. Further, I also jotted down key statistics related to that issue as well as some good quotes which I can then use in my essays. All this might seem to be a herculean task, but, believe me, it will be worth it! This is because, the same notes will add to your answers in the GS papers as well thereby fetching you those "extra marks" that you really need to go ahead of other candidates.

4. Practice, practice and practice. Write a lot of essays on various topics and do get them evaluated to get external feedback.
5. In the exam, select a topic with which you are most comfortable with and have good content to deliver. Do not take extreme risk by going into unchartered territories as you might do more harm than good.
6. Use interesting and catchy introduction. I usually began my essays with some short stories which could be from Ramayana, Mahabharatha, World History or even my own creations. The intro should be such that it catches the attention of the examiner and makes her keen on reading the essay.
7. Ensure that everything you write in there is relevant to the topic. Please do not stray around.
8. Finally give a positive and optimistic conclusion to the essay. The conclusion should reflect your solution oriented as well as futuristic approach as an administrator.

Don'ts

1. Don't start writing the essay without proper planning. Before writing, always give at least 10-15 minutes to plan out a schema of how you are going to organize the essay and what all areas are you going to touch. This will ensure that your essay is coherent and has proper flow.
2. Avoid making grammatical mistakes.
3. Do not consume your entire time in writing the first essay only. Many students end up with very less time for the second essay during the exam. Remember that both essays carry equal marks. So devote equal time to both.
4. Avoid political or religious biases or extremes. After all, you are going to be a civil servant who is bound by the conduct rules!
5. Do not unnecessarily use ornamental words. You do not need to be Shakespeare. Simple effective communication will do the work for you!

I hope that this write-up would be of some help to you. Trust yourself and practice hard. You will surely do wonders. Best of luck!

❑❑

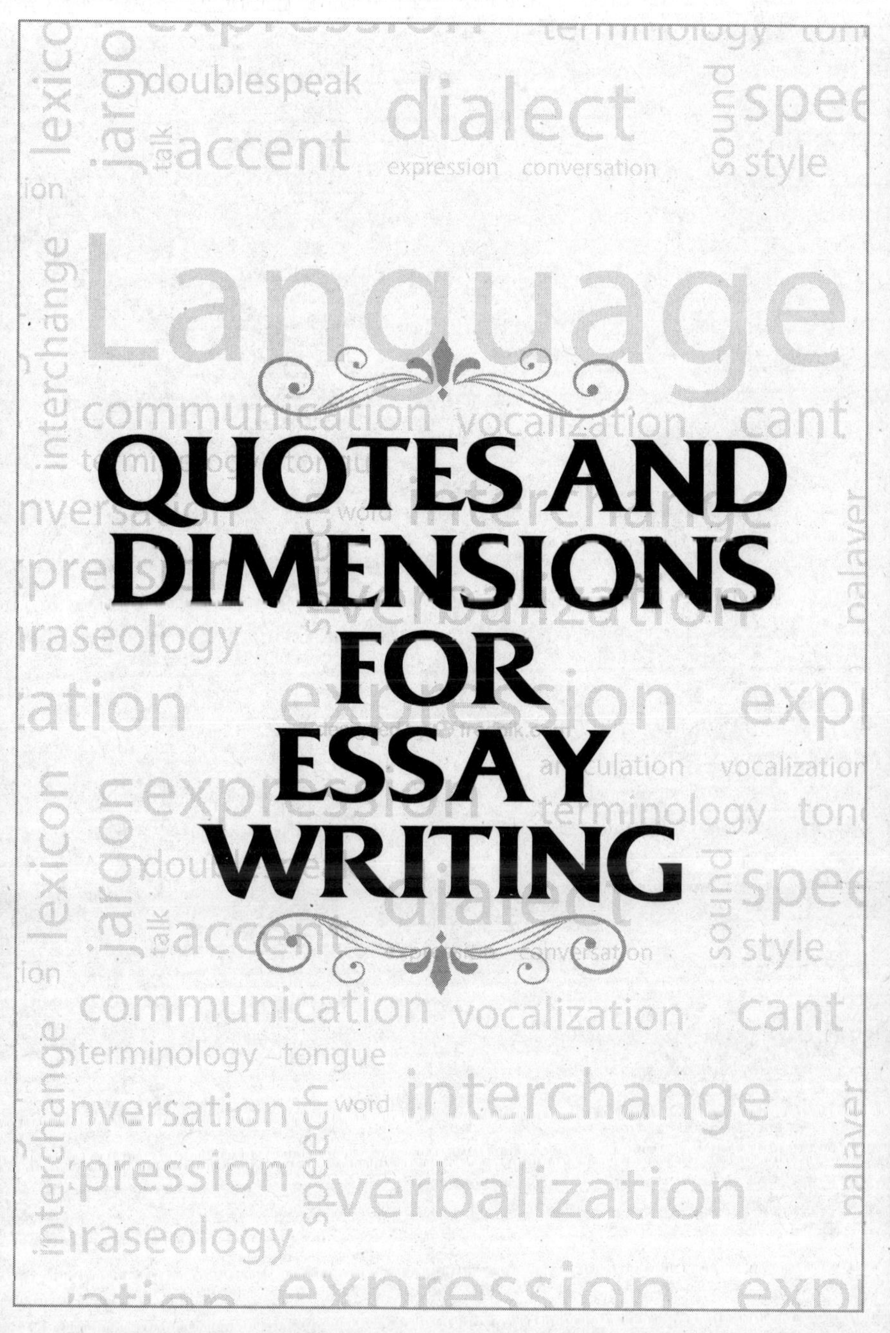

QUOTES AND DIMENSIONS FOR ESSAY WRITING

Quotes and Dimensions for Essay Writing

QUOTES FOR ESSAY WRITING

Corruption

Righteousness is the foundation stone of peace and good governance.

–Confucius

Corruption is like a ball of snow. Once it sets rolling, it must increase.

–Charles Colton

Power tends to corrupts, and absolute power corrupts absolutely.

–Lord Acton

Power does not corrupt. Fear corrupts, perhaps the fear of a loss of power.

–John Steinbeck

Peace

When the power of love overcomes the love of power, the world will know peace.

–William Gladstone

Peace and justice are two sides of the same coin.

–Eisenhower

Democracy

I do not agree with what you have to say, but I'll defend to the death your right to say it.

–Voltaire

I understand democracy as something that gives the weak the same chance as the strong.

–Mahatma Gandhi

Pillars of democracy : 3D .i.e. Debate, Discuss and Dialogue
Revolutions are the locomotives of history.

–Karl Marx

From each according to his abilities to each according to his needs.

–Karl Marx

History repeats itself, first as tragedy, second as a farce.

–Karl Marx

Science vs. Religion

All thinking men are atheists.

–Ernest Hemingway

Our scientific power has outrun our spiritual power. We have guided missiles and misguided men.

–Martin Luther King

Science without religion is lame and religion without science is blind.

–Einstein

Education

Education is the most powerful weapon which you can use to change the world.

–Nelson Mandela

Literacy is a bridge from misery to hope.

–Kofi Annan

Live as if you were to die tomorrow. Learn as if you were to live forever.

–Mahatma Gandhi

Education is the manifestation of perfection already in man.

–Swami Vivekananda

An investment in knowledge pays the best interest.

-Benjamin Franklin

Success is walking from failure to failure with no loss of enthusiasm.

–Winston Churchill

Gender Equality/Women

A gender-equal society would be one where the word 'gender' does not exist: where everyone can be themselves.

–Gloria Steinem

I measure the progress of a community by the degree of progress which women have achieved.

–B.R Ambedkar

Women are the largest untapped reservoir of talent in the world.

–Hillary Clinton

You educate a man, you educate a man. You educate a woman, you educate a generation.

–Brigham Young

No one cares how much you know, until they know how much you care.

–Theodore Roosevelt

Whatever is begun in anger, ends in shame.

–Benjamin Franklin

If you want something said, as a man; if you want something done, as a woman.

–Margaret Thatcher

Poverty

Poverty is like a punishment for a crime you didn't commit.

–Eli Khamarov

Best way to help poor is not to be one of them.

–Carnegie Mellon

Poverty is the worst form of violence.

–Mahatma Gandhi

Health

It is the health that is real wealth and not pieces of gold and silver.

–Mahatma Gandhi

Environment and Climate Change

What we are doing to the forest of the world is but a mirror reflection of what we are doing to ourselves and to one another.

–Mahatma Gandhi

We do not inherit the earth from our ancestors, we borrow it from our children.

–David Brower

There are no passengers on spaceship earth. We are all crew.

–Marshall McLuhan

There is a sufficiency in the world for man's need but not for man's greed.

–Mohandas K. Gandhi

In an underdeveloped country, don't drink the water; in a developed country, don't breathe the air.

–Jonathan Raban

We're in a giant car heading towards a brick wall and everyone's arguing over where they're going to sit.

–David Suzuki

Ethics

Happiness is when what you think, what you say, and what you do, are in a harmony.

–Mahatma Gandhi

We must become the change we want to see.

–Mahatma Gandhi

An eye for an eye only ends up making the whole world blind.

–Mahatma Gandhi

Peace is it's own reward.

–Mahatma Gandhi

The mind is everything. What you think, you become.

–Buddha

May your choices reflect your hopes, not your fears.

–Nelson Mandela

Nearly all men can stand adversity, but if you want to test a man's character, give him power.

–Abraham Lincoln

Injustice anywhere is a threat to justice everywhere.

–Martin Luther King JR

Greed has poisoned men's souls.

–Charlie Chaplin

The best test of a man is authority.

–Anonymous

I fear the day when technology will suppress human interaction and the world will have a generation of idiots.

–Albert Einstein

Science and Technology

I fear the day when technology will suppress human interaction and the world will have generation of idiots.

–Albert Einstein

Social media is reducing social barriers. It connects people on the strength of human values, not identities.

–Narendra Modi

The internet is becoming the town square for the global village of tomorrow.

–Bill Gates

Human spirit must prevail over technology.

–Albert Einstein

The real danger is not computers will begin to think like men, but that man will begin to think like computers.

–Sydney Harris

Agriculture

If agriculture fails, everything else will fail.

–M.S. Swaminathan

Children

If we have to bring real peace in the world, we must begin with children.

–Mahatma Gandhi

Child is the father of man.

–William Wordsworth

It's the greatest poverty to decide that a child must die so that you may live as you wish.

–Mother Teresa

Small hands can handle a pen better. Lend your support to abolish child Labour.

A child is meant to learn, not to earn.

Public Participation

The ballot is stronger than the bullet.

–Abraham Lincoln

Democracy is the road to socialism.

–Karl Marx

The education of a man is never completed until he dies.

–Robert E. Lee

Education begins in womb and ends in tomb.

If you think in terms of a year, plant a seed; if in terms of ten years, plant trees; if in term of 100 years, teach the people. (importance of human capital)

–Confucius

The illiterate of the twenty first century will not be those who do not read or write but those who do not learn, re-learn and un-learn.

–Alvin Toffler

If the ability of a fish was measured by its ability to climb a tree, then fish would have lived its whole life believing that it is stupid.

–Albert Einstein

Emotional Intelligence

A leader is a dealer in hope.

– Napoleon Bonaparte

Media

Whoever controls the media, controls the mind

–Jim Morrison

The man who reads nothing at all is better educated than the man who reads nothing but newspapers

–Thomas Jefferson

Development

An honest man's the noblest work of God.

–Alexander Pope

No legacy is so rich as honesty.

–William Shakespeare

You cannot have peace without security and you cannot have security without inclusive development.

–Kofi Annan

Honesty

Honesty is the first chapter of the book of wisdom.

–Thomas Jefferson

Honesty is the best policy when there is money in it.

–Mark Twain

Integrity

If you tell the truth, you don't have to remember anything.

–Mark Twain

A lie can travel half way around the world while the truth is putting on its shoes.

–Mark Twain

The truth is rarely pure and never simple.

–Oscar Wilde Truth

Men build too many walls and not enough bridges.

–Joseph Fort Newton

Compassion

Knowing yourself is the beginning of all wisdom.

–Aristotle

The only true wisdom is in knowing you know nothing.

–Socrates

Courage

Courage is grace under pressure.

–Ernest Hemingway

If you are not willing to risk the usual, you will have to settle for the ordinary.

–Jim Rohn

Learn from yesterday, live for today, hope for tomorrow. The important thing is not to stop questioning.

–Albert Einstein

Take up one idea. Make that one idea your life -- think of it, dream of it, live on that idea. Let the brain, muscles, nerves, every part of your body be full of that idea, and just leave every other idea alone. This is the way to success.

–Swami Vivekananda

Sometimes you can't see yourself clearly until you see yourself through the eyes of others.

–Ellen DeGeneres

All our dreams can come true if we have the courage to pursue them.

–Walt Disney

Miscellaneous

It does not matter how slowly you go, so long as you do not stop.

–Confucius

Someone is sitting in the shade today because someone planted a tree a long time ago.

–Warren Buffett

Don't cry because it's over. Smile because it happened.

–Dr. Seuss

You only live once, but if you do it right, once is enough.

–Mae West

Opportunities don't happen. You create them.

–Chris Grosser

Once you choose hope, anything's possible.

–Christopher Reeve

Try not to become a person of success, but rather try to become a person of value.

–Albert Einstein

There is no easy walk to freedom anywhere, and many of us will have to pass through the valley of the shadow of death again and again before we reach the mountain tops of our desires.

–Nelson Mandela

It is not the strongest of the species that survive, nor the most intelligent, but the one most responsive to change.

–Charles Darwin

The best and most beautiful things in the world cannot be seen or even touched – they must be felt with the heart.

–Helen Keller

Great minds discuss ideas; average minds discuss events; small minds discuss people.

–Eleanor Roosevelt

The best revenge is massive success.

–Frank Sinatra

The difference between winning and losing is most often not quitting.

–Walt Disney

I have not failed. I've just found 10,000 ways that won't work.

–Thomas Edison

A successful man is one who can lay a firm foundation with the bricks others have thrown at him.

–David Brinkley

No one can make you feel inferior without your consent.

–Eleanor Roosevelt

The whole secret of a successful life is to find out what is one's destiny to do, and then do it.

–Henry Ford

You miss 100 percent of the shots you don't take.

–Wayne Gretzky

The way I see it, if you want the rainbow, you gotta put up with the rain.

–Dolly Parton

You can't please everyone, and you can't make everyone like you.

–Katie Couric

There are two types of people who will tell you that you cannot make a difference in this world: those who are afraid to try and those who are afraid you will succeed.

–Ray Goforth

Start where you are. Use what you have. Do what you can.

–Arthur Ashe

The two most important days in your life are the day you are born and the day you find out why.

–Mark Twain

All progress takes place outside the comfort zone.

–Michael John Bobak

We become what we think about most of the time, and that's the strangest secret.

–Earl Nightingale

Do one thing every day that scares you.

–Eleanor Roosevelt

The only place where success comes before work is in the dictionary.

–Vidal Sassoon

Nothing great was ever achieved without enthusiasm.

–Ralph Waldo Emerson

Twenty years from now you will be more disappointed by the things that you didn't do than by the ones you did do. So throw off the bowlines. Sail away from the safe harbor.

Catch the trade winds in your sails. Explore. Dream. Discover.

–Mark Twain

Keep your face to the sunshine and you can never see the shadow.

–Helen Keller

If you always do what interests you, at least one person is pleased.

–Katharine Hepburn

If you want to make a permanent change, stop focusing on the size of your problems and start focusing on the size of you!

–T Harv Eker

Success does not consist in never making mistakes but in never making the same one a second time.

–George Bernard Shaw

Be yourself. Everyone else is already taken.

–Oscar Wilde

Non-violence is A Weapon of the Strong.
An Eye for an Eye will only make the Whole World Blind.
Non-Violence requires a Double Faith, Faith in God and also Faith in Man.
Whenever you are confronted with an Opponent, Conquer him with Love.

–Gandhiji

DIMENSIONS FOR ESSAY WRITING

LOVE

Possible Dimensions:

1. Retributive justice vs. reformative justice.
2. SC mandating the use of death penalty in the rarest of rare cases.
3. Dealing with radicalisation, xenophobia, communalism, extremists, separatists - use of strictest crackdowns (justified all the time?? Are there adverse effects of AFSPA, Public Safety Act?).
4. Persuasion and behavioural change for sustained peace - e.g. ending untouchability and caste discrimination, gender discrimination (in the long run).
5. Addressing inequality cannot be through Maoist thought but by progressive expenditure and regressive taxation.
6. Democratic transfer of power vs. French revolution type transfer (which can bring sustained peace??)
7. Spirit of tolerance for differing cultures vs. subjugation of one culture by another (real or perceived and neglected) (example. partition of Pakistan 1971, Sri Lankan Civil War, Issue of Catalonia, Demand for Gorkhaland in India).
8. Diplomacy vs. wars to end wars (American misadventures in Vietnam, Afghanistan, Middle East).

9. Anthropocentric view of environment and ecology - altering species that are dangerous for humans (mosquitoes so that they become extinct) for short term human benefit without understanding their wholesome role in ecosystem, damming and interlinking rivers without proper understanding and rehabilitation of its after effects.

Do we, in the course of our lives, light lamps, or do we snuf out the lamps or candles that exist?

Purpose: GS1, GS2, GS3, GS4 and Essay

1. Work ethic and diligence.
2. Education pedagogy - encouraging curiosity or curbing it.
3. Ethics in public relations, public service, personal relations.
5. Humility in public service - not self promotion.
6. Governance - outcomes more important than procedures ... does it help the needy?
7. Culture and tradition - civilizational values vs. obscurantism, orthodoxy.
8. Compensatory afforestation as a replacement for forests - does it really help the environment.
9. Idea of justice - social, economic and political.
10. Criminal justice system - retributive or reformative.
11. Politics - field of ideas fulfilled by gaining power or power for the sake of power.
12. Democracy - majoritarian or empowering the last person in line???
13. State - welfare state of equity or laissez faire of competition and inequality.
14. News media - as a means of education and public service or as a way of political partisanship (paid media).
15. Social media - a pillar of democracy or as a way of rumour mongering and a way to boost egos and conceit.
16. RTI - means of transparency or a way of harassing honest bureaucrats.
17. Judicial activism vs. judicial overreach.
18. Extremism, fundamentalism in the name of religion and secularism.
19. Lynchings in the name of nationalism and patriotism deterring dissent and free speech.
20. Globalisation and its ill-effects on the marginalised - women, children (forced labour or underpaid labour), tribals (biopiracy and loss of tribal knowledge), seniors citizens (loneliness as children go away).
21. Wars for peace.

Nations without vision will perish

Purpose: GS1, GS2, GS3, GS4 and Essay.

1. For dreams kind of essay and answers.
2. Policy-making to be broad-based and policy makers should be visionary.
3. Society - values of inclusion, peace and brotherhood to be incorporated in the vision for tolerance to be the norm as seen in fundamental duties and preamble.
4. Constitution makers' vision incorporated in the preamble.
5. Politics - a field of ideas to realise the vision of political parties incorporated in the manifesto.
6. Leadership of a movement has to have a vision for change and course correction to make democracy vibrant (example RTI, Jan Lokpal Act).
7. Vision for sustainable development (Rig Veda, Gandhiji's idea of need vs. greed).
8. India's vision of Vasudhaiva Kutumbakam guided our policy of non-alignment and gave us a unique place in global arena.
9. Economic vision - faster, sustainable, inclusive equitable economic growth incorporated in the budget.
10. Every culture has a vision for the civilization it comes from and helps sustain and develop the social capital in the civilization.
11. Productive and regulated use of technology (social media, AI, BD, AR, VR) possible only with individual, organisations, society, nations and world community has a vision.

Good governance depends on ability to take responsibility by both administration as well as people

Purpose: GS1, GS2, GS3, GS4 and Essay

1. Citizen centric governance.
2. Idea of fundamental duties for citizens and DPSPs for government leading to good governance overall.
3. Responsibility of citizens to vote and not go by money power or muscle power or cult of personality or casteist, sexist criteria.
4. Social audit - to be done by the people actively and facilitated by the bureaucracy responsibly.
5. Implementation of citizens charter by the bureaucracy in letter and spirit and demand of the same by an active citizenry.
6. Constitution's success will depend on the people implementing it.
7. Results of government schemes depends on the administration implementing them and citizens' participation (e.g. give it up).

8. Collusive corruption can be stopped only by combined effort of both administration and the people.
9. Coercive corruption can be contained by ethical bureaucracy and aware citizenry who can use PoCA (report after giving bribe).
10. Role of media (and civil society as large) as a pillar of democracy to keep government and bureaucracy at its toes by using RTI.
11. Role of media to bring to fore issues of marginalised (e.g. movies like Traffic Signal, Pink, etc.) and change narrative in society leading to putting pressure on government.
12. Role of media to report positive outcome of government initiative to people dispelling a cynical attitude that society holds by and large.
13. Responsibility of people to not spread rumours and forward fake news to prevent rumour mongering and prevent adverse law and order situations like riots and lynchings.
14. Role of SHGs and NGOs as partners in implementation of government schemes and as on-field partners of government.
15. Public discussion of proposed legislation and rules e.g. net neutrality.
16. Participation in mohalla sabhas to provide feedback to the government.
17. Paying taxes.
18. Role of society to not normalise corruption with a 'chalta hai attitude' and bring a 'badal sakta hai' attitude.
19. Affirmative action - government taking responsibility for the marginalised.
20. Indian version of secularism - government taking responsibility for the suppressed.
21. PIL and judicial activism - judiciary taking pro-active responsibility for the neglected.
22. Pre-LPG vs. Post-LPG - government changing roles realising responsibility varies as a provider (pre-LPG) and a regulator and facilitator (post-LPG).
23. Voluntary disclosures mandated under RTI as responsibility of government.
24. Peoples police not politician's police and community policing.

To give pleasure to a single heart by a single act is better than a thousand heads bowing in prayer

Purpose: GS1, GS2, GS3, GS4 and Essay

1. Service of the weakest is the true service to God.
2. Religion has no value if it cannot better your society and help the poor, depressed and disadvantaged; pitfalls of orthodoxy.

3. Social reform - with or without vedas, Gandhiji said ignore vedas if the sanction untouchability.
4. Compassionate society from morals as against communalism, xenophobia, caste and untouchability in the name of religion.
5. Politics - cult of personality, money and muscle power vs. politics of ideas that bring happiness to people.
6. Trusteeship rather than having an army of servants for ego boosting.
7. Environmental - Frugal and minimalist lifestyle better than consumerist lifestyle of buying stuff as status symbol.
8. Redistributive justice vs. inequality caused by accumulation of wealth by a few just for pride, greed and vanity.
9. Connecting and helping friends and family on a personal basis rather than likes, shares and follower culture of social media (mostly strangers).

Whoever controls the media, controls the mind

Purpose: GS1, GS2, GS3, GS4 and Essay

1. Article 19(1)(a) and freedom of speech and how it is subtly manipulated.
2. Fake news - penetration of all stratas of media and resultant crimes like lynchings.
3. Effects on democracy - Cambirdge analytica US elections of 2016.
4. Opinion polls and strategic voting.
5. PR teams maintained by most political parties.
6. Paid media.
7. Self control and regulation of media ... Why??
8. Right to information and its use by the news media.
9. Soft power and use of media to promote it (display of western culture in Indian media and movies – tribal and traditional culture of India).
10. Use of media for ICE campaigns.
11. Neglect of certain sections of society by media and poor discourse in society as such - PwDs, Dalits, Transgenders, Senior Citizens vs intense coverage of mainstream sections (bollywood and sports stars).
12. Perception of government, politicians and bureaucracy in society despite several honest and well meaning officers and politicians.
13. Advertisement campaigns feeding consumerism... making you buy stuff you do not need with money you don't have.
14. Gender stereotypes being promoted in advertisements.
15. Crimes inspired by movies - Bunty aur Bubly, glorification of stalking as in Raanjhanaa, glorification of smoking (under some control now).

16. Movies that talk of social issues - bringing neglected issues to attention of society e.g. PINK (LGBTQ issue), Lipstick under my burkha, trapped (lonely life in metropolitans), Citylights (inequality).
17. Glorification of Vietnam war in US hiding the human rights violations and tragedies (e.g. movies like When we were Young)
18. Control of media in China and USSR (murder, imprisonment of journalists).

True compassion means not only feeling another's pain but also being moved to help relieve it

Purpose: GS1, GS2, GS3, GS4 and Essay

1. Definition of compassion.
2. Welfare state as seen in Indian constitutional ideals of justice, equality.
3. Protection of rights of minorities in a democracy which at a bare-bone level works by the logic of majority.
4. Welfare of animals laws like Prevention of Cruelty to Animals Act.
5. Gandhiji's Talisman.
6. Citizen Centric governance.
7. Citizens charter and social audit.
8. Right to Service Delivery Act.
9. Spirit of CSR and social service.
10. Idea of vasudhaiva kutumbakam - Gujaral doctrine, Global welfare organisations like WFP, Doctors without borders, etc.
11. Idea of progressive taxation.
12. Gandhian idea of trusteeship and sarvodaya.
13. Assistance to the marginalised sections of society - women, senior citizens, children, differently-abled, etc.
14. Jain ideals of ahimsa and parasparopagraho Jīvānām.
15. Vedic tradition of living in harmony with all life forms to WHO's modern concept of one health.

An ideal society should be mobile, should be full of channels for conveying a change taking place in one part to other parts

Purpose: GS1, GS2, GS3, GS4 and Essay

1. Migration - rural to rural, rural to urban, urban to urban and international for business, studies, marriage, etc.
2. Changing values of a society and society being tolerant to new values e.g. Section 377.

3. Political education of masses to graduate from a representative to participatory to as much direct democracy.
4. Penetrating start-up culture in the country, acceptance in society that it is okay to fail and learn.
5. Vocal for local and local for global-making indigenous methods, innovation as well as local solutions across the country recognised nationally and globally adapted.
6. Secularism - acceptance and celebration of different cultures and building a composite culture by learning from best in every way of life.
7. Social capital.
8. Collective action for common problems of all so that the energy of the masses can be leveraged by jan bhagidari model leverage by IEC of masses.
9. Role of society in adapting to changing needs of time and inculcating new values to children.
10. Public morality to evolve to meet the goals of constitutional morality and if need be vice versa via (amendments).
11. Development of technology and its effect on human geography and society, society to collectively ponder on its effects and ensure that adverse effects are nullified, mitigated or adapted to in an inclusive and progressive manner.
12. Evolving definition of social contract and laws to be framed and amended keeping mind newer challenges posed by changing values, lifestyles, cultures, technology, etc.
13. Faster, more sustainable and inclusive growth but not decimate of indigenous cultures - tribal panchsheel.
14. New models of cities - rural, urban, metropolitan, 15 minute city (Melbourne targeting the idea) and ways to ensure that social interactions and liveability is ensured.
15. New models of family - joint to nuclear to live-in-relations but ensuring as they penetrate the society interests of all are ensured (especially women, senior citizens).
16. New types of jobs in economy - gig economy penetrating across classes but ensuring those employed have social security too.

Schooling confuses teaching with learning, Grade Advancement with Education, a Diploma with Competence and Fluency with the ability to say something new

Purpose: GS1, GS2, GS3, GS4 and Essay

1. Commercialization of education.
2. Difference between literacy and education - development of knowledge vs. character.

3. Role of family, society, peers to inculcate values, civic sense.
4. Nai taleem of Gandhiji.
5. Rote learning, marks rewarded for reproducing what is taught not understanding why? Less emphasis on the intellectual and spiritual role of education in Indian education system.
6. Mismatch between curricula and industry's needs.
7. Educated practicing patriarchy and caste system.
8. Flaws in Indian R&D system which lets plagiarism happen.
9. Continuing learning not emphasised in our education system.
10. Low value given to research vis-à-vis package.
11. Start-ups being seen as undesirable endeavours by parents and failure of them seen as taboo in society.
12. Disagreeing with teacher is seen as being rude but education should teach dissent.
13. Schooling promoting materialism.
14. Need for adaptive learning, knowledge creation by children and learning by doing for children.
15. Education to instil constitutional morality into pupil, role of education to inculcate values of public service, sympathy, empathy, compassion, integrity, honesty, tolerance, justice, truthfulness, love caring, humanitarianism, trusteeship, social unity, altruism, equity, redistribution, benevolence, philanthropy and in the students.
16. Aware and mature electorate through political education of masses - not go for vote bank politics.
17. No detention policy and its flaws; need for CCE, AAAC along with NDP.

At his best, man is noblest of all animals; separated from law and justice, he is the worst - Aristotle

Purpose: GS1, GS2, GS3, GS4 and Essay

1. Dictatorship (arbitrary use of power) vs. representative democracy (peaceful transition of power) vs. direct democracy
2. Rules banning the use of chemical, biological weapons and war crimes vs. peaceful settlement of disputes via negotiations.
3. Desecration of environment caused by materialism vs. environmental conventions to protect it like UNFCCC, CCD, CBD vs. tribal cultures of animism and sacred grooves.
4. Data privacy - pre and after EU GDPR.

5. Outer space treaty vs. space race.
6. Taxation laws - avoidance need for adaptation of laws to avoid BEPS vs. progressive taxation vs. bali in ancient egalitarian society.
7. Reform of election laws to face challenges of social media, paid media, money and muscle power vs. direct democracy.
8. Laws to control anti-competitive practices e.g. CCI in India, EU's fines on google, antiprofiteering authority of GST.
9. Nuclear umbrella, nuclear race vs. new NPT.
10. Gujaral doctrine and Panchsheel vs. debt trap diplomacy by China (absence of legal framework to control neo-colonialism).
11. Indian secularism with right of government to intervene for social welfare, ancient varna system vs. obscurantism and caste system.

Not let dignity be the domain of the few and injustice the everyday of the many

Purpose: GS1, GS2, GS3, GS4 and Essay

1. Compassionate society.
2. Social justice - minorities, untouchability, inequality, gated communities, ghetos, slums, homeless on roads, beggars, PWDs, oldies and destitute.
3. Fraternity, brotherhood and inclusive society.
4. Right based approach.
5. Inalienable human rights for all.
6. Food security for antyodaya.
7. Article 21.
8. Reducing inequality.
9. Climate justice and associated deprivations to poor and LDCs.
10. Universal Basic Income.
11. Client patron attitude of bureaucracy.
12. Role of society in instilling values in children.

Abraham Lincoln - nearly all men can stand adversity, but If you want to test a man's character, give him power

The essence of government is power, and power, lodged as it must be in human hands, will ever be liable to abuse

Lord Acton - Power tends to corrupt and absolute power corrupts absolutely

Edmund Burke - The greater the power, the more dangerous the abuse

Edmund Burke - Power gradually extirpates for the mind every humane and gentle virtue

Purpose: GS1, GS2, GS3, GS4 and Essay.

1. Need for democracy and failing of dictatorship.
2. Rise of caste system by asymmetric distribution of power among various varnas.
3. Power distribution in families and rise of patriarchy.
4. Humility in success and equanimity.
5. Loss of humility in civil servants and politicians - sometimes due to enormity of what they do.
6. Abuse of power in society by dominant sections.
7. Majoritarianism in democracies.
8. Subjugation of minorities - social, cultural, lingusitic.
9. Cult of personality in politics and eventual dicatatorship.
10. Capitalism (power to upper classes) => imperialism, colonialism and militarism.
11. Colonial mentality and client patron relationship.
12. Destruction of environment (flora and fauna) by the most intelligent animal.
13. Discretion (power) - transparency - accountability = Corruption.
14. Climate injustice by first world.
15. Neo-colonialism.
16. Change of Chinese stance since Deng Xiaoping (hide capabilites, bide time and never claim leadership) to Xi Jinping (claim at cost of other's right and global laws) - Belt and Road of China, South China Sea.
17. Gandhiji said political power is like crown of thorns, not as an asset, discharged with nishkam and detached way not getting enticed.
18. Alleged abuse of laws – AFSPA, UAPA, Public Safety Act, National Security Act, EIA, LARR, FRA.

Rivers do not drink their waters themselves, nor do trees eat their fruit, nor do the clouds eat the grains raised by them. The wealth of the noble is used solely for the benefit of others

Purpose: GS1, GS2, GS3, GS4 and Essay.

1. Jack Ma - When you are a billionaire, it is the trust of the society, it is the society's money... not your own.
2. Benevolence, generosity, charity, trusteeship.
3. Educated should help others.
4. Each one teach one.

5. Wealth can be any asset, skill, gift, talent - use it for greater good.
6. Socio-economic justice.
7. Corporate social responsibility.
8. Progressive taxation regressive expenditure in a welfare state.
9. Gandhiji's talisman.
10. Detached possession and nishkam karma.

One has to carry people with one - Pandit Nehru

1. Financial Inclusion.
2. Inclusive growth and development.
3. Poverty alleviation (poverty anywhere is a threat to prosperity everywhere).
4. Balanced regional development in a country or it will lead to separatism.
5. Protection and development of marginalised and minorities (else communalism and partition).
6. Consensus building and public discussion under EIA, LARR Acts.
7. Negotiations - insurgency, militancy, alienation of minorities, tribals @ LWEs.
8. NGOs and civil society.
9. Participatory democracy and universal adult franchise.
10. Progressive taxation and regressive expenditure.
11. Transparency and accountability.
12. Each on teach one.
13. Public participation in government initiatives - jan andolan.
14. Utilitarianism.
15. Social justice and equitable access to all to public goods.
16. Justice done and seen as done.
17. Tribal Panchsheel.
18. Vasudhaiva Kutumbakam.

The only real victory was one in which all were equally victorious and there was defeat for no one

Purpose: GS1, GS2, GS3, GS4 and Essay.

1. Negotiations - Diplomacy is not a zero sum game.
2. Consensus building in case studies.
3. Behavioural change by suasion not force.
4. Tolerance, accommodation, resilience of peace thus obtained.
5. Diverse pluralistic society, devoid of extremism and fundamentalism.

6. Dignity of all not a few.
7. Middle path - golden mean.
8. Social justice by compromise - Gandhiji wanted to pursuade the sanatanis and not overpower or subjugate them.
9. Inclusive politics while allaying the fear of minorities with pandering or appeasement.
10. Neither capitalism nor communism but democratic socialism.
11. Balance achieved in land acquisition in LARR and between environment protection and unavoidable degradation in CAMPA Act.
12. Mosaic of cultures - unity in diversity that is India.
13. Tribal development as per their own genius rather than 'modern' culture being forced on them.
14. Redistributive justice - progressive taxation and regressive expenditure.
15. Affirmative action.

Nations that forget history are bound to lose the power to create it

Purpose: GS1, GS2, GS3, GS4 and Essay.

1. Institutional memory in bureaucracies.
2. Intergenerational transmission of knowledge in cultures, traditions, lawmaking.
3. Value of precedents in criminal justice system.
4. Life is too short to learn from own mistakes.
5. Tribal knowledge - Traditional Knowledge Digital Library and biopiracy, AYUSH.
6. Vedic maths.
7. International relations and historical precedents - learnings from World War.
8. Deterioration of society from vedic age to later and then post-vedic age to age of Mahajanapadas to Gupta and Medieval Age leading to dark ages of superstition and being colonised.
9. Neocolonialism.
10. Traditional values and declining morals of society and challenges associated with mindless copying of the west.
11. Resorting to personality cult in politics for winning elections and deterioration of democracies to autocracies.
12. Forgetting vedic wisdom of worshiping environment and its consequences (e.g. sacred grooves).
13. Sanskrit being forgotten in India and being researched in NASA.

14. Soft power of history and culture being left unutilized - e.g. Yoga.
15. History of syncretic culture being degraded to communalism leading to civil wars, violence (Kashmiri Pandit issue) and partition (India, Pakistan) - people suffering, opportunity for prosperity being missed.
16. Traditional cures for modern diseases e.g. Turmeric (Curcumin) for cancer ... being researched.

Earth provides enough to satisfy every man's needs, but not every man's greed.

Distinguish between real needs and artificial wants and control the latter

Possible uses: GS1, GS2, GS3, GS4 and Essay

1. Sustainable development, expanding ecological footprint and earth overshoot day.
2. Intergenerational equity, balanced use of resources to counter inequality.
3. Climate justice.
4. Trusteeship.
5. Economic reasons of middle class as a base of communalism.
6. Quest for dominance and hegemony as root of international conflict, unilateral aggression (South China Sea, American lifestyle and war instigated in quest of oil, etc.).
7. Consumerism vs. Minimalism.
8. Conscience as a guide to see salvation and spiritual upliftment does not lay in materialism.
9. Temperance as a virtue.
10. Detached possession to achieve goal of justice, peace, social well-being.

Gandhiji - If I have the belief that I can do it, I shall surely acquire the capacity to do It even If I may not have it at the beginning.

Rabindranath Tagore - Everything comes to us that belongs to us if we create the capacity to receive it.

A.P.J. Abdul Kalam - You can't cross the sea merely by standing and staring at the water.

F.A.I.L. means "first attempt in learning"; E.N.D. means "effort never dies"; N.O. means "next opportunity".

If you want to shine like a sun, First burn like the sun.

Without your involvement you can't succeed. With your involvement you can't fail.

Man needs difficulties in life because they are necessary to enjoy the success.

All of us do not have equal talent. But , all of us have an equal opportunity to develop our talents.

Swami Vivekananda - arise, awake, and stop not till the goal is reached.

1. Initiative and solution to collective action problem - Corruption, Cleanliness, Health, Education And Demographic Dividend.
2. Vision, progressive building, positivity, hope, optimism.
3. Equanimity in the face of troubles - determination, perseverance, will power.
4. R&D.
5. Reform - Social, economic and political justice is needed to realise that - example affirmative action, scholarships, subsidy.
6. Case studies for motivating someone demotivated.

Bad Laws are the Worst Sort of Tyranny

Relevance: GS1, GS2, GS3, GS4 and Essay

1. Procedure established by the law and due process of law.
2. Hasty laws leading to extreme actions by executive
3. Emphasis of not rushing legislation.
4. Colonial laws like Rowlatt Act, Section 124A before Kedar Nath case, AFSPA before SC guidelines.
5. Institutionalization of injustice.
6. Extreme justice => injustice.
7. Capital Punishment.
8. Section 66A of IT Act (struck down by SC of India).
9. Aadhaar Act - provisions struck down.
10. Public consultation in law making.
11. Referring Bills to the Standing Committees.
12. Judicial review.
13. Participatory democracy - initiative where people can initiate legislation.

The purpose of a government is to make it easy for people to do good and difficult to do evil - Gladstone

1. Deterrent role of law - power of state to use violence for the greater good, power vested in governments under social contract - Institutions and government structures to provide stable life.
2. Citizen centric governance.
3. Deter corruption not create gray areas to promote it!
4. Labour laws - Licence, permit, quota and inspectors - for pro-poor inclusive growth not rent seeking or regulatory cholesterol.
5. Ease of doing business.
6. Electoral reforms to increase honest voting in elections.
7. Laws and constitutional provisions for social justice - Indian definition of secularism.
8. EIA, SIA provisions in LARR; Laws like Forest Rights Act.
9. Citizen Charter.
10. RTI.
11. Social Audit Laws.
12. Right to service laws.
13. Grievance redressal mechanism.
14. Ethical governance, 8 pillars of good governance.
15. Efficiency of judiciary - cost of delays.
16. Reduce the incentive for tax evasion and increase the cost.
17. Policy implementation - for the good of the people and not harm them despite good intentions - Aadhaar and exclusion due to fingerprints being unreadable.

Have faith in humanity. Humanity is like an ocean; if a few drops of the ocean are dirty, the whole ocean doesn't become dirty

Possible Uses: GS1, GS2, GS3, GS4 and Essay

1. Foundation of social contract - base of human existence and society - sense of good and conscience distinguishes us from the wild animals.
2. Role of society in imparting values, society as a teacher.
3. Positive ending for answers about society, humanity for emphasizing virtuous nature of human beings.
4. Reverse of collective action problem - motivation for social service - be the change.

5. Bringing about change in people by information, communication and education campaigns - people behave properly once they understand the need for it.
6. Working of democracy - masses rejecting unfit leaders as a whole.
7. Countless examples of people from different communities helping each other even during riots.
8. Good Samaritans - take an example from them.
9. Sensitisation for social change and not force - as emphasised by Gandhiji - since he believed in inherent goodness of all.
10. Non-violence for changing the behaviour of adversary.
11. Criminal justice system - even though some might be given capital punishment rarest of rare - but the design overall is reformative.
12. Systems like plea bargaining and community service as punishment to get offending people to do good for society in turn bring out the humanity in them.

To be outspoken is easy when you do not wait to speak the complete truth

Relevance: GS1, GS2, GS3, GS4 and Essay

1. Not bowing to peer pressure, going by the promptings of ones own conscience.
2. Not bowing to patriarchal injustice.
3. Claiming the right for social justice in the face of debilitating norms - e.g. Rosa Parks (African American) did not give up her seat on the bus for white man, Mahatma Gandhi's movement against racism in South Africa.
4. Rise of right wing extremism, fundamentalism and xenophobia.
5. Value of every single vote in a democracy.
6. When there is corruption in institution and you are alone (e.g. for case studies regarding nepotism in appointments).
7. No excuse for not acting honestly (a pusillanimous civil servant abets corruption at the behest of political boss, even though he may be honest himself).
8. Public participation in procedures like EIA, SIA.
9. Yellow journalism and paid media.
10. Independent directors failing in their roles.
11. (Alleged) Biased behaviour by institutions - Election Commission, Judiciary, League of Nations, WHO and other UN bodies.
12. Countries siding with one or the other superpower despite the ill-effects of Cold wars - e.g. global arms race, countries being used as props to show supremacy of either powers.

13. Speaking truth to power (DIG D. Roopa when she was posted as prison in-charge where V.K. Sasikala was jailed).

Know thy self, know thy enemy. A thousand battles, a thousand victories

Possible uses: GS1, GS2, GS3, GS4 and Essay.

1. Evidence based policy making.
2. Planning, strategising.
3. SWOT analysis.
4. Iterative improvement in laws and policy as seen in GST.
5. Managing the process of urbanisation rather than getting trapped in rigid master plans.
6. Public discussions, putting draft bills on website, transparency - know thyself.
7. International data sharing - know thy enemy better in security issues.
8. Intelligence regarding terror.
9. Power of introspection and constructive criticism.
10. Flaws of our society and reform by consensus.
11. Reform of government work culture in India - openness and colonial mentality.
12. Need for a proper census.

We have just enough religion to make us hate, but not enough to make us love one another

Relevance: GS1, GS2, Essay and Interview

1. Radicalisation based on religion; misinterpretation based on jihad.
2. Cow vigilante violence - where were these when cows were being washed away in floods.
3. Communal violence - true reason for communalism is economic inequality and not religion.
4. Sectarian conflict@ middle east
5. Extremism, fundamentalism and nationalism of the bad kind.
6. Caste orthodoxy, dalit marginalisation, khap panchayats.
7. Vote bank politics.
8. Rohingya issue.
9. Sri Lanka - Tamil and Sinhala - based on language ... religion can be replaced with culture and linguistic protests against impositions - gorkhaland, Karnataka, TN.
10. Misinterpretation of religious values - peace and love for all lifeforms is the base of all religions.
12. Truth and non-violence as the base of all religion.

Enacting of a law but tolerating its infringement is worse than not enacting a law at all

Possible Uses: GS1, GS2, GS3, GS4, Essay and Interview

1. Law enforcement - justice delayed = tolerating its infringement.
2. Fundamental rights - speech, religion, equality; SC, STs - Prevention of Atrocities Act, Protection of Civil Rights Act, Manual Scavenging, Child labour, Sexual Harassment at Workplace Act, Minimum Wage, Forest Rights Act.
3. Environmental Laws - Air Act, Water Act, LARR Act (EIA and SIA provisions).
4. Credibility of state, trust of people, violation of the rights of the stakeholders.
5. Withdrawal of people from the state.
6. Abuse of Article 356.
7. Creates an environment of impunity, anarchy and lawlessness.
8. Grievance Redressal Mechanism.
9. RTI - transparency and accountability.
10. FRBMA - fiscal deficit.
11. Independence of Media.
12. Independence of Institutions.

We have been all the way to the moon and back, but have trouble crossing the street to meet the new neighbour - Dalai Lama

Possible Uses: GS1, GS2, GS3, GS4, and Essay

1. Materialistic world + Mad dash for success.
2. Loss of compassion, social capital, sympathy, empathy, human touch.
3. Loss of social capital.
4. Social media replacing face to face interaction and hence EI - new neighbour can be replaced with another human being.
5. Against virtual reality, augmented reality and Artificial Intelligence in essay ... we want to see a fictitious virtual world but chose to ignore the beggar on the street in front.
6. Rising divorces.
7. Lack of attention to children and declining role of families in value development of children.
8. Marginalisation of minorities and their alienation and radicalisation.
9. Mental health issues due to loneliness in young as well as seniors and consequent suicides, depression etc.
10. Shift of Indian towards individualism (urban life) from collectivism (rural life).

An ounce of practice is worth a thousand words

1. Intellectual Integrity.
2. Development of work culture.
3. Leading from the front.
4. Social influence by demonstration - Be the change.
5. Role of family in value development of children.
6. Religion vs. Spirituality - pompous festivals and fests vs. following principles in life.
7. Policy implementation.
8. Diplomacy and negotiations.
9. Transparency and accountability in practice.
10. Justice should not only be done but also seen as done - long judgments vs. effect on field.
11. Citizen centric politics and ethics in governance.
12. Trust of people in government specially in LWE areas.
13. Elaborate constitutions vs. those implementing it.
14. Detailed laws vs. efficient delegated legislation with an ethical executive.

Better than a thousand hollow words is one word that brings peace - Buddha

1. Diplomacy.
2. Consensus building.
3. All party talks @ insurgency and separatists.
4. Communication in relations should be honest, frank and non-adversarial.
5. Constructive criticism.
6. Anger should not inform speech.
7. Alphabet soup of schemes vs. one comprehensive step.

The punishment suffered by the wise who refuse to take part in Government, is to suffer under the government of bad men - Plato

Possible Uses: GS1, GS2, GS3, GS4, Essay and Interview

1. Public participation, role of civil society, awareness generation and demanding accountability.
2. Core functioning of democracy - chance to everyone to participate and elect desirable people unlike dictatorship.
3. Role of press in keeping the government under check through critique of governments' steps.

4. Standing up for the rights of others or else no one will be left to stand for you.
5. Criminalisation of politics and the attitude of people that it is a dirty profession and hence decide not to vote or participate as candidates.
6. Controlling corruption and not accepting it as a part of public life or else it will always be.
7. Capable people joining bureaucracy.

Man's capacity for justice makes democracy possible, but man's inclination to injustice makes democracy necessary - Reinhold Niebuhr

King was the fountainhead of justice but with the limitation that even he was obliged to rule according to the Dharmashastras - Kautilya's Arthashastra.

Democracy is the worst form of government except for all those other forms that have been tried from time to time - Winston Churchill

Democracy as a means to bring about a significant change in the living conditions of the depressed without resorting to bloodshed - B. R. Ambedkar

Indian independence is an opportunity to build a "prosperous, democratic and progressive nation and to create social, economic and political institutions which will ensure justice and fullness of life to every man and woman – Jawaharlal Nehru

Possible Uses: GS2, Essay and Interview

1. Democracy - way to realise social, economic, political justice short of John Rawl's veil of ignorance - precocious India (Economic Survey 2016-2017).
2. Absence of democracy = authoritarianism = leads to injustices.
3. Ancient democracies in egalitarian societies - sabha, samiti, vidhata, gana - even the king was held accountable.
4. Empowerment of the weakest, upliftment of the poor - specialty of democracy.
5. Protection of minorities.
6. Modes of accountability in modern democracy - Parliamentary oversight, judiciary, elections in India.
7. Free media - essential part of democracy => enabling voice & justice to the marginalised.
8. Checks and balances by representative and participatory democracy.

Drawbacks of democracy

1. Consensus building = slow tedious process.
2. Social demand - education and heath on an infant state.

3. Parliamentary politics of stymieing bills for political gains.
4. Consolidating votes necessary as democracy runs on numbers => Vote bank politics, freebie politics.
5. Possible degradation to majoritarianism.
6. Allegations of minority appeasement.
7. Coalition and associated instability.

Gandhiji-

1. Whatever you do will be insignificant, but it is very important that you do it.
2. You may never know what results come of your action, but if you do nothing there will be no result.

Possible uses: GS4, Essay **("let us vow to.." kind of ending in conclusion of essays)**

1. Leap of faith; do your best, god will take care of the rest.
2. Nishkam karma.
3. Humility and necessity of service.
4. Taking initiative as a leader.
5. Collective action problem vs. smallest contribution can be worthy - education - each one teach one, cleanliness (what difference does it make if one litters will not work), paying taxes on time, civic sense.
6. Social influence to change society by peer effect.
7. Resisting corruption.
8. Human effort, perseverance, incrementalism.
9. Curtailing carbon emissions.
10. Value of a single vote in a democracy.
11. Value of smallest donation.
12. Not wasting resources - food, water, energy.
13 Fiscal consolidation - curtailing inefficient revenue expenditure by each government office(r).

When the rich fight (compete) the rich, it is the poor who die (suffer)

Possible uses: Essay, GS, Answer Conclusion

It is advisable to give a compassionate and humanitarian touch in each essay at 2-3 places ... such thoughts help to give such a touch ...

International Relations-

1. Cold war - nuclear weapon testing and its pollution effect on Marshall Islands.
2. World War II and the death of people in colonies due to famines.
3. Imperialism, colonialism and militarism.
4. Scramble of African Continent during competition among imperial powers.
5. Terrorism in Afghanistan and Taliban, role of west in Middle eastern crisis.
6. Soft power of western cultures competing for global hegemony obliterating local cultures.

Environment-

1. 80 people die in NCR everyday due to air pollution= SUVs (status symbol in India) are 2.5% of the fleet cause 60% of the pollution.
2. Quest to provide better lifestyle in Developed countries - coral bleaching, islands accumulating plastic debris; e.g. Great Barrier Reef off Australia, Henderson Island = most polluted island.
3. Climate Change = major per capita polluters countries competing for sophisticated life => Maldives submerging.
4. Mineral extraction for lifestyle in cities = displaced and uprooted are the poor tribals and farmers (tribals form 7.5% of Indian population, yet form 50% of the total number of displaced people).

Economy-

1. Globalisation = impact on tribals, exploitation of informal workers, environment.
2. Global financial crisis = lending by major banks like (Lehman Brothers) to make profits = poor lost savings.
3. Acquiring land under the concept of eminent domain from poor farmers.
4. Thomas Piketty - international competition for capital exacerbates income inequality.

Political -

1. Vote bank politics by cash rich parties - hollowing out democracy instead of issue based and development based politics.

The late B. R. Ambedakar: Bhakti in religion may be a road to the salvation of the soul. But in politics, bhakti or hero-worship is a sure road to degradation and to eventual dictatorship

Possible Uses: GS1, GS2, GS3, GS4 and Essay

1. Politics of authoritarianism - disintegration of USSR.
2. Need for public participation, checks and balances, Separation of power.

3. Accountability.
4. Feudal organisation of state and dark ages in Europe.
5. Theocratic state and degradation of society.
6. Caste discrimination leading to disintegration of society in the name of religion (higher castes to be venerated and have all political and economic power and lower castes to be exploited).

Be more dedicated to making solid achievements than running after swift but synthetic happiness

Possible Uses: GS2, GS3, GS4 and Essay

1. Slow and steady wins the race in GS4 case studies.
2. Planned and though out policies and IMPLEMENTATION and not half baked legislation in response to public pressure.
3. Avoid knee jerk reactions - Interpersonal relations via communication.
4. WORLD NEGOTIATIONS to reach long lasting solutions.
5. Constructive peace building through alleviation of insecurities.
6. Use of excessive force for peace does not work - AFSPA, curfews, sanctions, coercion and blockades.
7. Conservation measures for environment - not harm the economy and vice versa (Environmental Kuznet's curve does not work).
8. Economic - debt fuelled growth leading to 1991 BoP crisis vs. growth with fiscal consolidation and macro-economic stability.

We can never guarantee our own security if we cannot assure that of others - Bertrand Russell

Possible Uses: GS1, GS2, GS3, GS4 and Essay

1. Financial security - GFC crash of Lehman brothers, propel financial inclusion to leverage small savings and hence capitalise banks, informal to formal to widen tax base and increase public investment.
2. Health - urbanisation => marginalization of tribals => pushed deeper into forests => Man animal conflict/ interaction => ebola = epidemic in cities too; COVID Pandemic wearing masks and physical distancing.
3. Environmental - climate change, man–animal conflict due to expanding ecological footprint.
4. Mental - people being radicalised => terror, communalism; Carnage of partition of India.
5. Cultural security - Partition of Pakistan, Sri Lanka - Sinhala Tamil issue, Insurgency in North-East India, Militancy of youth in Kashmir (paranoia regarding cultural subjugation and economic dimensions).

6. Economic - jobless being prone to crime and violence as paid for mercenaries.
7. Inequality - social, economic, biological dimensions.
8. Physical - peace and security in society as a whole.
9. Global - ISIS + terrorism.
10. Food insecurity and consequent riots.
11. GS-4 - benevolence, welfare, rationalism and categorical imperative for a stable society.

Very important - A similar topic appeared in UPSC CSE Essay 2018 - "Poverty anywhere is a threat to prosperity everywhere"

Civilization is the encouragement of differences.

No culture can live, if it attempts to be exclusive.

Intolerance is itself a form of violence and an obstacle to the growth of a true democratic spirit.

Honest differences are often a healthy sign of progress.

Possible Uses: Essay, GS1 – Society, GS4 – Consensus building in case studies

1. Society, secularism, in/tolerance.
2. Growth of science.
3. Inclusiveness, xenophobia, regionalism, Rohingya violence, minorities, Tamil Sri Lankan issue, Partition of India in 1947 and Pakistan in 1971.
4. Preamble, Article 51A(e)
5. Public consultation, consensus building, Democratic decision-making.
6. Obscurantism vs. Renaissance, Enlightenment and Reformation.

Freedom is not worth having if it does not include the freedom to make mistakes

Possible Uses: GS2, GS3, GS4 and Essay

1. Start-ups.
2. Role of society - differentiate between honest mistake and predetermined malice.
3. Liberty.
4. Constructive criticism for children rather than damaging their self-esteem.
5. Live and learn.
6. Governance - Prevention of Corruption Act, Distinguishing between malfeasance and misfeasance.
7. Research and development, innovation - risky new projects.
8. Education - learning by doing, adaptive learning - involves making mistakes.

The difference between what we do and what we are capable of doing would suffice to solve most of the world's problems

Possible Uses in Essay and GS-

1. World negotiations - climate change, crisis in middle east.
2. Policy implementation, development.
3. Red tape, CORRUPTION, Delays in projects.
4. Leadership - breach the gap b/w what we do and what we are capable of doing.
5. Dedication to work, diligence in work, work ethic.
6. Cleanliness.
7. Demographic Dividend.

Victory attained by violence is tantamount to a defeat, for it is momentary

1. Retributive justice and its limitations - against capital punishment.
2. Uselessness of war for peace until life is in danger (war is last resort; solution comes from negotiations).
3. Cracking down on those with radical mindset for peace is counter-productive; Reaching out to marginalised communities and trust building should be the way ahead.
4. Behavioural change by IEC not punishment.
5. Social reform cannot be by violence (like Gandhiji said co-opt and convince the Sanatanis).
6. Sectarian violence.
7. Very much useful in ethics case studies.

Every saint has a past, every sinner has a future

GANDHIJI

1. Hate the sin, love the sinner
2. The weak can never forgive. Forgiveness is the attribute of the strong.
3. Non-violence is a weapon of the strong.
4. An eye for an eye will only make the whole world blind.
5. Non-violence requires a double faith, faith in god and also faith in man.
6. Whenever you are confronted with an opponent, conquer him with love.
   1. Reformative justice, not retributive justice, vengeance, retribution.
   2. Juveniles in conflict with law + Juvenile Justice Act.

3. Non-violence.
4. Moral strength needed and developed by forgiveness.
5. Ethics in human actions.
6. Radicalisation, alienation, communalism.
7. Persuasion.

❑❑

EXAMPLES FOR ESSAY WRITING

5 Examples for Essay Writing

Agriculture and Food Security

Examples-

- Karnataka's Crop Loan Waiver System - details such as Aadhaar, land survey, ration card numbers, bank data and digitised land records (Bhoomi database) and ration card records - saved in 4000 crores in double payments since Dec. 2018 to June 2019।
- Helped eliminate 8 lakh loans as non-farm.
- Farmers of northern districts of Haryana - crop diversification scheme called 'Jal Hi Jeevan Hai' - HR gov. - diversify paddy area into maize, arhar dal (pigeon pea) and soybean@ 7 dark zone blocks - 50000 ha
- Maharashtra State Agricultural Marketing Board has appointed trade representatives in other states to help farmers sell their produce in markets outside the states. As of now only the traders understand the supply chain, demand of the markets, know the key players. Farmers can tie up with agencies like Mother Dairy that run retail fruit and vegetable shops in NCR. Officers liaison with their counterpart and it ensures timely payment. Contacts developed by officers were shared with farmers online. Board will also provide farmers with road transport subsidies to carry out trade outside Maharashtra.
- Berhampur, Odisha Milk ATM - vending machine for fortified milk - eliminate the use of single use milk packets - by IAS Vijay Amruta Kulange.
- Andhra Pradesh gov. - e-Rythu App - mobile platform - farmers to market produce at reasonable prices.
- Sikkim - World's first totally organic agriculture state - Farmers traditionally never used chemicals for cardamom - Sikkim's main cash crop
- Traditional knowledge for conservation - Orans of Rajasthan
- Food Safety-
  - State Food Safety Index (SFSI) - FSSAI.

- Raman 1.0 by FSSAI - hand-held battery operated equipment for rapid detection (in less than 1 minute) of economically driven adulteration in fats, ghee and edible oils.
- Food Safety Magic Box - do-it-yourself food testing kit with manual and equipment to check for food adulterants.
- Eat Right Awards: Instituted by FSSAI.

- SMART project in Maharashtra villages
  - State of Maharashtra Agri-business and Rural Transformation (SMART).
  - 10,000 villages trained in sustainable farming.
  - Focus at villages facing the worst agriculture crisis and suffering from lack of infrastructure.
  - Assured value chains.
  - Facilitated agri-business investment and stimulated SMEs.
  - Supported resilient agriculture production systems.
  - Expanded access to new and organised markets for producers.
- Million Farmers' School in Uttar Pradesh
  - Rigorous training of staff by proper trainers.
  - Structured training modules for farmers.
  - Kisan pathshalas at campaign mode.
- Agri R&D- Investment in research has led to the development of Pusa Basmati 1121 and 1509. Basmati exports range between $ 4 - 5 billion annually.
  - Sugarcane variety Co-0238 in Uttar Pradesh - recovery ratio has increased from about 9.2 in 2012-13 to > 11% today.

NGOs

1. Microsoft India, NITI Aayog pact for AI tools in agriculture to provide Farm advisory services.
2. Consultative Group on International Agricultural Research - HarvestPlus programme - fortify major staples with micronutrients - released iron-rich pearl millet in India.
3. All India Kisan Sangharsh Coordination Committee - march to Parliament to press its demands in Dec. 2018.
4. FarmerUncle - Gurgaon-based online direct-to-consumer fruit trading platform.
5. Cooperative-based dairy activities (Saras in Rajasthan and Amul in Gujarat).
6. Zero Budget Natural Farming - Tohu village in Himachal Pradesh's Hamirpur district
   - increased wheat productivity by three times
   - reduced urea consumption by soil health cards SHCs
   - increased their income by ₹ 5,000 to 6,000 per acre.

7. Thirunelly Agri Producer Company Ltd. is a farmers' collective in Kerala's Wayanad district. It works on conserving and propagating traditional rice varieties by organic methods. Procuring them from members at a premium + selling end product at affordable price after value additions.
8. Kerala group farming system
9. Yavatmal, Maharashtra - Cotton district battled pesticide poisoning with the NGO Dilasa
   - From 22 deaths per year to 0.
   - 28,000 safety kits — masks, gloves and synthetic aprons — were distributed free of cost to farmers.
   - Awareness drive in villages.
   - Timely treatment.
   - Dedicated wards in government medical facilities with dedicated staff.
   - Cases against companies, dealers & individuals for violating provisions of the Insecticides Act.
   - Advised farmers to spray at the time insect was laying eggs => 8/10 sprays vs. 15 last year.

International

Agriculture

- Uberisation of agriculture - by developing an App based support system for custom hiring of happy seeder being used in Nigeria, Rajasthan, MP, Gujarat, Uttar Pradesh and Bihar.
- Scottish farms growing salt tolerant crops with sea water.
- Dogs helping farmers in US detecting diseases in crops.
- Farmers across China, Japan, Iran and France are using ducks instead of pesticides as they eat insect and weeds.
- German supermarket SirPlus sells food rejected by other shops due to minor defects.
- Desert control has developed a technology called Liquid Nanoclay. It is a mixture of clay, nano particles with water added onsite. The product is then directly applied on site. It works by creating a 20 inch thick soil strata that acts as sponge to absorb nutrients and water; it lasts 5 years and reduces water need by 50% thus improving the yield quality.
- Dutch Tomato cultivation
  - Hydroponic system (uses 90% less water) - Tomatoes are grown in small bags of rockwool substrate. It is made by spinning together molten basaltic rock

into fine fibres. It contains nutrients, allows plants to soak up water even when moisture levels are low (Rockwool - lightweight hydroponic substrate is made from spinning molten basaltic rock into fine fibers - formed into cubes, blocks, growing slabs and granular products.).

- Uses geothermal energy (to heat greenhouses).
- No pesticides used.
- Farms circulate waste CO_2 into the greenhouses from a local Shell oil refinery. Plants need it to grow and this reduces CO_2 released into the atmosphere.
- Maximizing yield-
  - Double glass roof to conserve heat.
  - LED lights - plants can keep growing through the night.
  - Precision farming.

- Open Agriculture initiative - open source digital library allowing you to download the specific conditions needed to grow each type of plant as efficiently as possible so you can grow them anywhere globally - saving on shipping.
- Persona group - HR firm in Japan converted its office building into city farm in lobbies, guest spaces, shelves, meeting spaces.
- Italy's underwater farm "NEMO'S GARDEN" - vegetables in airtight pods anchored to seabed; sunlight heats the interior to the right temperature to grow. Seawater in pods evaporate; condenses on roof; drip as freshwater and feeds the plants; Pods are sealed - no pesticides are needed; They are maintained by scuba divers.
- Nyon, Switzerland - Agriculture scientists fly a drone to study nitrogen level in leaves, not at farm level but at each individual plant level.
- China sent science students to live with farmers to help farmers to provide them scientific inputs; Customised guidance was provided to every farmer as per local soil and weather. From 2005-2009 the wheat yield increased by 22%, corn by 29% in Quzhou; Students got hands-on experience.
- Plant based meat - 95% less land and 74% less water.
- Urban farming - uses rainwater, heat from building's cooling system warms green house. Harvested food gets on to the shelf an hour later.
- Singapore - urban farm on top of a mall. Food cultivated using hydroponics. It does not use soil or chemicals/pesticides; Better nutrition value as the vegetables are locally produced not transported.
- AeroFarms New Jersey-
  - 95% less water than normal farms

- plants cultivated in a tray under purple LED lights - most efficient absorption of nutrients by plants, light is customised to meet the needs of plants.
- computer monitored to give exact nutrient/ water needed to each plant.
- no pesticides.
- no time need for soil rejuvenation.
- roots sprayed with nutrient mist - 40% less than hydroponics.
- vertical farming.
- food produced closer to consumers - reduces transport emissions.
- Abu Dhabi doing it in shipping containers
- 390 times more crops per sq^2 than traditional; seed to harvest 3 times less time than traditional.
- But
  - ENERGY - high energy input needed
  - Economically viable only for leafy green as need less light and have good margins
  - Investments by - Musk, Bezos
  - Only premium markets as of now.
  - Qualities of crop needed - high edible mass %, low plant height, fast growing cycle, suited to hydroponics, low shelf life, electricity access

- Food Wastage-
  - People led redistributive justice - UK - Community fridges where people donate leftover food, and the needy can borrow and thus ensures food security and reduces food wastage.
  - Startup Apeel - innovative way to make food last long by using a coating made from natural peel made from fatty acids found in peel; Food wastage = $2.6 trillion per annum; Food rots as moisture goes out and oxygen gets in.
  - France wastes 1.8% food. First country globally to adopt and anti-food waste law. Supermarket banned from throwing away unsold leftovers - They are required to give it to charities. Restaurants give carrybags for leftovers.
  - Reduce waste by root to stem cooking-peels of fruits and veggies are nutritious. They have vitamins and minerals. We can use greens to make dips, salads and dals; Fruit peel can be used to make tea. Fruit seeds have vitamins and minerals. Zest can be made from peels of citrus fruits.

- Wefoods supermarket in Iceland sells out of date food; run by volleys and profits go to charity. 30-50% discount; foods have minor flaws incorrect labels damaged packaging, and tried to reduce wastage; 800 million go to bed hungry. May be we can do this for marriage parties and party foods.
- China - kitchen waste is fed to cockroaches (50 tonne waste is fed to 1 billion cockroaches). They are used as a source of protein for pigs and livestock, medicines and beauty products @ city of Jinan
- U.K. appointed leader to tackle food waste - Ben Elliot - campaigned to reduce food binned every year by restaurants, supermarkets and manufacturers.
- Ooze company which sells smoothies - buys local organic food no matter how disfigured it looks; 40% food wasted in UK due to improper looks.
- Wasteless app - AI based app that works out which food need to be eaten based on which is approaching expiry date. This reduces prices of food stuff in real time as they approach expiry date.

Innovative Ideas-

- Impossible Foods and Beyond Meat - plant based meat can avoid corona like crises and also resource efficient, ethical protein for hungry; 95% less land, 74% less water, 87% less GHGs.
- Finnish Scientists created new protein food using hydrogen and bacteria - could replace palm oil and reduce deforestation. It begins with getting hydrogen by splitting water. It is fed to bacteria that produces protein flour; It has no taste and can be used in bread, animal feed and can compete with soya, replace palm oil.
- Refugees in Jordan and scientists from the UK are growing fresh food using old mattresses - using them as substrate and hydroponics for nutrients.
- Vertical farming - 350 times more food per acre, 1% water year round; company Plenty - 6m high towers, food grows on hanging structures using LED lights.
- Seaweed - food for the future-nutritious => iron, fibre, calcium, folic acid => low in fat and calories
    - Flourishing sustainable ecosystems - fish + mussels + seaweed
    - fish waste provides food for mussels
    - powdered mussel shells are fed to the fish => symbiotic relationship
    - fish exhale CO_2 which makes seaweed grow

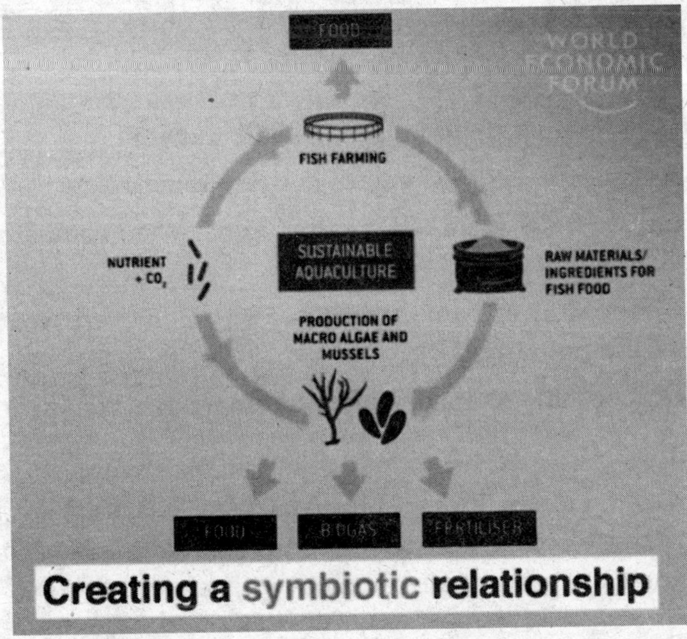

Child

Health - Nutrition and Vaccination

Examples-

- Birhors - a nomadic hunting, gathering tribe at Koderma district of Jharkhand. 5 years ago - no immunization or healthcare for pregnant mothers and newborns.
  - ICDS was introduced but Anganwadi workers of so-called upper caste refused to touch kids.
  - Rashtriya Jharkhand Seva Sansthan (RJSS) of Child Rights and You (CRY) suggested to hire a member of the community.
    - Increased awareness about hygiene procedures.
    - Vaccination.
    - Institutional deliveries.
- TN government - Noon Meal Scheme led to better nutritional, educational and inter-caste harmony outcomes in the State. Supreme court made it a mandatory policy for all States.

International examples-

- Schools in Ecuador are swapping burgers and pizza for quinoa and corn based traditional meals which are high in nutrient and low in fat, sugar, calories. They take the knowledge home. This same idea has helped Japanese kids to cut obesity and grow taller.

Marriage

Example-

- Karnataka - has made child marriage null and void.
- Madhya Pradesh - Lado scheme to curb child marriage.
- West Bengal - 'Kanyashree Prakalpa' initiative to combat child marriage and ensure education to the girl child.
  - Cash deposited in bank account of girls for every year they remained in school and unmarried.
- MWCD's proposal - to make make child marriage 'void ab initio' pending.

NGOs-

- Young Lives India's 'India Child Marriage and Teenage Pregnancy Report' mentions that secondary schooling completion rate is much higher in unmarried girls in the 15-19 years of age group.

Child Labour

NGOs-

- Kailash Satyarthi-
  - Kailash Satyarthi Children's Foundation
  - Bachpan Bachao Andolan (BBA)
    - Protection of children
    - Works with law enforcement agencies and policymakers.
    - Several laws for protection of child's rights.

Criminal Justice

International-

- Brazilian Open Jail - inmates have keys to their cells, no guns with guards, no inmate numbers as it depersonalises them, provides them education and skilling and ability to develop hobby => 20% of the inmates reoffend as opposed to 70% globally; jail is run at 33.3% cost; The model is one of trust and responsibility on the inmate. It was proposed by Valdeci Ferreira.
- Malaysia recently abolished capital punishment.
- Norway uses arts, cookery, yoga and education to turn violent criminals into model citizens. Inmates encouraged to study, socialise. Wardens and inmates eat and exercise together.

Culture

NGOs-

- India Pride Project - protecting Indian antiquities and involved in repatriation of works.
- Indian Trust for Rural Heritage and Development (ITRHD): preservation of Indian Heritage and Culture in Rural India.

International-

- Mindfulness and meditation is a part of curriculum in 370 schools in England.

Differently-abled People

- Willem Johan Kolff is the father of artificial organs and pioneer of hemodialysis was dyslexic.
- Helen B. Taussig founded the field of paediatric cardiology. As an adolescent she struggled with dyslexia.
- Supreme Court mandated those with colour blindness should not be discouraged from taking the MBBS exam.
- World's first IT campus for diffrently-abled people has been set up in Hyderabad.
- Varun Khullar was paralysed waist down by an accident in Manali in 2014 and became wheelchair bound. He studied music and is now a resident DJ at a club in New Delhi.
- Divyanshu Ganatra was 19 when glaucoma claimed his eyesight. Today he runs an adventure sport company.
- Nidhi Goyal lost her degenerative eyesight to disorder at 15. She converted her subsequent dating misadventures into an internationally acclaimed stand-up comedy sketch.
- MA Johnson rendered immobile by polio at 6 months of age. Yet he could pioneer in the manufacture of LED bulbs in India. He runs an electronics industry and a network of service centres across the Kerala.

International-

- Camphill Movement has 100 communities globally. In a Scottish Village called Newton Dee people with learning disabilities live with carers. They help their housemates to develop careers and do productive work in a supportive community like working on a farm, garden, houses, cooking clean and machine skills, social identity.

NGOs-

- Sambhavna filed a case in Delhi HC to redress the fact that in JNU no post reserved for PWDs - Delhi HC case.

- National Centre for Promotion of Employment for Disabled People (NCPEDP) has shown that 84% seats reserved for PWDs in higher education institutions are vacant.
- Disability Rights India Foundation (DRIF) conducted a study of Rights of Persons with Disability Act across 24 States and found out that more than half have not notified the State rules.
- Bhagwan Mahaveer Viklang Sahayata Samiti has lauched India for Humanity initiative with MEA and is distributing artificial limb fitment camps world over.
- Buddhist Association for the blind, Saavi Foundation and Swagat Thorat are working on first ever constitution in Braille.
- Anuprayaas has been the driving force behind India's first blind friendly station.

ECONOMY

Government-

- Affordable housing by Gujarat government for migrant labourers in Bhuj so that they can save more.
- Hunnarshala Foundation.

NGOs-

- Ministry of Rural Development + Maruti Suzuki India Ltd. - MoU for Training Rural Youth for Skill Development under Deen Dayal Upadhyaya-Gramin Kaushal Yojana.
- Champion Employers and Industry leaders are providing training and captive employment to Deen Dayal Upadhyaya-Gramin Kaushal Yojana candidates (DDU-GKY), strategic alignment of objectives of DDU-GKY with HR strategy of organizations.
- Infosys has launched a digital learning platform, offering curated content to engineering students in their 3d and 4th years. The idea is to create more industry ready talent among fresh graduates.
- Lego foundation and education charity Porticus have invested $ 8.8 million in playlabs - Uganda, Tanzania, Bangladesh. In these playlabs, kids choose own activities from reading stories together, painting and drawing, playing outside. This helps them develop self expression by dance, songs, stories, crafts - labs are operated by NGOBRAC.
- CII launched Fiscal Performance Index which incorporates qualitative assessments of revenue & capital expenditure, revenues, fiscal prudence and level of public debt.

International-

- Singapore most competitive economy - skilled workers, cutting edge infrastructure, openness to immigration, business friendly laws and tax policies.

- What Bangladesh did right to achieve rapid economic growth - demographic dividend, digital tech, garment industry and knowledge based society - tech hub in Dhaka; tax breaks to entrepreneurs, 100 SEZs.
- France and Germany have enacted right to disconnect laws
  - In France employees unreachable on smartphone outside of work hours cannot be tagged for misconduct.
  - In 2015, EU mandated time spent in commute (to and from work) as work.

Innovative Ideas-

- Eco-tourism - esnure boost to local economy and ensure their participation, use the proceeds to conserve species. Also use it to run schools and health clinics.
- NZ companies are giving a four-day workweek - 20% more productivity.
- Time banks where you can have account for hours of services rendered and get the services you need in return whenever you need it so there is no problem of double coincidence of wants as there used to be in barter system.

Education

Government

- Project Second Innings in Dahod (an Aspirational District) drafting retired teachers to sign up voluntarily for remedial classes where they can learn reading, writing and maths
- Delhi
  - happiness curriculum
  - entrepreneurship mindset curriculum.
  - special classes for academically weaker students
  - exams practice
  - home counselling to improve attendance
  - better training for teachers and administrators
  - Improved physical infrastructure
- Welfare of migrant children-

- Punjab-
  - Cash awards given to teachers at learning outcomes
  - ₹ 900 crore smart school projects
- Karnataka school teachers were given instructions to improve students' strength or get transferred; Report cards were given to teachers based on the performance of students.
- MP - Digi enabled teaching at 15000 schools.
- Roping in social groups to improve facilities at school, Government Primary School at Berkhedi-
  - Perfect execution of community participation model.
  - Headmaster Prakash Musre - quality education to the students and increasing student enrollment.

NGOs-

- Vijaya Mulay was an icon of educational technology
  - She was a pioneer of animated films for children. Her short film, 'Ek, Anek Aur Ekta' - Internet became a hit.
  - She warned against the tendency of using technology for replicating and magnifying entrenched systemic weaknesses.
- Banka Unnayan Abhiyan-
  - Interactive online and offline study method.
  - Interactive concept videos, real-time doubt-clearing, examination and digital report card generation.
  - Teaching Class IX and Class X students through smart classes and Eckovation app.
  - Banka district's 70 schools under a project that was started in August 2017.
  - Replicated by Unnat Bharat Abhiyan in schools of about 5,000 villages across the country.

International-

- Ecole 24 - school in Paris which does not have teachers, a fixed curriculum; It works on a co-learning model where students teach each other.
- Brown university is ending the culture of student loans. Best education for less wealthy students; students assessed academically and at success given a grant for education fees.
- In Iceland people give each other books on Christmas eve then spend the night reading them - it is the 3rd most literate country.
- Denmark schools where students grow their own food in large rooftop gardens. Food grown is used in cookery classes.

- Shanghai model of inclusive education - class does not advance until every kid has finished the task.
- Finland is teaching children the skills of future – collaboration, communication, diversity, tolerance and creativity.
    - Kids start school at 7. They spend early years playing at subsidised pre-schools based on learning through playing. One standardised test is conducted at end of high school. Otherwise teachers set their own grading system. Teachers have masters degree in education. They can develop flexible education strategies best suited to children.
    - Students choose between 2 paths for high school. University or vocational education comprising of apprenticeships and can switch between the two too. University education is free. Adult education is promoted and subsidised.
    - Education is free for all. Equal access to education is a constitutional right.
- Why kids in Estonia do better in learing and education-
    - Teachers are required to have masters degrees, and are paid handsomely.
    - Teachers have freedom to design their own pedagogy within the confines of a curriculum
    - Adopting digital tech + put digital skills in the curriculum; by 2020 every school must use only digital learning materials
    - Free books, transport, lunch
- UK is shifting maths classes outdoors. Closer to nature kids concentrate more, learn better. Teachers enjoy more. This leads to better health and creativity.
- Norway - Kindergarten kids spend 70% school time in the summers outside; Finland, Singapore too.
- In Japan school kids help prepare, serve and clean up their school lunches and use the veggies grown in terrance gardens - learn about healthy eating and responsibility. Subsidised lunches are mandatory. Balanced meal created by nutritionists.
- South Korea - Fail expo where people are taught it is okay to fail. The idea is to change attitudes towards failure. Meet other job seekers and entrepreneurs who have struggled and learn about the schemes that could support them. Inspired by Finland's International Day of Failure, Museum of Failure in Sweden.
- UNESCO Asia Pacific Regional Bureau on Education's Happy School Project and Happy School Framework
    - Launched in cooperation with MGIEP
    - Social & emotional learning curriculum - Libre
        - Critical inquiry
        - Mindfulness

- Compassion
- Empathy

NGOs-

- ASER
- Sonam Wangchuk - the educational reformer and muse for 3 idiots movie led the Ladakh Students' Education and Cultural Movement of Ladakh to coach Ladakhi students under the name - Operation New Hope. Before that 95% students used to fail the government exams.

ELECTORAL DEMOCRACY

Govt.

- State Election Commission of Maharashtra
  - June 2013 order: if NOTA gets the highest number of valid votes then elections to the particular seat is countermanded and fresh elections are conducted; However the same candidates are allowed to contest new election.
- State Election Commission of Haryana - if all contesting candidates individually get less votes than NOTA then none is declared as elected and all the contesting candidates are ineligible to recontest re-election.

Examples-

International Examples-

- Lessons which India can adopt from Bhutanese Election System
  - Election Commission of Bhutan (ECB) provides for public campaign finance
    - allocation of finances
    - monitoring, auditing
    - strict penalties for misuse
  - Election Act 2008 bars religious personalities from joining a political party participating at electoral process.
  - ECB provides for common fora for parties to address electorate at specified venue for electioneering.
  - 2 public debates - presidents of parties/ nominees take part.
  - Strict guidelines for all media outlets - submit undertaking on responsible reporting and create a level playing field.
  - Social media rules and regulations ensure accountability and responsibility.
  - Election advertising, media coverage of elections rules and regulations, code of conduct for media persons ensures check on misuse of mass media.

- 70% of the voters in the 18 constituencies in Chhattisgarh that went to polls in Nov. 2018. In districts marked as the worst affected by Maoist violence in the country - voters voted in with the conviction saying how many fingers can dadalog chop off?
- UK - independence of the Speaker is secured - no party contests against Speaker in the next general election.

NGOs-

- #PowerOf 18campaign: by Twitter India - encouraging youth to conduct public debates and civic engagement for the 2019 general elections. Resource platform for youth to find information on elections, social causes and join public conversation.

Innovations-

- AI Biometric voting machine which can be directly linked to the aadhaar details of a person. It will use the finger print to verify identity. This will help to void fraudulent voting; It helps voting in the city of your residence without having to travel to the constituency where you are registered.

Energy

Examples-

Government-

- Punjab - farmer given refund for the units of free electricity they didn't consume.
- Jharkhand - 249 remote villages powered by solar microgrids.
- Indian Railways to run on 25% solar power by 2025.

International

- S-Park - It's system that consists of a front bicycle wheel, and bike rack. As a rider bikes around, the spinning front wheel stores kinetic energy in batteries. When the bike is parked at the S-Park rack, that energy flows out to the area's electric grid.
- Company Ten Fold Engineering - house that is an elaborate mechanical system and can unfold in less than 10 mins; foldable units can expand to 3 times the size. Uses sunlight and heat during the day by unfolding and traps heat inside by folding in the evening.

International

- Scotland putting giant turbines at the bottom of the sea to generate energy from the power of ocean
- Tesla by Elon Musk - 100MW battery system online in South Australia can store and sell energy now.

- American Cities putting turbines in water pipes to generate clean energy - Portland in areas of gravity flow, Riverside (California) powers the water system, powers street lights.
- Renewable energy is Germany's 40% source of power; 65% by 2030.
- World instals 70,000 solar panels every hour over the next 5 years; China is leading by installing 50% of new solar capacity in 2016 due to low cost, high efficiency, political will.
- UK in April 2017 ran without coal for the first time since industrial revolution; In June - wind, nuclear and solar energy output was more than natural gas and coal; UK has been able to wean itself off of coal but is dependent on natural gas as an energy source; Contribution of renewable energy in UK's energy mix has been more than coal for 90% of 2017.
- China
  - Invested $130 billion in 2017 in clean energy, Increased by 24% compared to 2016
  - More investment in wind, solar and hydro power than any other
  - Solar plant over man made lake over collapsed coal mine - reduces land required, cooling increases efficiency
  - Produces 66.6% of world's solar panels
  - Doubled solar capacity in 2016
- Since 2017 - 50 coal fired power plants in US have shut, creating 1,10,000 new renewable energy jobs.
- California-
  - New homes mandatorily need to have solar panels
  - Public buses are being transformed in zero emission
  - Building massive battery storage system - renewable energy gives 44% of state power
- Half of all cars sold in Norway in 2018 were electric - free parking, access to bus lanes, tax incentives.
- UK is the first G7 country to have a net zero emission target by 2050 enshrined in law now.
- Sweden is using heat from servers to heat the homes and offices by circulating water to extract the heat from the servers and then heating houses.
- Steps taken by Netherlands towards circular economy
  - Bike lane has been made out of used and recycled toilet paper. The paper is dried, sterilized and bleached. The fluffy stuff with high cellulose content is extracted and it replaces plant based cellulose in asphalt. Dutch have more bicycles than people. It has 35k km of bike lanes.

- Bike path made out of recycled plastic.
- Dutch companies are making phone called Fairphones. These are built to last. They can be repaired and recycled easily. Their components is responsibly sourced.
- The Edge is a series of smart sustainable building which have solar panels power phones, laptops, electric vehicles. They have upto 30000 sensors which continuously track movements and temperature and thus optimize energy usage based on need. They use 70% less electricity than peers.
- Netherlands is producing 100% carbon neutral electricity.
- It intends to halve its usage of raw materials by 2030.

Innovative Ideas-

- Vertical faced windmills - reduce bird hits and group efficient.
- Smart flower - flower made of solar panels follows the sun throughout the day to ensure maximum clean energy is produced.
- Solatube is a daylight system which uses roof-mounted domes which use refraction to get light into windowless rooms. Light travels in thin tubes lined with special materials that reflects 99.7% of the natural light. It brings natural light indoors by redirection and tube is also fitted with solar cells.
- Kids used solar panels to generate electricity, and then passed the electricity through sewage water to decompose it into hydrogen and oxygen gas.
- Microgrids enable the people to become prosumers (producer and consumer). Microgrid controllers - enables decisions regarding net metering modulated by demand of prosumers. The system also uses weather forecast and projected trends of energy production. Thus, it can adjust intake and outgo of energy.
- Smart grids to adjust prices to keep up with supply and demand by learning about peoples consumption habits. People even get messages in their thermostat/ smart devices that they could financially benefit by delaying consumption.
- Smart distribution system - shows us how and when what amount of energy is moving around.
- Ways to storge energy compressed air, batteries, hydropower.
- Organic solar cell or plastic solar cell is a type of photovoltaic that uses organic electronics - conductive organic polymers or small organic molecules, for light absorption and charge transport to produce electricity from sunlight by the photovoltaic effect. Most organic photovoltaic cells are polymer solar cells.
  - They have lower efficiency (33.3%), lower stability and lower strength vs. inorganic photovoltaic cells aka silicon solar cells.
  - Lightweight, disposable and inexpensive to fabricate (can be fabicated using even printed electronics), flexible, customizable at molecular level, less

adverse environmental impact. They exhibit transparency. and hence can be used even on windows, walls, flexible electronics.

- But with leaf design efficiency can be increased by 47% (10-15% needed for commercialisation); In leaf design wrinkles and folds relieve mechanical stresses from bending.

ENVIRONMENT

Air

Examples

- Bhubaneswar has become 0.5°C hotter due to urbanisation between 2000-2010.
- Electric scooter sales doubled in 2017-18 vs. last year. Car sales halved in the same period. Charging cost of 2 wheelers are about 10% for same distance.
- e-rickshaw 'Namma Auto' - launched to promote the shift to less polluting autorickshaws in Bengaluru. Model for adoption EVs:
  - Systematic adoption of EVs by coordination of urban planning, transportation and power sectors.
  - Center for Study of Science, Technology and Policy (CSTEP) has developed suitable routes for e-buses in city.
  - Analysed constraints:
    - Location and size of depots
    - Schedule of buses
    - Electrical loading of the distribution network
    - GIS platform and incentives
- Jharkhand government introduced EVs for official use.
- Odisha - Public bicycle sharing system - 'Mo Cycle' system.
- Delhi government launched an Open Transit Data Platform for real-time data for use by 3rd party app developers and researchers. They use the data to develop transport solutions. Geo-coordinates of all bus stops, route maps, timetables and locations of all buses with 10 sec lag GPS feeds.
- India to make every public vehicles electric by 2030 - Bengaluru home to India's first and largest electric only cab service.
- MoEFCC
  - Harit Diwali-Swasth Diwali" campaign
  - "Green Good Deed" movement - Idea is of social mobilization for preserving, conserving and protecting environment
- Genetically modified common indoor plant - Pothos plant ivy
  - Removes pollutants in the air in the house

  - Benzene or chloroform gas
  - Concentration of chloroform dropped by 82% and became undetectable by day six
- Gujarat launched India's first trading programme to combat particulate air pollution - PAT kind of model.

NGOs-

- No Burn Farm campaign works to communicate to farmers that crop burning is not the best method.

International

- UK first G7 to have a net zero emission target by 2050 - enshrined in law now - as of now cut 80% by 2050 with respect to 1990.
- Car free zones-
  - Australia is building neighbourhoods where you do not have to use a car called 20 minute neighbourhood in Melbourne - work, medical help, education and recreation are just 20 min away - foot, bike or bus.
  - NY Times square - once a congested area now a car free pedestrian zone.
  - Barcelona is targeting to be a post car city
  - Hamburg, Germany - 40% of the road area by bike and walk ways.
  - Open streets movement - take cars off the road for one day for about 120 km stretch in Bogota on Sunday - instead of cars there is imaginative community type use of roads like fairs and gatherings.
  - Oslo - removed parking spaces in the downtown area and build benches, tiny parks and bike lanes.
  - Paris goes car free for one Sunday every month.
  - Brussels is cutting 25% of its on street parking places - providing extra space for pedestrians, cyclists and public transport.
  - Banning polluting vehicles - Madrid (from city centre), Paris, Brussels, Copenhagen.
  - Partial ban on polluting - New York and Portland.
  - France wants to triple the number of cyclists. 350 million euros have been invested in new bike paths. New ones have been connected to old ones. New buildings will have bike parks. By 2022 every high school will offer cycling lessons. Tax incentives are being provided by purchasing cycles. Paris - 400 miles of bicycle lanes in 2007; Developed bike sharing programme. Vélib is the largest and most used at West.
  - Norway witnesing a boom in electric cars due to the efforts of the government.
    - 30% of all new cars being sold in Norway are electric as opposed to 2% in Europe and 1-2% in U.S.

        - Subsidies and perks are being given to the buyers.
        - Target is to sell only zero-emissions cars by 2025.
        - Government waived hefty vehicle import duties, registration and sales taxes.
        - Exemption from road tolls and free use of ferries, bus lanes in congested city centres.
    - Parts of Tokyo and Kyoto - pedestrianized certain streets.
    - Copenhagen has banned motorized vehicles in the 1960s. 200 miles of bike lanes have been developed in the city and 50% of the population bikes to work.
    - São Paulo has banned Sunday movement of motor vehicles on Paulista Avenue (marker of Brazil's economic vibrancy and rising global stature). It has given booster shot to city's cultural scene and has helped breaking barriers between people.
- England has targeted to achieved zero emissions in double-decker bus by retrofitting them to run on hydrogen.
- Scotland has launched 1st hydrogen powered seagoing ferry.
- Japan is promoting and using hydrogen powered vehicles and is working on increasing hydrogen refueling stations.
- Norway's steps to promote sale of electric vehicles:
    - No sales tax
    - No annual road tax
    - Lower tolls on roads
    - No parking fees in public car parking
    - They can drive in bus lanes
    - Installed charging points all over the country
- Europe - sleeper trains are making a comeback as alternative to flying; Austria launched one - Vienna to Brussels, UK - London to Scotland; Sweden has coined a word for flight shame - flygskam.
- Netherland has more cycles than people and quarter of all trips are by bicycles - government support by tax free incentives for work commutes and infra (cycle lanes, parking spots, carriage racks on buses.

CLIMATE CHANGE IMPACTS

- Melting glaciers can destroy villages on coast by giant waves even tsunamis. Innaarsuit island in northwestern Greenland next to 100 m high glacier.
- Munroe Thuruthu, Kollam district is slowly going under water, fleeing residents are becoming climate refugees. Climate change is forcing someone to flee home every 2 secs creating a refugee crisis.

- Forest fires within the Arctic circle are increasing.
- 2019 was one of the hottest years on record, wild fires in Portugal and Chile.
- 2017 was the most expensive hurricane season on record, flooding affected millions in South Asia.

Government

- NIT Rourkela, Odisha - discovered a marine bacterial strain (Citrobacter species) that can produce ethanol directly from fruit waste.

NGOs-

- Non-State Actor Zone for Climate Action (NAZCA) has been working with UN and has been able to get 12,500 pledges by 2,500 cities, 209 regions and more than 2,100 firms and 500 investors for actions to reduce carbon emissions.

International-

- Mexico producing plastic and biofuel from cactus
- AI can help fight climate change by monitoring deforestation to designing low-carbon materials.
- NZ is putting climate change at the heart of every decision. The idea is to judge any new policy by how it will affect the planet. Net zero emission by 2050, 1 billion trees by 2028. Banned new offshore oil and gas exploration.
- Whales are vital in the fight against climate change as they store a lot of carbon in their bodies. There is carbon worth about a 1000 trees in 1 whale. It helps phytoplankton grow.
- EU's GHG emissions down by 23% since 1990, GDP up by 62%.
- US cities and states remain committed even after Trump pulled out of the Paris Accord.
- Bologna - incentivises people with beer and ice cream for people who walk, bike or use public transport. The app uses GPS to log credit points.
- Beijing and London - Empowered city mayors and local councils to combat climate change.
- Shenzhen - first city in the world to electrify 100% of its buses. Now it is doing same with taxi fleet (as of now 65% in Jan 2019) bus charging points, subsidies to public transport companies has led to rapid sales growth.
- Karachi's public buses to run on biogas - 3,200 tonnes of dung to be used to run the zero emission Green Bus Rapid Transit (BRT) network. The network has 200 buses fuelled by biomethane.
- Germany has launched the world's first hydrogen powered train. It emits steam and water. It is cheaper to run but expensive to buy.

- Luxembourg to make public transport completely free including trains, trams, buses.
- Transit based development based on metro. However, there is last mile connectivity issue. For this, Netherlands has developed bicycle parking station underneath the Utrecht railway station hub - 6000 bikes.
- Sweden built a road that can charge electric vehicles so that vehicles go long with small batteries.

Innovations-

- AirCarbon - a polyhydroxyalkanoate (PHA)-based thermoplastic. - High-performance plastic made with carbon captured from emissions; Uses biocatalyst that combines air and methane, reassembles carbon, hydrogen and oxygen molecules into a thermoplastic - makers call AirCarbon.
- Zelfo Technology - engineers cellulosic and ligno-cellulosic fibres from a wide range of sources including industrial, agricultural and horticultural waste streams to impart user specific fibre properties including a high degree of defibrillation. It multiplies the binding capability of the material by a factor of several thousand. It stores carbon at the same time.
- Wooden skyscraper-
  - Wooden HoHo tower is a hotel, residential and commercial building in Vienna - 84 m and 24 storey.
  - T3 project in Minneapolis
  - Sakyamuni Pagoda in China is the oldest wooden building (about 900 years old).
  - Globally concrete and steel are responsible for 8% and 5% emissions respectively.

LAND–

Government

- Miyawaki method of afforestation in Japan-
  - Build dense, native forests
  - Plant growth is 10 times faster + 30 times denser
  - Planting dozens of native species => maintenance-free after 3 years.
  - Create such forests in small urban spaces~ 30 sq. feet.
  - Telangana green drive at Telanganaku Haritha Haaram (TKHH), Khammam is following this method.
- Sustainable approaches to land and forest conservation in Mendha-Lekha village in Maharashtra.
- Van Dhan Yojana by the Rajasthan can be scaled up towards building a green mission to save our non-protected forests (outside the existing national parks and sanctuaries).

- India in green mission-
  - MP planted 66 million trees in 12 hours, 1.5 million volunteers broke the world record at the expense of $6.2 billion in 2017.
  - Target to increase the forest cover to 95 million hectares by 2030.
  - Kerala–10 million trees planted in the green carpet initiative to promote ecotourism and carbon neutrality.
  - Bengaluru council has developed an App for people to order free saplings.
  - Uttar Pradesh planted 50 millions trees in just 24 hours in 2016.

NGOs-

Cultural religion in India - guidelines to counter the recklessness in the name of development.

- Hindu Vedic principles of Satya Dharma (moral duty of communities to maintain cosmic natural order); Myth - Krishna punishing the serpent Kalia who polluted the river Yamuna; Mythical mountains Meru and Kailash - centre and axis of the world habour soil, vegetation and water.
- Sikhism (integrated approach to life and nature).
- Islam and Sufism (tawhid - all things in the world are related to one another and are as aspects of God, valuable and worthy of preservation).

International

- 300 cities studied in US - areas with more trees had less theft and crimes. Urban crime drops around tress, plants and grass as people are happier, less stressed leads to less aggression which in turn leads to less crimes.
- National parks are worth $6 trillion to our mental health, creativity, anxiety and depression, sense of belonging, lower anti-social behaviour and workplace productivity; Psychological healing, oils the trees release into the air - kill germs and protect trees from diseases and insects. Doctors in UK are pre... 'nature' now. Finland, US, Canada have a culture of forest bathing too. ... has special therapy forests called for forest bathing - where peo... get closer to nature and de-stress to escape the rat race. Reduces ... sure and heart rate, boosts immunity.
- Afforestation
  - China - building vertical for... ng began in 2007. The project cos... ...ce 60 kg O_2 per day. The towers are home to 1100 tre... ...ing the benefits. It has been able to g... ...ney absorb 25 tons of CO_2 ... year; Similar forests ... ...aly in 2014. ...vated dry land.
  - Great ...

- Italy's Milan has vertical forest. They have planted 3 million trees by 2030 including flat rooftops (total target area is 10 million m²), disused railway networks, school courtyards. They purify the air, counter climate change, they absorb 5 million tonnes of CO^2 pa and 3000 tons of PM 10 in 10 years. They reduce the temperature by 2°C; Other cities doing the same globally are Seoul, Athens (protect from flooding and storm surges), Melbourne.
- Costa Rica almost doubled rainforest area in 1 generation by restricting logging permits; paying land owners who conserve their land; overseas investment at ecotourism and pharmaceuticals lead to both jobs and healthy forests.
- Kenya airdropping seedballs coated with charcoal to enable germination while preventing animals from eating them.
- Iceland is planting 3 million trees a year with 10% forest target.
- Urban forests - Milan's vertical forests - 20000 plants on 2 tower blocks.
- Senegal has planted 80 million mangrove trees - getting benefits already.
- Copenhagen is planting fruit trees in street for all to enjoy fruits - parks, playgrounds, churches.
- Philippines - students have to plant 10 trees before they graduate. Culture - plant a tree when you move to a new phase of life.
- Drone that plant trees are 150 times more faster than traditional methods; Seeds are put into a pod that is biodegradable and has all the nutrients that the tree needs to grow. Uses automation and digital intelligence that combines the right location and the right species. This data is fed to the drone which follows the path.
- For more than 100 years Sweden has been planting more trees than it cuts off. Swedish economy is based on environment. Forest is a national resource for the country.
- France encouraging living walls and opening vegetable gardens in schools.
- [Ma]lawi planting bamboo to fight climate change. It grows quickly, takes [...] years to mature, harvested again and again for 80 years. It absorb carbo[n] [...]
- Trillion tre[e] [...] stops landslides.
- [...] wants to plant that number by 2050.
- Singapore to unve[il] [...] [...]round Master Plan in 2019.

Innovative Ideas-

- Citizens groups like prakri[...] [...] [...]en action leading to community governance for environmental [...]
- Urban landscaping with fruit trees t[...] [...]d sewage effluent.

- Studies have shown that extra 10% of green space in cities could help compensate for climate change
- Artificial leaf developed by the University of Illinois at Chicago. It can take up to 10 times the CO_2 from air compared to natural leaves and convert them to carbohydrates.

Waste Management

Government

- India - NCR - Ghazipur trash mountain - growing 10 m pa and will be taller than Taj Mahal - 40 football fields.
- Kerala Tourism launches app to find nearest toilet.
- Bengaluru - wet waste collected by door to door collection every day. Dry waste twice a week. Mixed waste will either not be accepted or accepted with steep fines. Targets to achieve 100% doortodoor collection and 90% segregation. Idea is to minimise waste @ landfills to 13-15% + zero tolerance for garbage black spots and plastic usage.
- Municipal Corporation in Ambikapur, Chhattisgarh the country's "Garbage Cafe" offers free meals in exchange for plastic or any kind of trash to ragpickers.
- Chennai - the waste is converted into ash and then this ash is used to make colourful tiles and bricks. It started as a pilot project at a city landfill.
- India has banned all forms of disposable plastic in NCR.
- Odisha to reward people returning plastic bottles.
- India has been making roads out of recycled plastic. Consequently, pollution has been reduced, jobs have been created. Waste-pickers collect plastic litter, shreded in machine subsidized by government and is sold to builders; Roads thus made are more durable in floods and extreme heat; India has made 33600 km roads out of plastic. Eg. Chennai's Jambulingam street is one of the... road uses 1 million plastic bags, saves 1 tonne of asphalt and c...

NGOs–

- Afroz Shah from Mumbai led waste clea... oceans and rivers. He organised th... in 2015. He transformed V... renewed turtle hatch... is mobilising ...
- Plas...

...km ...ss.
...stic from going into
...ach clean-up in Mumbai
feet high waste pile up to
g on the 17 km of Mithi river. He
...bachao - helped reduce the use
in a year. Selling cloth bags for ₹ 5 ...
to veggie markets, langar plates and ...
Facebook and YouTube

- Hair used by start-up "matter of trust' to clean up oil spills. Woven into mats. Catchment cages of storm water drains to be lined with these mats to absorb oil that rainwater collects from the streets.
- Recycling - Jodhpur firm Priti International turns junk (old trucks, cars, bicycles and various machines) into tables, chairs, wine racks. Jodhpur has a big defence installation and a military auction house. The firms purchases old trucks and machines auctioned there (A good example of location of industries).
- *HelpUsGreen:*
    - Collects flowers from temples and mosques and recycles to natural incense, organic fertilizers and biodegradable packaging material.
    - 1,260 women in UP work in this initiative who used to be manual scavengers.
    - Provides livelihood to total of 5,100 women and recycles 51 tonnes of temple waste daily by 2021.
    - Preventing chemical pesticides from entering the rivers with temple waste.
    - World's first profitable solution to the temple waste problem.

International

- Operation Straw - a group of Australian divers dive to fish for straw. They call it strawkling - snorkelling for straw, plastic bags, fishing gear.
- Denmark - You can go boating for free if you pick up floating trash. You are given boat, vest, trash picker and can by GreenKayak; Similar initiatives are being taken in Norway, Germany, Ireland.
- Germany has converted exhausted open cast mines in lakes with beaches and camp-sites in Lusatia, Saxony and Brandenburg; Old giant excavators are now part of open air Ferropolis (Iron City) museum.
- New York reinventing the milkman to reduce the plastic waste problem. You order shampoo, milk, cereal etc. They are delivered at doorstep. You give empty containers which are reused. 90% of the plastic doesn't get recycled. Loop is N...art-up running this business and is a partnership of several global brands. comp... ...ifts the responsibility for packaging's after-life from customer to ...ompany is required to collect the used containers.
- Tokyo Ol... ...be a 100% renewable energy event, turning old phones into medals, ...goods used in the games will be reused or recycled, driverless taxis fo... ...cross venues giving foreign language support and carrying bags fo... ...illage plaza is built from reusable timber - will be dismantled af... ...used again. Japan will offset all the carbon emissions caused b... ...ill be made of recycled plastic. Torches made from Fukushi... ...om recycled e-waste, all raw materials have been sustain...

- Germany now reuses half of all used clothing. Start-ups are encouraging renting and not buying.
- Global food wastage is the third largest green house gas emitter as a country in country rankings. A British pub serves beer out of discarded toast is helping tackle food waste.
- UK - more and more people are buying second hand clothes; exporting too.
- In Rome we can pay metro train tickets with plastic bottles.
- EU wants to introduce one charger that works for every phone thus reducing e-waste; but abrupt shifting might cause more waste too. Hence it should be done slowly.
- Classrooms made out of plastic waste in Ivory coast - by making bricks out of plastic. These rooms are fire retardent and water proof, do not require any cement or sand. Students of Graphics era university developed a car C-zero. The body is made out of papers, weighs only 35 kg, costs 90% less and does 108 km/ KWh.
- Toronto, New York City, Los Angeles are turning food waste into fuel. Garbage trucks collect food scarps which are subjected to anaerobic digestion. This is used to extract renewable energy in the form of natural gas that is used to fuel the trucks themselves, homes, businesses.
- Sweden has a shopping mall for recycled products. You bring in products for restoring, they repair and sell it. The ideas has been adopted from India's jugaad and repair culture.
- Biodegradable plates made of wheat bran. They degrade in 30 days.
- In Mexico waste from food processing is being turned into bioplastic.
  - Waste from Avocado is being converted into straws and cutlery.
  - Waste from Sugarcane and Corn starch into bags and containers
- Innovative climate change summit by Marshall Islands carbon neutral.
- Curitiba city in Brazil has been recycl... borne diseases by 99%.
- Refuse derived...
- Plas...

online =>
reduced mosquito-
bricks and energy and water.
...a cup but lease it for 1 Euro, which is
...model is followed in Norway.
...zil and Philippines to collect plastic gar...
...have to pay to throw the trash away if th...
...source - more effective than taxing.

- Plastic eating fungus in Pakistan. It breaks down non-biodegradable plastics in weeks - Aspergillus tubingensis - rubbish dump in Islamabad - usually found in soil; live on plastic surface - breaks down bonds b/w molecules; 2014 - we made 311 mt of plastic.
- In Indonesian city of Surabaya people can pay for bus and movie tickets with plastic bottles, In Beijing, people can use plastic bottles to pay for his subway tickets.
- Norway has developed reverse vending machines where you can put in plastic bottles and get money.
- Iconic polo T-shirt has been re-made entirely of recycled plastic bottles. It is dyed by a process that uses zero water. It's called Earth Polo.
- Plastic recycling by turning it into ropes, robes (monks in Thailand) and bricks.
- Waxworms caterpillars can degrade plastic found recently. We produce 80 mt of polyethylene plastics a year globally, 150 mt single use.
- Portuguese airline Hi Fly conducted a test flight without a single piece of single-use plastic item on-board. The flight was from Lisbon to Natale, Brazil – no plastic cups, no plastic silverware, no plastic cocktail stirres and no plastic containers.
- Company TerraCycle collects and reuses, recycles and upcycles waste. Its free recycling programs are sponsored by brands, manufacturers and retailers. The collection points have been set up at homes, schools, offices. Courier collection service also provided. It recycles industrial waste. It gives out shipping labels for free as part of courier collection services.
- Alliance to End Plastic Waste (AEPW) is an allliance of 30 Global companies which has invested $1 billion and plans to eliminate plastic waste.

Inno[illegible]tive Ideas

- Start-u[illegible] learning [illegible] de[illegible]zes, five years - 'shoes that grow' can be adjust to expand by 5 sizes and last 5 years thus reducing wastage invented by Kenton Lee.
- Spill Waste P[illegible]lic' - large scale disposable and waterproof leaf plates - Lights show the c[illegible]dition of India. system for remote [illegible] [illegible]d with an ultra sonic sensor, LED and buzzer. [illegible] light turns red when full. Adding a [illegible] bins utilized.
- Recycled High Density [illegible] These tiles crafted out of plastic waste such as polyba[illegible] bottle caps. They are weather resistant, chip re[illegible] [illegible]al stability, cheaper.

- Larvicidal cakes that can attract and kill mosquitoes built from cigarette butts. These cake use nicotine. Its toxicity can kill the mosquitoes and their larva and the left over cake can used as fertilizers.
- An Indonesian start-up has developed Edible packaging material. The bottles are made of algae jelly. They are chilled in a bottle shaped mould and it needs liquid to hold the shape. It decomposes as soon as it gets empty so you can even eat it or dump it.
- We can increase price of products sold in non-recycled/non-recyclable packaging (10%) and vice versa. We can raise tax on trash going to landfill and reduce on recycling plants.
- Bill and Melinda Gates Foundation.
  - reinvented toilet and attached an omni processor waste treatment plant with it. They can be used in small towns in a cluster approach (2/3 families can together to share treatment plant).
  - pledged $200 million to incubate new technologies to scale up sanitation.
- Plastic-
  - Bioplastics
  - Ecohike-t-shirts made out of recycled plastic PET bottles.
  - Bioplastic made from fishing waste-fish scales and algae. Does not pollute, is stronger than standard plastic, can be used for variety packaging, edible, solves waste problem.
  - Recycled plastic can be used to make flash graphene. R&D by Rice University charging up high voltage capacitors with electricity then unleashing it all at once onto any carbon containing material like coal, plastic, food waste; current pass through target material. Thus, heating it to 3000K and breaking every C2C bond in the process. Non-carbon elements sublime out while the C atoms rearrange themselves as graphene, excess energy is dispersed as light thus forming flash graphene. Change can take place in 10 ms, quick, cheap; produces turbostratic graphene. The layers are not in ordered alignment. The layers can be separated using solvents but as of now only makes small flakes and not large sheets. This can be used in concrete as well and could boost cement strength.
  - Adidas making shoes out of recycled plastic.
  - Filling and heating thermoplastic to repair the potholes of a road.
  - MIT has developed a way of turning plastic into super strong concret... at is 15% stronger than normal. Making concrete produces about 4.5% c... CO_2 emission. Flakes of plastic subjected to small amount of rad... then crushed and mixed with cement paste and flyash.
  - UK has banned microbeads in cosmetics.

- Kwinana city, Australia is using giant plastic nets to trap wastes in drains and let's water filter through.
- Start-up called Bamboo House India in Hyderabad-
    - is developing plastic tiles for paving at the cost of 600 bags/tile; Thus the tiles costing less than < $1 each
    - House made of plastic provides good insulation in summer and winter thus saving on heating and cooling costs.
- Drinking water fountains to reduce demand of use and throw plastic water bottles.
- Manchester University has developed Graphene sieve. It uses oxidised membrane with tiny holes to filter and turn sea water into potable water. UN says 1.8 billion will suffer from water scarcity in 2025.

WATER

Govt.

- Best practices of decentralised planning of Hiware Bazar, Maharashtra.
- Swajal model of community based drinking water in Uttarakhand.
- Local approaches to developing infrastructure for storage of water-
    - Dewas model by M.P. Government for rehabilitation of farm ponds. It gave support to build ponds for storage and supply to farms. This lead to a 6 to 40 m rise in the water table; 120-190% rise in irrigated area.
- Gureh village, Banda district 5 pronged plan-
    - Kuan Talab Jiao Abhiyan - Drafted men to clean silt and debris to revive wells; water showed up even before an ancient well was fully cleaned.
    - Dig ponds and sell top-soil.
    - Wealthy non-resident villagers have funded digging ponds.
    - MGNREGA - ponds planned based on analysis of catchment area, study of inlet and outlets and storage.
    - Apna Talab Abhiyan.
- Mission Kakatiya in Telangana - restoration of irrigation tanks and lakes/minor irrigation sources built by the Kakatiya dynasty.
- Bengaluru working on reclaiming Kundalahalli lake (once a landfill) by CSR funds in a PPP model.
- Haryana - paddy farmers requested to switch to maize and told that the government would procure it and give a ₹2,000 per acre subsidy. Resulting in 18,000 hectares of land transferred from paddy cultivation to maize.
- Maharashtra - Seeing sugarcane cultivation is the largest water guzzler - so no sugarcane could be grown without precision drip irrigation. This has led to a saving 75% of water required in cultivation.

- Mansa district Punjab is using soak pits to store, clean water and recharge groundwater.
- Ice stupa artificial glacier by Sonam Wangchuk to save water in winter and use it till late spring (July).
- Water management model of Surat
- Jal Bachao, Video Banao, Puraskar Pao contest: MoWR,RD & GR.
- Thenmala dam has been made 70 km from Munroe Thuruthu, Kollam, Kerala in the 1960s for the Kallada Irrigation Project. It blocked the flow of fresh water and sediments from the Kallada river which has been determinantal to land's fertility. As a result, whole area has turned saline.
- Best practices of decentralised planning of Hiware Bazar, Maharashtra.
- Uttarakhand - Swajal model of community based drinking water management.

NGOs-

- Water crisis in TN lead to clashes erupt in Chennai, which in turn IT firms cutting down operations. This shows how environmental destruction and ensuing crisis can threaten the very economic growth in the name of which environment was polluted in the first place.
- Swachhagrahis - Army of grassroots motivators on water conservation and sanitation.
- Bill Gates promoted fund has developed solar panels that can make water out of air and sunlight. Each one of these panels can produce 10 lt. of water per day.
- Solar panels that can make water out of air by Zero Mass Water Inc.
- Laporia village in Rajasthan did not have a single drop of water 40 years ago. Laxman Singh started working on water harvesting and groundwater recharge. Today, Laporia is water secure.
- Even Chennai droughts Sriperumbudur - Oragadam belt - companies and manufacturing units maintained production due to efficient water management practices. Rain Water Harvesting pond and all buildings have artificial groundwater recharge.
- Start-up ocean cleanup's fleet of solar powered interceptors to clean rivers.

International

- Israel treats 100% and recycles 94% and this meets 50% of irrigation needs.
- Israeli start-up has developed AI algorithm to detect leakages thus helps in conserving water and preventing damage in commercial and government buildings.
- Peace ambassadors' appointed by UN have helped ease water conflicts in Kenya. They teach villagers about sustainable farming and how to share resources thus reducing wastage and using water efficiently.

- In Cape Town, South Africa water saving is being driven through the concepts such as Day Zero and prompting better and more efficient use of water.
- In China sponge cities (like Hebi City has earmarked a pilot area 30 km^2 for sponge city construction) are being developed to protect against flooding. Architects are turning cities into giant sponges. The city absorbs rainwater and stop floods; China, Russia, Indonesia, US-gardens, restoring wetlands, riverbanks, sponge cities, Porous asphalt permeable pavements, green walls, green buildings, underground tanks and tunnels; floods have increase by four times since 1980s; Only about 20-30% rainwater infiltrates in urban areas.
- In Mexico city new executive position of a "resilience officer" has been appointed to save its sinking urban sprawls.
- Warka water in Ethiopia.
- Bangkok's innovative park stores 3.8 million litres of floods water in tanks underneath it and uses it for 20 days of watering.
- Palau island nation in Pacific makes tourists pledge (stamped on passport) to protect the environment. It has turned most of its waters into a marine sanctuary. The idea is to tread lightly, act kindly, explore mindfully and banned tourists from taking marine animals as souvenirs, cannot damage or touch the coral.
- Singapore has developed a water treatment system which has reservoirs and 2/3rd of the city-state's surface area is the catchment areas of the treatment.

Innovative Ideas-

- Smart water pump switch - This device will function to "Switch on" the water pump when the tank is empty and "Switch off when the tank is full.
- Smart water dispensor - allows you to set how much water they need, the device then automatically stops the tap or motor once the water is dispensed.
- Local underground grey water treatment plant - then use the water for fountains to cool the area and the local irrigation.
- Papyrus grass is planted in bio fizzes and then it is soaked down in the water. They biofilter the water by nutrient uptake thus improve the water quality even more.

WILDLIFE

Govt.

- Animal underpasses on Maharashtra highways have become a life saver for tigers and they are turning out to be regular users on NH 44 - Tiger T1 used pass 9 atleast twice in March to May.
- WCCB has launched a scheme to enroll willing persons as WCCB Volunteers.
- Wildlife Crime Database Management System by WCCB has developed an online system to get real time data and analyze trends in crime, devise effective measures for helping put in preventive measures and carrying out operations.

International

- Eastern seaboard of USA is a dead zone for sealife; It has become four times now compared to 1950 due to human actions due to chemical runoff from agriculture and climate change. This has led to migration of fish to other areas. Solution is to cut fossil fuel use, water pollution, create protected areas for fish avoiding dead zones, track and predict future dead zones.
- Thames river was a dead zone and was resurrected.
- Nepal is the first country to double its tiger population. It used local communities to look after forests and to report and check illegal activity. They also used drone to monitor trafficking routes and turned 25% of land into conservation reserves.
- Jamaica - divers are growing baby corals in underwater nursery and when they become the size of hand they bind it to a rocky outcrop. Then the coral attaches itself and grows into a new reef. Corals cover 0.1% of the ocean floor, but support 25% of the marine life.
- Dutch city of Utrecht covered hundreds of bus stops with green roofs, turning bus stops into bee stops.
- Dutch engineers build artificial islands to bring wildlife back to an archipelago of 5 islets. It attracted greylag goose, common tern and several species of waders.
- Israel has developed a state of the art centralised water management system and desalination plants. They use waste water for farming.
- Galapagos island bans noisy fireworks in a move to protect unique wildlife.
- French tech company Sigfox developed a bite-size tracker that can be inserted on the horns of rhinos to monitor and protect the endangered species.

NGOs-

- World Animal Protection has launched Global Ghost Gear Initiative (GGGI) to collect ghost fishing gear from oceans all over the world.

Innovative ideas-

- Dr. David Vaughan's technique of micro-fragmentation to grow coral. Fragments of a coral grow to the original size within weeks. The plan is to plant 1 lakh corals in florida.
- LED lights in nets to scare off by catch marine creatures like turtles but fish aren't put off.

Fundamental Rights

Examples-

Good-

- Upholding right to speech-
  - Chakyar Koothu, Ottan Thullal art forms satire is the dominant idiom

- Nehru asked Kesava Sankar Pillai the pioneer of the Indian political cartoons not to spare him in his work-done!!

Bad-

- Denying fundamental rights
  - Journalist Prashant Kanojia was arrested by UP Police for sharing on Twitter a video pertaining to CM Yogi Adityanath.
  - Kerala Lalit Kala Akademi was asked by the state government to review its decision to award a cartoonist due to objections from a section of Christian clergy. This issue is regarding a cartoon on Father Fraco Mulakkal, accused of rape. The cartoon targeted only the person not values, institution or religion.

Governance

Examples-

- Greater Bengaluru Governance Bill, 2018-
  - Expert Committee has been made for Bruhat Bengaluru Mahanagara Palike Restructuring.
  - Greater Bengaluru Authority headed by a directly elected Mayor has been made for planning of Greater Bengaluru.
  - Powers for interagency coordination and administration of major infrastructural projects has been given to the Greater Bengaluru Authority in Urban local bodies area.
- Back to the Village of Jammu and Kashmir – 4500 officers from PS to entry level gazetted officers will visit every panchayat, stay overnight and listen to people's grievances and needs, also participate in various activities - energizing panchayats, feedback on delivery of government schemes, capturing specific economic potential, and undertaking assessment of village needs.
- Online portal ~ "Grievance Against Misleading Advertisements" (GAMA) where complaints relating to misleading advertisements can be lodged.
- #Self4Society app by PMO for Corporate professionals wanna do volunteer work.
- Niramala Sitharaman to crowdsource ideas for her first budget as Finance Minister - inclusive and participatory governance.
- In Maharashtra citizens seeking data from the government under RTI can stop by concerned office on Monday afternoons and study files.
- Experiment on Universal Basic Income in Madhya Pradesh with SEWA. This model shows improvement in nutrition, sanitation, health and health care, school attendance and performance, women's status and well-being, position of disabled and vulnerable groups.

- Assam-
  - Only state in India with Citizens Budget presented in public domain.
  - Only government conducts budget awareness campaigns across 17 districts.

NGOs-

- Dainik Bhaskar is promoting "SDG chaupals" in Indian villages.
- National Campaign for People's Right to Information filed an appeal with the central information commission about more than > 23,500 pending appeals, complaints, sought filling up of vacancies.

International

- Local Self Governance in U.K. - 'City Deals' - agreement between central government and city economic region. This has been modelled in 'competition policy style' approach. The city economic region has been represented by a 'combined authority' under a statutory body set up through national legislation. A group of councils collaborate decisions and is steered by a directly elected Mayor. The idea is to further democratise and incentivise local authorities to collaborate and reduce fragmented governance, drive economic prosperity, job growth, etc. 'City Deals' move from budget silos and promote 'economic growth budget' across regions. U.K. has established 9 such combined authorities.
- Nigeria sent a delegation to study Swachh Bharat Mission - 4 pillars of success – political leadership, public financing, partnerships and people's participation.
- How UK reduced smoking - from 80% in 1940s to just 15%
  - Banned smoking in public places
  - Plain packaging and health warnings
  - Services to help people quit
  - Future - sanction on tobacco companies and services targeting specific groups like teenagers and construction workers, etc.
- Germany integrated 4 lakh refugees in the job market
- Japanese Tsukuba city works with scientists to make laws - policy based on evidence and scientific background - mobility robots (dedicated experimental street), blockchain voting, leading in algal biomass energy, nanotechnology.
- GiveDirectly handed $1000 to 10500 homes in rural villages in Kenya. People in neighbouring villages benefited too. $1 give => $2.6 in additional spending and income. This exercise led to 0.1% inflation only; It also lead to rise in permanent assets and per month spend even after 3 years.
- Denmark's "Festival of Politics" works to deepen democracy where every leader comes and people challenge them in an informal setting; It is conducted in a remote island away from capital.

- New Zealand has embarked to transform politics to focus on kindness, empathy and well-being. Well being budget has been initiated where ministers who want to spend money will have to prove that their initiative will improve inter-generational well being - focus on societal not just economic well being.

Health

Examples-

Government-

- Maharashtra Health Dept. has launched a scheme to appoint specialists in rural areas, offering contracts with performance based cash incentives.
- Mother's milk banks have come up at government hospitals in Maharashtra.
- Odisha success in reducing malaria - efforts by government, political and bureaucrats.
- Accredited Social Health Activists - worked on the following heads
  - Swachh Bharat Mission
  - Trianed ASHA in EDCT using rapid diagnostic kits - incentive of ₹ 75 per positive test reported
  - DAMAN initiative - controlling malaria in remote locations - mass screening camps - twice a year + entire population screened
  - Indoor residual spray - residual insecticide is applied to inner walls and ceilings of houses
  - 1.1 cr long lasting insecticide nets - ASHA explained people how to use the nets
- Chhattisgarh and Assam
  - 3 year trained physician are called LMPs (Licentiate Medical Practitioners). They have been given training to handle basic public health issues in rural areas.
  - Public health practitioners to address infectious diseases and public health requirements of the rural poor.
- IIT Delhi developed Naso filters. These can we worn in the nose to filter out particulate matter in the air we breathe. They can be used for about 10 hours and are available for ₹ 10 per piece.
- Healthcamps run by Karnataka government.
- Telemedicine for OPD care patients in UP by docs in Andhra.
- Maharashtra - animal drug stores to stop selling antibiotics to farmers without prescription.
- Odisha's per capita income is lower than that of Gujarat but has a better nutritional status due to

- Better network of ICDS
- Public health facility/workforce per lakh population
- Educational attainment in women

- Delhi government - Zero Fatality Corridor
- Odisha vs. Haryana - malnutrition in Haryana's (34% stunting and 29.5% underweight) agriculturally-developed districts like Karnal, Panipat, Sonipat, Rohtak, Gurugram is higher than average of Odisha.
- Indian Air Force has launched a mobile health app to provide health information to the users, including first-aid and other health and nutritional topics.
- Loo Review campaign under Swachh Bharat Mission by MoHUA and Google.
  - Locating Public Toilets on G-maps.
  - To encourage all local guides in India to rate and review public toilets on Google Maps.
  - 500+ cities in India; More than 30,000 toilets named SBM Toilet are live.
  - Awareness and ease of locating public toilets across India.

International

- Hospital ship of Bangladesh - using waterways to access and serve remote areas
- Ebola experience of Sierra Leone and Liberia have taught us that not big hospitals but strengthening community health is the key to contain epidemic.
- Spain has the highest organ donation rate 47/ million. They have an opt out system rather than opt in system (idea developed from the concept of behavioural economics).
- Portugal decriminalised drug use and possession in 2001.
  - lowest rate of drug-related social costs of death and crime in EU.
  - redeployed the investment for enforcement to the support of addicts.
- Thai model of state health insurance coverage reduced out of pocket expenditure spending down to 18%.
- West Africa's 2013 Ebola virus outbreak and Latin America's 2015 Zika outbreak have shown that proactive sharing of data can help. During the Ebola epidemic 80% of the epidemiological modelling studies used only open data.
- Bridge courses world over to practitioners to deliver primary health-care service at grassroot level.
  - US - Physician Assistant-paramedics, nurses
  - UK - Physician Associate - 2 years training
  - NZ - centre for rural health development - Physician Assistant in clinical role

- China - Associate doctors
- South Africa - clinical associate
- Bangladesh - 3 year training - 89% health@ rural (SACMO)
- Malaysia - Associate medical officer

- University of New Mexico - ECHO model - Extension for community health outcomes.

NGOs-

- Shraddha Rehab. Foundation where psychiatrist Bharat Vatwani who works for mentally ill street people in Mumbai.
- SNEHA Chennai based suicide prevention hotline saves more than 1 lakh a year.
- NGO working for TB patients
  - TB Mukt Vahini-Bihar
  - Stop TB Partnership, Geneva
  - Global Coalition of TB Activists; Rainbow TB Forum, Tamil Nadu
  - Journalists against TB, Bengaluru
  - Doctors w/o borders
  - Microsoft India, NITI Aayog pact for AI tools in healthcare - Healthcare screening models to screen patients at Primary Health Centres.

INTERNATIONAL RELATIONS

Examples

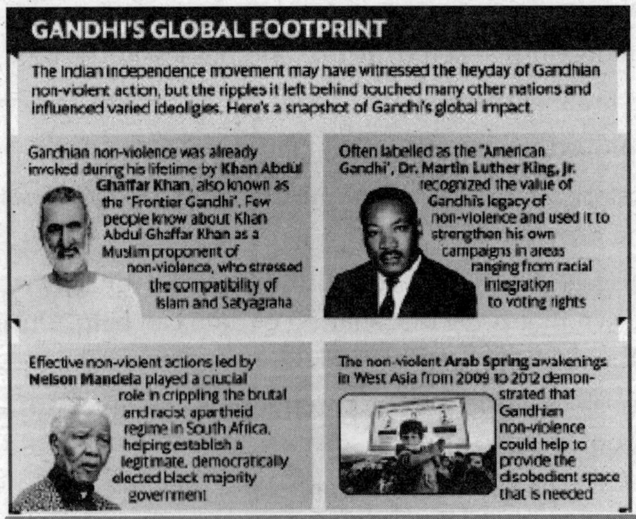

- Non - violent uprisings in Serbia, Ukraine, Georgia, Myanmar, Iran, the Palestinian Territories, Egypt, and Tunisia.

- Protectionism - Canada wants to take in 1 million immigrants in next 3 years ~ 1% of population - 2036 dependency ratio of 2.
- Football-
  - 10% world cup footballers are migrants
  - 30%, 62%, 90% respectively in teams of Portugal, Morocco, Belgium.
  - Swiss team has 30% and the coach says cultural diversity is the reason for success.
- Rehabilitation of Refugee rehab-
  - Lego Foundation and Sesame street has invested in Syria and Rohingyas entertainment in "play labs". The labs teaches to read and write by using toys, games and videos. They help how to manage stress of displacement. They help to reduce trauma (50% of 68.5 million refugee-kids).
  - Za'atari Project has painted murals on wall around camp.
  - Exile Voices has been teaching Syrian kids and trains them in photograpy.
  - Germany has been training refugees to become train drivers. It has till yet integrate 1 million displaced people.

Justice

- Nagaland Tourist Police ensures safety and security of tourists and report crime to the nearest police station. The police has set up an Integrated Police Control Room for tourists.

Media

- Virus movie dealing with deadly Nipah virus outbreak in Kerala
  - How to deal with adversity using public knowledge + workforce.
  - Role played by the local media in preventing panic and disseminating information.
  - State machinery - defence to tackle grave situation.
  - Meticulous planning by many individuals.
  - Women were key players under the leadership of K. K. Shailaja, Kerala's Minister of Health and Social Welfare.
- *Kabir Singh* - a movie that glorifies toxic masculinity, intimidation of women and sense of entitlement which some men have given themselves. It glorifies stalking and even ownership of women by men; so did *Dabangg* and *Tere Naam.*
- Kumbalangi Nights - story of 4 unsuccessful oddballs and women in their lives that creates a nurturing loving community of love.
- Social media platform Instagram has induced an AI powered prompt to reconsider offensive language offers online abusers a shot at redemption.

Feature restrict allows users a degree of control over their terms of engagement with their abusers.

- Movies - stereotypical dalits - powerless, wretched and dependent on morality of social elites - Bandit queen, Lagaan, Aarakshan; complex characters - Newton, Rajneeti, Sonchariya, Masaan
- Rumours' effect - Alimuddin Ansari, Dadarao Bhosale, Nilotpal Das, Tribal Madhu - lynched on rumours.

Debunking fake news-

- Altnews.in - video showing a Hindu girl being attacked by a Muslim mob 2 year-old clip from Guatemala.
- SM Hoax Slayer - WhatsApp forward of the Indian flag flying atop the Israeli Parliament was fake.
- Check4Spam.com - digital rumours of 200 child kidnappers having arrived in Bangalore.
- Facebook has given 10 easy tips and a "forward" warning as way of identify rumours.
- Poynter's International Fact Checking Code of Principles to be able to detect fake news.
- Spot fake news on the internet - head of Wikimedia - few handy guidelines-
  - If there are too many adjectives in a sentence - chances are the author is trying to convince you of something
  - Read more critically - check the citations
  - Is the source reliable - who published it, when and why? what incentive do they have?

International-

- Sri Lanka enacted a Law on fake news: Sentencing 5 years in prison for fake news and hate speech.

Law And Order

Government-

- Cop connect app by Telangana police. It is basically a whatsapp for police
- Partnership between sex workers and anti-human trafficking units to root out exploitative practices
  - Success stories at country's largest red-light district of Sonagachi in West Bengal. Self-regulatory body of sex workers since 2001 has been tracking entry of minors and has helped in identifying traffickers.

- Model has been emulated in Sangli in Maharashtra and has helped anti-human trafficking unit and workers to rescue minors and prevent trafficking.
- Telegram group called National Police Group has been made only for constables, head constables, Assistant Sub-Inspectors, Sub-Inspectors, and Inspectors from 28 states to help crack cases by information sharing and informal level cooperation.

International examples-

- Scotland - Glasgow - most violent city in the developed world - police realized the reasons.
  - poverty, inequality, toxic masculinity, alcohol abuse.
  - treated violence as health problem like obesity and smoking; City enlisted social workers and doctors and staff to work on defusing tensions, stopping revenge attacks and offering therapy, educated children about knife crimes, helped violent offenders get jobs, housing, education on leaving prisons.

NGOs-

- Shakti Vahini, a Delhi-based NGO that resulted in the landmark Khap Panchayat case
- Utthan - a trafficking survivors' collective groups
- Lawyers Collective - NGO working on human rights issues
- Common Cause filed a PIL in Madras High court, resulted in the judgment madating one day week holiday for all police officers
- Amnesty International working in the domain of Prison reforms
- Sex workers' group-VAMP (Veshya Anyay Mukti Parishad) + NGO Sangram conducted a study called Raided from 2005 and 2017.
  - They traced the lives of 243 released "rescued" women
  - 79% or 193 stated at the time of raid that they were in sex work voluntarily and did not want to be 'rescued'.

Poverty Alleviation And Welfare

Financial Inclusion

- Kenya model of digital empowerment - M-Pesa mobile money service
  - Can be used to store monetary value on phones and transfer via SMS
  - This financial inclusion uplifted 2% of Kenya's households out of poverty
  - Female beneficiaries have benefitted in social, economic spheres
  - This has also brought about savings behaviour
  - This has altered occupational choices from subsistence agriculture and multiple part-time jobs to business ownership
  - Direct access to remittances through M-Pesa and hence increased agency

NGOs-

- Nirman Kusuma programme in ODISHA gave financial support to children of construction workers, trained them in ITIs and polytechnics
- Timbaktu Collective of Telangana ensured decent livelihoods for tribals by promoting their craft through small scale manufacturing.
- Kudumbashree (Kerala) has worked on skill training and poverty eradication of women.
- In Yelagiri hills, Tamil Nadu MAHALIR MANDRAN POONGANUR has been maintaining a tourist spot.
- SEWA, Lizzat papad has helped in promoting entrepreneurial culture among women.
- Tamil Nadu SHGs helped inculcate sanitation habits among the community people.

Sport

NGOs-

- Sports: A way of life has filed a PIL to make sports a fundamental right - 21A, DPSP and FD

Society

Examples-

Govt.-

- Scheduled Castes - Gobindpura village (1/144 total) Nabha Tehsil Patiala district ended separate cremation grounds for Scheduled Castes; former MP used carrot and stick approach using MPLAD funds for villages for renovation of cremation grounds. Now members of all communities attend funerals together.
- Drug Abuse - Excise Department of Kerala has launched a mission to fight drugs grassroots by forming a Vimukthi Sena of young volunteers 18-40 years at the ward-level. Kerala State Mission for Deaddiction has launched awareness campaigns against alcoholism and drug abuse.
- LGBTQ - NALSA campaigned for the transgenders right to be called the third gender, separate from male and female and seek legal, political and economic rights, and remedy against discrimination.

NGOs and Non-Government examples-

- In tolerance
  - Muslim Manganiar folk singers singing songs of exquisite beauty to Krishna - they follow Islam but they sing Hindu devotional songs

- Akhil Bharatiya Marathi Sahitya Sammelan (All India Marathi Literary Meet)- Nayantara Sahgal speech for Marathi Sahitya Sammelan: 'In some cases, it's our duty to hurt sentiments'. She got uninvited.
- Wendy Doniger's book The Hindus: An Alternative History - withdrawn from circulation.
- A.K. Ramanujan's essay 'Three Hundred Ramayanas' - dropped from a Delhi University syllabus.
- Perumal Murugan's book Madhorubagan (One Part Woman) - withdrawn by author but resurrected by Madras HC.
- Manipur law passed a law to prevent mob lynching.
- SC gives an 11-point prescription: Preventive, remedial and punitive steps

- Loyalty to Muslims to the country for when extremists question-
  - Brigadier Mohammad Usman (Dogra Regiment) was highest-ranking officer killed in the India-Pakistan War of 1947-48.
  - Havildar Abdul Hamid (Grenadier Regiment) - destroyed Pakistani tanks in the battle of Khem Karan. This was the most decisive encounter of the 1965 India-Pakistan war.
  - Captain Haneefuddin (Rajputana Rifles) was killed at 18,500 ft. during the Kargil conflict in 1999 when he led the eviction of enemy from a strategic position.
- Racism-
  - Turkish-origin footballer quits German team due to racism.
  - A RBI board member said Kerala flood is wrath of God for allowing women entry in Sabarimala.
- Messages being spread on social media warning people against contributing on CMDRF as the money might go to minorities and invite the wrath of God.
- Tribals_- Jiban Sampark Project of Odisha working for welfare of PVTGs; in association with UNICEF. Awareness amongst the PVTGs about their rights.
- Casteism-
  - Dalits of Hulikal village in Arkalgud taluk travel about 8 km to get a shave or a haircut.
  - National Campaign Against Mob Lynching (NCAML) has been campaiging for a law against mob lynching.
  - Sangham Radio - India's first community radio experiment run by Dalit women.
  - Rashtriya Dalit Adhikar Manch - Azadi Kooch after Una flogging.
  - Rashtriya Garima Abhiyan + MoSJE - manual scavenging census.
  - Veerammal

  - Founded Annai Ashram.
  - Started a school for Dalit girls in 1950s near Tiruchi. It conducted classes up to 12th standard.
  - Started an ITI; Children's home
- Kandan was from small village of Vanjinagaram, Melur in Tamil Nadu
  - Took on caste oppression
  - Led a movement to draw water from public well and pressed for rights.
  - 1987 - Kandan was hacked to death.

- Bhasha Mukherjee crowned Miss England in 2019 rather than being brand ambassador for various causes for global organisations; leaving her crown behind to go back to work as a doctor and help during the Covid-19 crisis.
- LGBTQ
  - Right wing opposition to Deepa Mehta's Fire on the topic of lesbian love 1998.
  - Puttaswamy case on Privacy focused preservation of personal intimacies, the sanctity of family life, marriage, procreation, the home and sexual orientation, right to be left alone.

International examples-

- Loneliness - Sidewalk talks are being done in 12 countries and 40 cities where volunteers often trained psychiatrists listen to you and make you feel valuable.
- Tolerance - studies on US expats shown that having close friends from different cultures gives us cognitive flexibility, makes us more entrepreneurial and enables us to develop different perspectives and innovative ideas.
- LGBTQ
  - Ireland legalised same sex marriage - first country globally to do so.
  - Naz foundation's Navtej Singh Johar case litigated in Supreme Court for striking down Section 377.
- Senior Citizens-
  - Living libraries of Malaysia are where young visit and learn from the old in retirement homes.
  - Japan has combined kindergarten with aged care homes for elderly. It reduces pace of mental decline of elderly, reduce blood pressure, risk of disease, stress, loneliness and boredom. Children are less likely to be ageist as they grow up. They encourage interaction between generations.
  - China's universities for the elderly are blooming. Reading 30 minutes a day can help live 20 months more.
  - UK has appointed Minister for loneliness.
  - In Italy young are moving in with the old so that they can get affordable housing and company.

- Homeless in Dublin are being trained as tour guides, in arts of creative writing, storytelling, etc. They get 50% of the ticket and the rest invested in scheme.
- New Zealand is measuring its success by the well being of its people and economic growth. Public investment in budget 2019 focused on quality of life - mental health, domestic violence, poverty, inequality + inter-generation well-being.
- Well-being buses: old condemned buses have been turned into a home for London's homeless - Occupants can sleep, dine and cook.
- Senior Citizens - Spanish city of Bilbao has put brain training games for elderly people in public parks - boost attention span, counter loneliness, memory, mental arithmetic.
- UK, Japan, French service called 'watch over my parents'. Relatives pay a fee to have postal staff look in on family members to fight loneliness and deliver groceries.

Innovative Ideas-

- TRIFED agreement with Amazon to use Global Selling Programme to market tribal products globally.
- Go Tribal Campaign: TRIFED is institutionalizing collaborations and partnerships with different organizations. The idea is to promote tribal products innovative activities to promote use of tribal handicrafts, handicrafts and natural products.
- Differently-abled people - Smart blind shoe - Internet of things enabled device; an interactive smart shoe can assist the visually impaired commute safely. IT has system that alerts the user with a buzzer and a vibration in the shoe upon sensing an obstruction in their path.
- IITD developed a smart cane that detects obstacles from knee to head height. It is a help for visually imparied. It works on ultrasonic transmitter receiver system, helps to change directions and find the alternative path.
- Social prescription - singing, dancing, drumming, volunteering and giving back to the community.
- Sesame street muppet show introduced a homeless character Lily to help children understand homelessness from the perspective of a child.

Tech

Apps and Websites

- Babasaheb Bhimrao Ambedkar University (BBAU) will use an ISRO-made app named 'Total Key Solution' under the Swachch Bharat Mission to maintain cleanliness of the campus. Students will take pictures and upload. App will show route map of the dump to supervisor who can send a sanitary worker to pick it up - worker to clean and upload pictures.

- Complaints against child pornography and SH received on www.cybercrime.gov.in
- Digital Detox App by SHUT Clinic - NIMHANS Bengaluru has developed a mobile app for people to reduce mobile usage.

3D printing-

- hearing aids
- corneas - Newcastle university scientists have successfully 3D printed the world's first human cornea in less than 10 mins. It is created by using a special bio-ink using stem cells mixed together with alginate and collagen.
- Human cartilage for use in arthritic joints.
- Model of a human heart complete with blood vessels but the size of rabbit's heart. It uses a bio-ink with human stem cells, hydrogel, polyester fibres to become tough enough for printing.
- MARSHA - 3D printed house for Mars. It is built using basalt and PLA (biopolymer). It does not use steel or concrete. It can be ground down after usage and re-printed using the same material. It is made in an egg-shaped to deal with the atmospheric pressure difference on Mars. It helps to deal with the wind and snow issues on Earth.
- Dubai made a 3D printed house-
  - Uses 50% less manpower
  - 60% less construction waste than normal
  - Cheaper and quicker
  - Rapid hardening concrete
  - Local materials
  - France, Haiti, El Salvador and Mexico have started trials for 3D printed shelters and affordable housing.
  - Mixture of industrial and construction waste, cement and a hardening agent; they are earthquake resistant and can be printed in 12 hours.

AI–

- Positives–
  - Cleaning space debris - AI can do the volume of processing required for thousands of pieces, which do not decay the way it happens on Earth. Once tracked, with AI engine training bringing in more accuracy, a 'netting' probe with an extended arms to collect debris can be positioned in the path of debris to be collected and cleaned, thus eliminates potentially dangerous targets by leveraging AI based technology.

- Help fight climate change.
  - monitoring deforestation and agri emission
  - designing low-carbon materials can replace steel and cement
  - using machine vision to monitor the environment
  - Predict extreme weather events
  - Make transportation more efficient
  - Reduce wasted energy from buildings
  - Geoengineer a more reflective Earth
  - Give individuals tools to reduce their carbon footprint.
  - Data analysis to find inefficiencies in emission-heavy industries
  - AI to model complex systems, like Earth's own climate
  - Forecasting electricity generation and demand - suppliers better integrate RE into national grids and reducing wastage
- AI program Pluribus beats professionals in 6-player poker. Earlier it was done in checkers, chess, Go and 2 player poker. AI algorithms can be used to solve a "wide variety of real world problems" that, like in poker, involve actors who bluff, or hide key information.
- Google's AI AlphaZero learnt hundreds of years of human chess knowledge in under 4 hours and then started inventing its own tactics. Now it is studying how proteins fold and could help cure Alzheimer's, Cystic fibrosis and Parkinson's.
- AI algorithms have been developed to detect precancerous cells with 91% accuracy as against only 69% by expert review.
- Boston runs school buses on an MIT algorithm. It has saved $5 million in a year. It has led to 1 million fewer miles driven every year and more efficient journey for 1000s of school-going children. It gets data from google maps to analyse traffic patterns and uses the data on which student needs to get where from information provided by schools regarding students. This has led to efficient trips with less miles and more kids in each bus, smoother planning by computer in 30 mins. what man did in weeks.
- AI robot of google learnt to walk by itself by a reinforcement learning plan for the robot made by the researchers so that it could learn from its mistakes.
- New AI tool can decode security captchas within 0.05 seconds.
- AI algorithms have been developed that beat doctors at detecting early stage of cervical cancer.
- AI has been aiding the search of child trafficking victims. It process through a database of hotel room pictures to match with online advertisements.

- Ai-Da-AI enabled humanoid sketch artist is able to draw creatively billed as one of the most exciting artists of our time.
- KP-Bot - India's first robo-cop launched by Kochi-based start-up, Asimov Robotics, Cyberdome (technology development centre of the Kerala police).
- In Chinese of Hangzhou city traffic is controlled by an AI brain that cut response time of emergency vehicles in half, eases congestion for drivers. The system uses data from cameras, Autonavi web mapping and navigation service.

- Negatives-
  - Nuclear wars - International Campaign to Abolish Nuclear Weapons has explained that hackers could breach A.I. technologies used in nuclear programs. They could use A.I. to dupe countries into launching attacks. For instance by using deepfakes, realistic-looking computer-altered videos to create a perceived threat that might not be there. A.I. could also be used to target nuclear arsenals or the people who manage them.
  - Robot read 3.5 million books and saw that we describe men and women differently in text. Adjectives like strong, rational, courageous and righteous are attached with men; Beauty is attached with women; Negative words for body are five times more frequent for women. Adjectives for women - focus on appearance and for men on behaviour. This has implication on AI, ML codes being developed using these texts.
  - Amazon used AI to help with recruiting showed bias against women as it used male dominated data to learn.
  - ProPublica was a risk-assessment software developed to forecast probability of reoffending by criminals showed a racial bias against black people.

Privacy issues

- Google contractors regularly listen to and review some recordings of what people say to AI system Google Assistant, via their phone/smart speakers - Google Home. The company acknowledged that humans can access those recordings after some of its Dutch language audio snippets were leaked.
- US regulators approve $5 billion Facebook settlement over privacy issues.

Navigation

- Google Maps launches 'Stay Safer' feature - alert and notify users travelling in taxis and auto rickshaws when their vehicle goes off route.

Computer Gaming-

- Gaming Addiction - Addiction to video game is bad for brain. WHO's next international classification of disease. Addictive gaming behaviour can impair life, personal, social and family relationships, depression and anxiety, behavioural changes and sleep disturbances, irregular dietary habits, insomnia, sleep apnea and nightmares. But it can help in improving reasoning, memory, perception and problem solving.

Robots

- Robots are being designed for HADR
    - European ROBOT project - autonomous robot on wheels
    - Boston Dynamics Wildcat - 32 kmph runner
    - Robot bushbaby - jumping robot with single leg - modeled after Senegal Bushbaby animal
- Chinese self driving car designed to be an office space as well - use 2 hours of commute to work.
- Feb 2019 - Kerala police inducted a robot for police work.
- Feb 2019 - Chennai got its second robot themed restaurant, robots serve as waiters and interact with customers in English and Tamil.
- Germany has developed ethical rules for autonomous vehicles that mandate human life be given much higher priority over property or animal life.
- December 2018 - cardiologist performed the world's first inhuman telerobotic coronary intervention on a patient nearly 32 km away.
- Indonesia has started using drones to deliver books, medicines to school children in remote areas to narrow inequality gaps between rural and urban areas.

Internet

- Internet (1969) changed the world in 50 years. It was developed by a US military research agency.

Space

- Cold war era spy satellite images repurposed to study ice loss in 650 glaciers.
- Odisha uses satellite imagery to create unique flood hazard atlas - uses flood inundation data from 2001 to 2018.

The atlas will help the authorities in several ways:

- To systematically plan flood control measures
- To control developmental activities on floodplains
- To carry out relief and rescue operations
- To plan relief shelters and health centres

Innovative ideas

- Bill Gates has suggested the idea of robot tax to help losers of automation.
- Jack Ma has advised to teach kids what machines will never learn - Value, believing, independent thinking, teamwork, care for others, sport, music, arts, soft power.

- Blockchains can store a person's digital identity like passports, exam certificates and financial histories. This can help refugees get jobs when documents are destroyed and help with payments reducing bank intermediary fee for transactions by 98%.

Terror, International Crime, Security

Examples-

- Greyhounds of AP
- Tripura Model
- Mizoram Model

International examples-

- Indonesia
  - de-radicalisation programs to tame terrorists in communities and families of reformed former terror convicts.
  - recruited young internet users with huge social media followings to spread the message of peace.
  - Philippine Military Recruiting Muslims into the military to counter terrorism on and religious and cultural approaches.
  - U.S. National Security Agency's programme of mass surveillance was examined by American court and found that of 50 instances of terrorist attacks prevented not even 1 successful pre-emption was based on the material collected from the NSA's surveillance regime.
  - Building a counter narrative to mis-leading radical interpretation of Islam - Singapore Internet Imam to counter the radical agenda online, answer queries and correct misunderstanding about jihad.

Women

Social Welfare

Government-

- Delhi government deployed bus marshalls on 60% of the city's buses to deal exclusively with women safety issues.
- DC Budgam Syed Sehrish Asgar ensured all Budgam schools, college have sanitary napkin dispensers, incinerators - thus addressing drop outs of girls.
- 'SHE Team' led by lady sub-inspectors have been deployed by Odisha's Gajapati district police
  - Patrol schools, colleges, local institutions and public places, where young girls and women are subjected to eve-teasing, stalking and harassment hot spots.

- Prevent sexual harassment at workplace and public places.
- Teach self-defence and cyber space safety to young girls and children.
- Visit child care institutions and make children aware about sexual abuse.

- Changing narrative on shaming women who suffer sexual assualt - Comic Shakti portrays a girl who got raped as a teenager, society and family blamed and banished her.. Hindu god Parvati came to her help.. helped her vanquish her assaulters and now she rescues other victims including trafficked people - by Ram Devineni.
- "Web - Wonder Women" campaign by MWCD to celebrate the exceptional achievements of women, who have been driving social reforms via social media.
- Kudumbashree by Government of Kerala in 1998 to wipe out absolute poverty by concerned community action and leadership of LSG.

NGOs-

- Women toilet masons of Assam - teams of women building toilets under SBM in Assam. They get employment and work gets done in a much more efficient and a timely manner.
- Foolmani Devi from Gutuatoli village, Ranchi, Jharkhand has benefited 400 people. She heads a team of 4 masons which has built 125 toilets under Swachh Bharat Mission trained under government initiative and has empowered women masons.
- #MeToo - Tanushree Datta, Sruthi Hariharan, Chinmayi Sripada vs. Alok Nath, Nana Patekar, Arjun Sarja.
- Indian Young Lawyers Association litigated the Sabarimala Case and ended gender discrimination in worship in that temple.
- Western Odisha Migration Network, Aide et Action, Global Alliance Against Traffic in Women, Aaina is working on developing a database of women migrant workers in the form of a register to track migrants.
- UNICEF 'super dads' campaign to emphasize father's active role in kids' life.
- Father's day is celebrated in 80 countries.
- Women's wall at DU has been made against patriarchy at the national capital and in solidarity with women who did the same in Kerala.
- Tarabai Shinde, Maharashtrian housewife - Stree Purush Tulana (Comparison of Men and Women) - protest against double standards of a male dominated society.
  - Young Brahmin widow sentenced to death for killing her newborn illegitimate baby
  - no effort to identify or punish father
- Begum Rokeya Sakhawat Hossain - Sultana's Dream

- was a short story and the earliest example of science fiction writing in India
- first by a woman author anywhere in the world.
- It reversed gender roles

- Sainik school in Mizoram admitted women on pilot basis

	Kerala	Tamil Nadu	UP	Bihar
Female literacy	92%	74%	42.2%	33.1%
Avg. age at marriage	21.4 (India-20.7)	21.2 (India-20.7)	19.4	19.5
TFR	1.7 (India-2.3)	1.6 (India-2.3)	3.1	3.3
% of women @ full antenatal care	61.2	45	5.9	3.3
NMR	6	15	>25	>25
Poverty alleviation	15 to 7.1	22.5 to 11.3	32.8 to 29.4%	41.4 to 33.7%

- Safety
  - UP Government recruited 1 lakh female special police officers as Power Angels to work for women's safety.
  - Hyderabad Police has set up Bharosa support Center for Women & Children. It is an integrated assistance where police, medical, legal, and prosecution, psycho therapeutic, counselling and rescue and rehabilitation services all are given under one roof.
  - Delhi Police's Operation Nirbheek to improve safety and security of girls in schools.
  - All women patrol van under Shishtachar Programme of Delhi Police.
  - Himmat app of Delhi Police.
  - Hawkeye app of Hyderabad Police.
  - Bangalore Police's Suraksha initiative.
  - Kangazha village in Kottayam, Kerala is the first local body to train all women aged 10-60 in self-defence under the Nirbhaya scheme in April 2017.

International

- Sorehara-
  - Japanese website for anonymous complaints about harassment and other grievances.
  - Abbreviation of the Japanese for "That's harassment" was devised by a 21-year old college student.

- Japan is giving empty homes to single mothers. Japan has a property surplus and 700000 single mothers with no place to live. NGO Little Ones buys, renovates and rents cheaply to single mothers using government subsidy.
- Scotland - first place to make feminine hygiene products free for all women.
- Gender neutrality-
    - Mexico - boys can wear skirts to school and girls can wear trousers and there are gender neutral toilets;
    - UK - pupils choose which uniform they wear
    - Wales - offer the same uniform to both sexes
- Finland considering paternity leave to 7 months; Japan gives 30 weeks.
- In Sweden schools do not use phrases little boy and little girl but little people. They have no presumption on behavior and toys. They avoid words that divide people by gender. Rather they emphasise the use of words like humans, kids, people, friends. Kids make fewer gender assumptions thus widen opportunities available and helps avoid stereotypes.
- Just 2% of advertising portrays women as intelligent, 3% shows them as leaders. This seeps into our consciousness. Gender stereotyping can be harmful to both men and women. It affects how we understand the relationship between sexes. Womens are portrayed in advertisement for cleansing products and men for cars, credit cards, housing, banks, etc. UN Women has been working with brands to end stereotypes. UK, in 2018, started cracking down on advertisement that use gender cliches. Eg. Outlawed advertisement that market different toys for girls and boys.
- Women paid more than men per hour on an average in Bangladesh.
- Project Ikumen project in Japan incentivize dads to devote time with kids. Stay at home dads and not suited salary man was promoted as a role model.
- In Finland the level education is higher in women than men; women are more than 50% of the graduates.
- In South Korea mothers and fathers take parental leave at the same time. It is extending paid leave for fathers with flexible work hours.
- Lithuania installed traffic lights featuring female symbols on the 100th anniversary of women getting the right to vote.
- UNiTE Campaign has been working for a world free from violence for all women and girls.
- Ireland criminalised emotional abuse. It has created a new offence called 'coercive control'. Non-violent emotional abuse in the form of fear and distress; France, England, Wales and Scotland also have adopted such laws. Worldwide 35% of women undergo physical violence and suffer from depression, HIV etc.

Economic

Govt.

- NITI Ayog has set up Women Entrepreneurial Platform
  - Women Entrepreneurial Platform Investment Council addresses funding related challenges faced by entrepreneur.
  - Women Transforming India Awards
- Womaniya on Government e Marketplace.
- Government's Trade Related Entrepreneurship Assistance and Development (TREAD).
- Firms in India are sanctioning menstruation leave (2 days/month).

NGOs

- Microsoft to Promote STEM education in AI studies and data sciences for women at NITI Ayog identified institutes.
- A start-up has designed a necklace that can be used to send SOS message to a friend when a person carrying it needs help.
- Project Sage - a private equity venture capital private debt funds helps women led enterprises mobilise funds.
- SAHA Fund - India's first woman's venture capital fund. It is for, by and of women entrepreneurs. Funds women led enterprises working in the domain of e-commerce, social media, education, healthcare, food technology.
- SonderConnect works on discovering, empowering and promoting Female Founders globally.
- Govt. - Kerala Tourism Development Corporation (KTDC) - India's first public sector hotel run entirely by women - 'Hostess'.
- National Forum for Single Women's Rights (NFSWR) – representing single women demands for enhanced budgetary allocation. Monthly pension and benefits for caregivers were also demanded.
- World Bank, SIDBI, UN Women and 10 wealth management firms and leading corporates have come up with a new social impact bond to offer credit to rural women entrepreneurs - Women livelihood bonds.
- Disha Project – UNDP India, IKEA Foundation and India Development Foundation has come up with - "Idea of Biz Sakhis"
  - To guide budding female entrepreneurs from rural communities multiple processes women.
  - Practical and psychological support.
  - Encourage rural women to undertake businesses by making them aware of entrepreneurship
  - Inform them about the benefits of own small businesses.

- Instrumental in the access to formal banking channels for loans.
- Information about schemes like Mudra Yojana Scheme.
- Give them inputs about access market linkages.
- Gives them inputs about variety of business models ideas to help them scale up.
- Helps small business owners develop their communication skills.
- Trains them to negotiate with stakeholders in ecosystem of businesses.
- Provides them with emotional and psychological support.

- Women in Cinema Collective - body formed by women to raise their collective issues.

International

- Alibaba has 47% women employees. Jack Ma - if you want to win in 21st century empower others make sure they are better than you are. Women think more about others than self.
- In Iceland it is illegal to pay men more than women for same work. It is the first country to make such a law globally. The companies will be fined otherwise. Companies have to prove innocence. It is a world leader at gender equality with a gap of only 12%. Both parents get equal parental leave.
- In Sweden parent's leave of 480 days can be split between mother and father. Dads to take at least 3 months off; Parents with kids less than 8 years have shorter working hours as a right; They can take time off work when child is sick for 80% of the wages, preschools are subsidised by the government; The government provides regressive subsidy;. The country has one of the best childcare systems in the world.
- **Norway**
    - first country in the world to impose a gender quota on companies - 40% seats in boardrooms
    - strong parental leave laws entitling upto 14 weeks of leave to both parents
    - Start and Improve Your Business Program (SIYB) of the International Labour Organisation

Political

Examples

- BJD in Odisha and TMC in WB fielded 33% and 50% women candidates in Lok Sabha elections of 2019.
- Odisha House passed 33% reservation for women.

International-

- UAE to double women's representation in Federal National Council to 50% from 22.5% from coming Parliamentary term.

- Ethiopia, Rwanda are one of the world's few "gender-balanced" Cabinets with 50% women.
- Rwanda–
  - women make up 61% of Parliamentarians
  - has seen a decrease in gender discrimination and gender-based crimes
- Finland-
  - First country in the world to award full political rights to women in 1906. The first country to have female MPs
- LEADERSHIP
  - Ritu Karidhal and Muthayya Vanitha - heading 2nd moon exploration programme of ISRO

❑❑

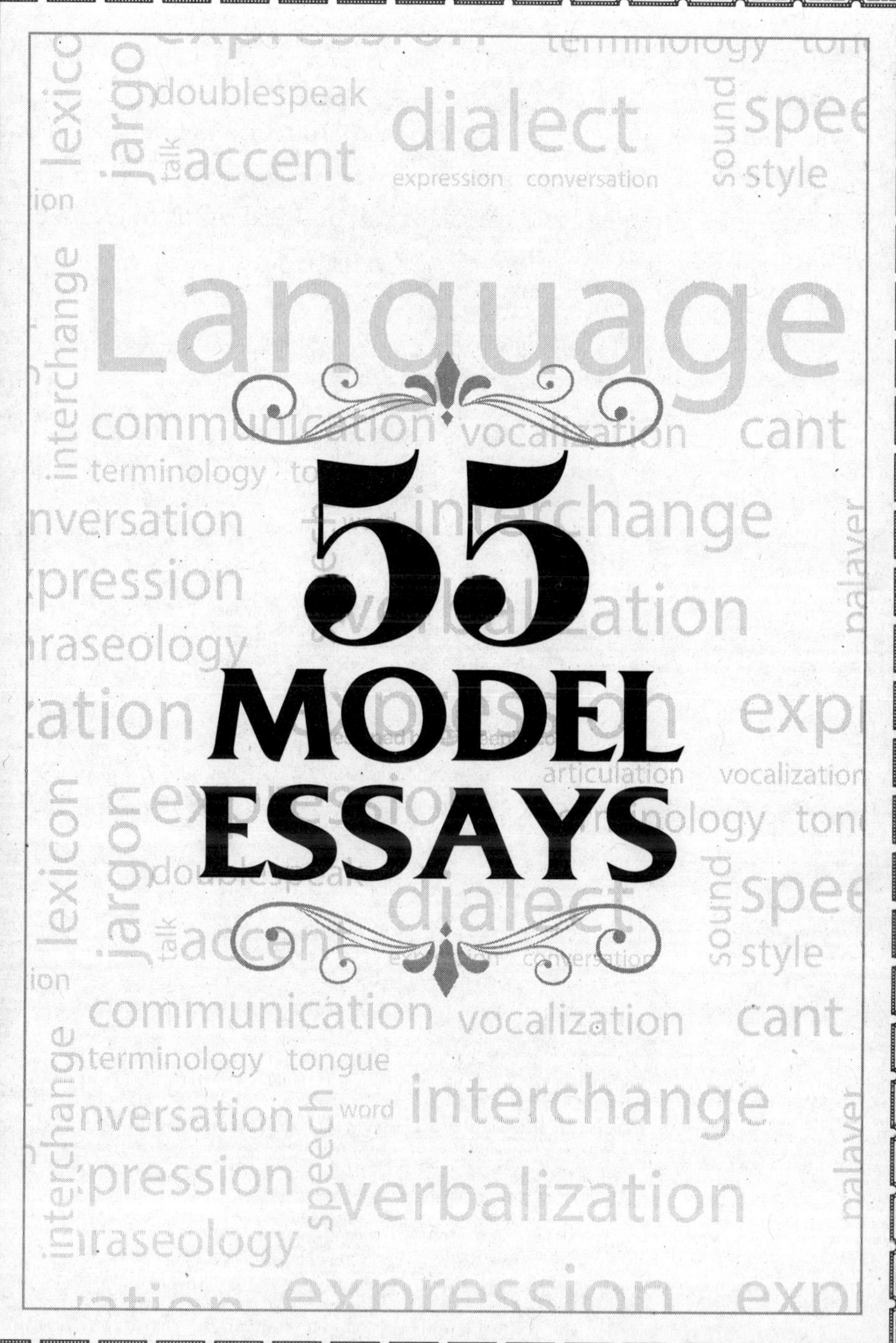
55
MODEL
ESSAYS

1 Artificial Intelligence: An End to Human Miseries or An End to Humanity Itself

Akshat Jain, IAS (AIR 2 CSE 2018)

Rewind the clock twenty years back, and one will find that the sci-fi film, 'Matrix', has caused quite a stir. The film takes us into a future where humanity has been enslaved by Artificial Intelligence. It revolves around humanity's struggle to retain its so-called place as the most superior species on the planet seemingly a childish fantasy at that time, fast forward to today, and all this appears a distinct reality.

Artificial Intelligence, or simply put AI refers to the capacity of a computer system to think and take decisions just like a human being. A development that started in the 1970s itself, has only now picked up pace. So rapid has been its rise that AI has become the talk of the tech-world. Every tech-giant is working on it and many nations are developing roadmaps on it. The who's who of tech-world is excited about AI, citing it as AN END TO HUMAN MISERIES. Their excitement and optimism is indeed justified for AI has applications in almost every field.

Perhaps the largest potential of AI lies in the economic field. AI is seen as the accelerator for building a global knowledge based economy. It has massive ability to boost the productivity and profits of companies. AI can help take more informed management decisions, improve manufacturing processes, perform redundant and high risk tasks, enhance customer interface. Its ability to streamline big data can help companies understand customer patterns and competitive behaviour more efficiently. In fact companies like Facebook and Amazon are already using AI to collect data sets on customers and introduce personal services.

AI can also provide a fillip to the banking sector in an almost identical manner. This can aid banks to take informed lending decisions, provide customized banking solutions, keep data secure. This can thus aid in financial inclusion.

The next important field being graced by AI is the domain of security. Self driven cars are being developed by giants like Google and Tesla, with an aim to reduce road accidents. For the armed forces, unmanned aerial vehicles (UAVs), drones, self-driven aircrafts and tanks are being developed. The idea is to reduce the role of humans on the battle-ground build a military deterrent. Apart from this, AI can also be used for policing and intelligence gathering.

Moving ahead, even Governments are thinking about the deployment of AI in political fields. It not only aids in policy making, but also provide public services, especially in rural and remote areas. It can act as banking correspondents, be used at Common Service Centres (CSCs), in infrastructure projects and for streamlining rigid bureaucratic procedures.

AI can even contribute in the field of healthcare. It has already been used to assist doctors in complex operations, perform surgeries by itself and for hospital management.

Even environmentalists are hoping that AI be used for advanced computing of meteorological data and study land from changes.

Last but not the least, AI can also serve as a companion to lonely individuals. Research is going on to develop AI-powered human bots, that can interact with humans as realistically as another human. The humanoid Sophia is just an example of the case in point.

Combining all this, it indeed looks true that AI can be the answer to all the miseries of human kind. But not all that glitters is gold. It is a natural law that excess of anything and everything, is bound to be dangerous. Even AI, for all its technological prowess, cannot escape this law.

The biggest fear comes from the unregulated and unethical use of AI. First of all, AI is an expensive technology to develop and thus risks the fear of becoming the monopoly of a handful of countries. Such a monopoly can never be fruitful.

One only needs to imagine the potential misuse of AI in the field of security. It is a technology that can wreak havoc in all the five theatres of war – land, air, water, space and cyber world.

Many organisations have pointed out to the development of AI powered Lethal Autonomous Weapon Systems (LAWS). These have the potential to kill thousands of people in one go. If such a technology falls into the wrong hands, the destruction of humanity is guaranteed.

There are further legitimate fears of uncompassionate policing, and above all, breach of privacy. AI can easily be used to infiltrate the digital footprints of an individual, thus compromising on this fundamental right.

AI is not an incorruptible technology and can become a victim of cybercrimes like hacking. This further aggravates all the above issues.

The threat is not restricted to the field of security. AI will impact the economic sector equally. It will increase the divide between rich and the poor. It can cause huge unemployment, as companies will look to cut down on costs not only in the manufacturing sector, but also tertiary. It also opens up space for unethical business practices, like obtaining customer data without consent. It will also put MSMEs at further risk of competing with MNCs. This will have huge repercussions in developing economies like India.

Moving on AI, can even put international and domestic governance at risk. It can provide a leverage for bigger countries over the developing and under-developed nations. This threatens the vision of a multi-polar world.

AI can be used to undermine electoral processes or threaten stability of regimes. For instance, AI can be used to infiltrate EVMs. All this will have huge geo-political implication.

It hence looks like it is better to let go-off such a technology, before we create a Frankenstein capable of ENDING HUMANITY ITSELF.

However, it is possible to create a balanced path that helps utilize AI for the betterment of mankind and reduce potential risks. It is imperative that the international community comes together on a single platform. The aim must be to distribute the fruits to all equitably. A rules based order needs to be established. Non-proliferation of AI into the wrong hands must be the priority. Further, organisations like the UN must work out to prevent any nation from developing lethal weapons and thus prevent what happened in the nuclear arm race.

For countries like India, who are developing their road maps for AI, the task should be to understand all dimensions holistically, including the ethical dimension. Further, India must be the leading voice of third world countries at international forum.

To conclude, only a rules-based order that is built on the principles of equality, security and morality, can ensure that AI be a boon for humanity.

The famous director, Steven Spielberg once said:

"Technology can be The Best Friend of Man,
But also His Worst Enemy"

Thus it is upto us to ensure that this relation be one of eternal friendship and peace, and let the wars be restricted to fantasy films and books only.

□□

2 Beware the Barrenness of Busy Life

Akshat Jain, IAS (AIR 2 CSE 2018)

As Ramesh opens the door and enters into his house, he is greeted by a silence, a silence only broken by the sound of the fan. Tired from his job, he calls out for his wife, only to remember that she was on a business trip. His elder son is busy on his laptop, unaware of Ramesh's presence. His younger daughter approaches, and asks him, "Daddy, Will you take me out for dinner today? You promised." "Sorry darling, but daddy has got a presentation to prepare for," Ramesh replies.

These kind of instances have become a common story in our households. Adults are occupied in their nine-to-five jobs, except that they hardly end on five. Children remain engrossed in their studies, and if not, then in their mobiles. The elderly remain lost, with boredom set to grip their final years of life. Has this become our fate-to be gone with the BARRENNESS OF OUR BUSY LIVES? How has it come down to this?

The reasons, for once, are not difficult to find. In today's era, the working population is involved in a rat race. At a time when jobs are hard to come by, and the costs of living keep on increasing every day, it is not surprising that these people lead busy lives. Globalization did bring in big and lucrative jobs at MNCs but they also brought in the obligations to work overtime, from home, at weekends. Whatever time is available, is spent on household obligations.

The children of today are not the same as before. Our educational system is such that the balance between studies and sports seems to have lost. With emphasis on getting marks and entering the best colleges, our childhood revolves around our school, tuition classes, and the coaching centres. Every child lives under the pressure that if he/she doesn't land a high paying job, they might not survive in this world. Due to all this, the once-put emphasis on physical activity, creativity, arts and innovation has evaporated. The neglect of parents further complicates the issue.

The present situation also owes much to technology. The purpose of technology was to free humans from the redundant tasks, and enhance the quality of their lives. Ironically, technology has only worsened the cause. Everybody seems to have their eyes stuck in their mobiles, even when someone is talking to them. The laptops ensure the work reaches out to every home, and is not confined to the office. The playground of the child has shrunk from the nearly park, to the play station. In fact, technology has only made us more lazy and resistant to spending time with others, physical activity, and to appreciate the natural beauty of this earth.

Probably, at the heart of all this has been a shift in our priorities and values. Materialistic possessions and a desire for wealth have eroded the real joys of life. Though it is not bad to pursue them, it certainly is unethical to make them the sole objective of our lives. This has been singled out by the Vedas as well.

However, one may still point out that life is still going on as before. They may say that all this is an exaggeration, and we still do spend time with friends and family. Well, the impacts of our busy lives point otherwise.

On an individual level, we find ourselves emotionally unbalanced. Our bank balances might have increased, but the happiness is not there. Children feel neglected by their parents; adults feel isolated from their loved ones and colleagues; while the elderly die in loneliness. The rising rates of suicides, juvenile crimes and old age homes are a testament to all this.

The institution of family, the cornerstone of human society, has also been affected. The rising incidences of divorces, single parent households, parent-children divide and fights between older and younger generation, all have destabilised our families.

The society has not been spared either. With declining levels of interactions, people have become intolerant and suspicious of even their neighbours.

All this has impacted our health as well. With low levels of physical fitness, and high level of mental fatigue, we have been pushed towards vices like alcohol and cigarettes. It is thus no coincidence that lifestyle diseases like cardiac arrest, lung cancer, diabetes and obesity are at an all-time high.

Finally, our democracy has also suffered. People are too busy to vote, care about national happenings and participate in nation building. After all, nation building is also about holding elected representatives accountable and developing a vibrant citizenry.

Amidst this abyss, are we set to become the slaves of our monotonous lives? Can this situation be reversed! Undoubtedly, yes!

We must start with reforming our educational system. So that each child gets the childhood he/she deserves. The curriculum must give proportional focus on studies, learning, physical activity and arts. Teachers and institutes must lead from the front, and actively encourage parents to spend time with their children.

Moving on, the work culture in our companies need to change. A company that gives adequate personal time to its employees, organises team trips and parties and doesn't intrude into their personal time always benefits from a happier and productive workforce.

The government must lead from the front here. A look at the labour laws may also help foster such an environment.

However, the ultimate one lies on the individual itself. Each of us should concern for our spiritual happiness, at least equally with that of materialistic pleasure. Spending valuable time with our dear ones, practising yoga and meditation, and building upon our relations with the society are some steps that we can take. These will only improve our productivity-economic, social and moral.

To conclude, it is high time that we realize where our true happiness lies. The human nature thrives when it connects to its own inner self and to other fellow beings. Therefore, the next time Mr. Ramesh says no to his daughter, we must all remind him

Beware The Barrenness of Busy Life!

❑❑

3 Industry 4.0 is the Biggest Game Changer of Present and Future

Jayant Nahata, IAS (AIR 56 CSE 2020)

Yuval Noah Harari in his book "Sapiens" has described the brief history of humankind from the Cognitive revolution to agriculture revolution to scientific revolution. The phases of the last two-three centuries of scientific revolution have seen astonishing progress. From the spinning jenny and power loom to telephone line, internet, micro-chips and supercomputing, the strings of achievements have been dizzyingly fast.

Now, (wo)man stands at the cusp of another great revolution i.e. the Industrial Revolution 4.0 which will "blur the lives" between the physical, biological and technological as we move into the future. It builds on Industrial Revolutions of the past based on "steam power", "electricity" and "electronics"/"Information Technology" yet very different and broader in scope.

Let's analyze, how Industrial Revolution 4.0 is set to be the biggest game changer of not present but future too. Whether it faces any challenges or poses any threats? Further, how can humankind reap the best dividends out of this great revolution that is unfolding.

Industrial Revolution 4.0 promises a future that is utopian to the least and impossible to grasp fully. It will involve technologies such as intelligent AI powered machines capable of human level cognition. We can imagine human cyborgs with chips inserted in the brain to argument our capabilities or 4-D printing in new ages factories of the future. From biotechnology to nanotechnology, from smart manufacturing to quantum computing, Industrial Revolution 4.0 is set to dazzle humankind.

No other revolution comes close. Any change of economic model such as *laissez faire* to welfare state and current neo-liberal, neither any changes in political agenda can hope to compete with the magnitude/scope of changes that Industry 4.0 promises.

In the economic sphere, we can expect to see ultra-high efficiency logistics due to predictive AI based technologies. Amazon has already rolled out the feature in some American towns where a product is pre-shipped to a location based on high probability that the customer will order it soon!

The industries will shift from current "assembly-line" manufacturing to decentralized, innovation driven 4D printed or 3D printed products. This will create complex, customer suited products like prosthetic limbs at fraction of environmental costs. It will boost productivity in the economy and reward talent.

Drone based technologies and nano-senors have already found their way to Netherland's farms. The real time data down to a 'single potato' about soil health, water requirements, optimum temperature is already revolutionizing concept of food security methods. Netherland shows the world a glimpse of farming of the future!

Outside industries and farms, the most important social domains of education, health and skills can be expected to see dramatic changes. Already China has deployed, AI powered robots as nursery classroom teacher assistants.

In India, NITI Aayog in a bold pilot, has partnered with Qure.ai company to deploy AI tools for TB screening in aspirational districts. Numerous studies have shown potential of AI based machines to diagnose TB, cancer etc. at a higher accuracy enabling faster diagnosis and speed to treatment.

The world of skills will see a change too. Not just the requirements of data scientists, biotechnologists etc. is set to proliferate, the task of skilling is set to see paradigm change from institution led to personalised, own-paced programs such as Massive Open Online Courses (MOOCs).

Industry 4.0 will not just change our exterior but ourselves too. With the ever closer integration of biotechnology in our lives apart from digicenticals (such as glucose monitoring chips embedded in body) and nano robots to deliver drugs, humans may soon become part of the revolution, quite literally. Technologies such as google glasses, virtual reality headgears, neuralink launched by Elon Musk (project in progress) show how technology might pair up with humans to script history of 21st century.

The political aspects of our lives can be enriched too. Instant, robust communication can boost participation of people in democratic policy making which is today restricted due to hassles of engaging directly with our political representatives. Not just the country, the world can come together overcoming the barriers of boundaries and check posts.

The borders may now irrelevant but with technologies like space based observation and surveillance drones, laser guided walls, robots manning the risky fences, security will undergo radical transformation leading to better safety and peace for the people.

However, 4th Industrial revolution brings with it host of unpredictability and policy/ moral/economical/environmental challenges.

Firstly, the pace of technological progress is unprecedented and even beats theories/ any past assumptions of gradualism. The future is here and now. We need to cope with it in real time.

Fourth Industrial Revolution and the flood of new technologies it entails, can further the inequalities already existing in our society. The Piketty papers highlighted that 1%

of Indians own 70% of all wealth in India. This gulf between the rich and the poor will/may get wider as the know-how, digital and financial literacy is enjoyed only by the few and only few can afford such technologies, inequalities even between nations maybe created, the Global North and Global South may further drift away in prosperity. We can already see China through "Made in China 2025" trying to get a lead in technologies like AI, robotics, SG, semi-conductors. This has precipitated the undergoing trade war that threatens peace across the world and lowers global growth prospects.

Further, a cocktail of futuristic technologies may go out of human control creating the "Frankenstein Monster" as shown in movies like Terminator and can threaten mankind itself. This raises serious moral issues. The recent episode of the Jiankui (China based researcher) who modified germline of living embryos in the quest of AIDS prevention shows the "regulatory headaches" the world is going to face going forward.

The environmental impact of 4th Industrial Revolution is really "the elephant in the room" as our previous experiments with steam engines and mass production in factories have today pushed mankind to the brink of civilizational collapse. IPCC predicts havoc with rising sea levels submerging islands and coasts, threatening our energy, food and health security.

As Charles Dickens eloquently put it in his novel "The Tale of Two Cities"- "It was the best of times, it was the worst of times". "It was on age of wisdom and age of foolishness". Similarly, the predicament facing humankind is based on how we choose to use these technologies and shape them. It can either be misused for geo-politics and breed inequalities or be used for astonishing results such as "knowledge economy", efficient production and argumenting human capacities to the fullest of its potential.

Since the scope of Industrial Revolution is global, the efforts to shape its future has to be global too. Governance models need to change for regulating technology use such as prohibition of human cloning/germline editing or offensive use of Artificial Intelligence.

For truly reaping the benefits of Industry 4.0, Amartya Sen's capability approach need to be used as the yardstick. Investments in upskilling and reskilling youth will truly reap demographic dividend else it might well turn into a demographic disaster – social unrest and protests. Tools of AI, robotics, tele-medicine can itself be used to prepare workforce for an era of Industry 4.0.

Investments on social security need to be made. The concepts of Minimum Basic Income need to be piloted as early as possible as automation is already risking jobs and threatening unrest. Education system needs to shift to "Continuous Learning Paradigm" such as recently started in Finland and National University of Singapore.

Micro, Small and Medium scale enterprises need to be integrated in formal sector, given technological capabilities and infrastructure/financial support to leverage the benefits of the Industry 4.0 which will essentially favour MSME-led decentralized product manufacturing.

Finally, as human revolutionary progress indicates, man has always longed for greater happiness and boundless productivity. With careful planning and capabilities, Industrial Revolution 4.0 will truly emerge as the biggest game changer for present and future.

"The future is now"

❑❑

4 Life Happens to All, Only Few Make it Happen

Jayant Nahata, IAS (AIR 56 CSE 2020)

Back in 18th century, there existed a sleepy town in the hinterland of present day U.S.A. The family by the name of Franklin had seven children with one particular short stature boy who was the youngest of the seven children.

The boy struggled with his limited means, received education in a local school and was often teased by his friends. But he was not like any other.

He possessed a kind of perseverance and passion few around him knew. At the day's end, he would open his diary, record his good habits and bad habits, during the day like reading books, showing punctuality, being humble etc. that he would sleep with resolve to make the next day better.

Throughout his adult phase, as he struggled with odd jobs like a newspaper printer, he never forgot to improve and learn each day. He grabbed an opportunity, expanded his networks and self-taught himself.

Slowly, he gained membership of legislature of American state, his scientific papers got published and he jumped into the American Revolution related activism and emerged as the tallest leader and father of Modern America. His name was Benjamin Franklin!

Thus, despite odds and circumstances, he built himself and made life happen! Not just for himself, but for his country!

Though, life in the form of birth happens to all humans, why are there only few Benjamin Franklin, Gandhi, Teresa? Does life happens to all truly?

We may argue that not all are fortunate to get a life worthy of its name. Some are unlucky and born as differently abled. Some lives are ended in the wombs by foeticide and some female children face the horror of infanticide by their unwilling parents.

Even after crossing the hurdles of mortality, not all get life in equal measure. Economic survey 2017-18 talks of "unwanted girls" born due to son-meta preference and thus facing neglect in education, nourishment and career.

Debt often leads to bonded labour and trafficking where freedom of an individual which is basic essence of human life is snatched away.

The present day ad-industry has its own way of curbing true choice by developing false needs of goods and values.

But the inspiring stories of Helen Keller (differently abled), Indira Gandhi (female), Rajnikanth (earlier a bus conductor) show how few individuals brave all circumstances in their way to truly make their life happen.

Life happens when one achieves individual success, pride, respect and glory. Life also happens in enabling the other individual by empowering him.

Stalwarts of fame made not only their life happen, but brought prosperity to an entire nation or steered the world to a better path.

History holds important lessons and is often told in reference of individuals such as Mauryan Empire, BC era as Before Christ, Gandhian phase of independence movement and so on. This shows their importance as "guiding light" to human race.

The lives of Gautama Buddha and Mahavira made life happen by wondering and contemplating the "Truth" to make society peaceful.

Traits define such great figures. Lincoln for example, showed festitude while engaging in the emancipation and the proclamation to outlaw slavery.

Mother Teresa had utmost empathy for diseases (leprosy patients for example). Gandhi, Martin Luther King and Mandela showed awe inspiring, leadership skills to sway masses towards the road to freedom.

Administrators like E. Sreedharan gained the repute of 'Metro Man' due to his sincerity and no non-sense attitude.

On the other end of the spectrum, the prodigies like Da Vinci and Picasso were gifted with 'creativity' while Einstein had an 'IQ' few could match. This led all these individuals to make life happen!

The common thread roaming through all such stories is the existence of a positive attitude towards life, perseverance and hard work and passion to achieve a noble vision.

However, what makes the other 99% fail to make life happen?

One may attribute it to genetic traits (such as high IQ of Einstein) not favourable as nature is random.

Others may agree that dire circumstances such as extreme poverty, birth in a black family or low caste or hindered by geography such as North-Eastern religion.

True, is there a 'level playing field' between an American white male born to Bill Gates and an Africa black female born in war torn Sudan?

On the other hand, it's equally true that 'making life happen' is no reserved for only few individuals who gain limelight.

A poor man toils throughout the day in the agricultural field with utmost honesty to make two meals possible and to get his children educated. Isn't he making life happen in his own way? Are soldiers on the borders or security guards at the colony gates not enabling others to make life happen?

Needless to say, some achieve more than others and for the right reasons. So it's prudent that the individuals learn from history and try to imbibe positive traits and methods to achieve similar results. Only then will society move towards the path of success.

Firstly, individuals need to gain objective understanding of their reality, their strengths and weakness. Then, they can begin developing positive habits.

As Benjamin Franklin said:

"Excellence is not an Act, It's a daily habit"

The role of states is very crucial to remove the external and internal impediments facing the citizens. The state should build capacity via investments in education, health, infrastructure, skills etc. The case of South Korea where 94% of citizens are skilled leading to prosperity and housing corporate giants like Samsung and LG proves that state has crucial role to make life happen to its citizens.

However, civil society and corporates have to share the burden equally with the state. Bill and Melinda Gates foundations exemplary work in Africa in fight against HIV proves that individuals who've made life happen to themselves can extend the helping hand to others left behind for society to progress as a whole.

Corporates need to reform their internal functioning to blur the 'glass ceiling' and give equal opportunity to all people to make good out of their lives. They have a role in environmental management and sustainable development for long term vitality of Earth.

The combined efforts of all actors will lead to true meaning of life unfolding for most in our society. With each individual outdoing herself/himself, expanding his frontiers of excellence and gaining success, the whole society will prosper. Life then will truly happen to all and all will be capable enough to make life happen to themselves.

"In the stirring lies the success"

❑❑

5 Nothing is Absolute, Subjectivity Applies Everywhere

Jayant Nahata, IAS (AIR 56 CSE 2020)

"There are no absolute truth... What we need is incredulity towards Meta-narratives".

–Lyotard

Lyotard was a post-modern scholar of fame. He warned of the dangers of sweeping generalisations and absolute ideologies instead calling for anti-foundationalism and anti-universalism.

But why was Lyotard so against absoluteness? Is nothing really absolute? Let's find out!

Absolute truths are those ideas, values, statements and beliefs where humans or society reposes blind faith and total acceptance.

For example, God is considered the highest authority according to most religions.

Subjectivity on the other hand implies difference of opinion and perspective on similar issues. The classic example is the "half-glass full" vs "half-glass empty" anecdote.

All through history there have been some or the other universal dogmas or beliefs that is, ideologies which have been used to articulate one's perspective and mobilise people around it.

While the Christians waged crusades in defence of their absolute belief in sayings of Bible, modern day world sees Jihad by extremist from Islam as waging wars to create an "Imagined Caliphate" in West Asia.

This absoluteness thus sparks conflicts between individuals, societal actors like corporates vs. government, between nations and clash of civilisation.

An individual's absolute trust on his argument during a road accident gets inflated into road rage killings/violence. A community's trust in its own superstitious beliefs/orthodoxy gets translated into our newspaper headlines talking of Khap panchayat sanctions, honour killings, witch huntings in Manipur etc.

Similarly, at the border, varying perceptions of the line of control results into ceasefire violations and killings of civilians/army men.

Thus, absoluteness of any kind seems to be causing weakening of social fabric and disharmony in the world.

Even Foucault, the great scholar of our times has analyzed ideologies and rejects absoluteness or discourses. He argues that there are no universal principle. We live in a social world where truth isn't discovered, its fabricated. Nietzche famously said that "God is dead" and there is no universal morality.

This can be analyzed even in various walks of life.

Subjectivity persists in religious beliefs while Jainism/ Buddhism preach against superiority of Vedas, Hinduism considers it sacred. The caste system has been interpreted by Manusmriti as "Dharma" or part of natural order while Ambedkar called for "putting dynamite" on the very same scripture. The concept of gender is also not absolute – ask a rural poor illiterate women and she would justify domestic violence by her husband in all probability.

Society has deep inter-linkages with polity. Though the world was divided into two absolute blocs of liberal west and Communist Soviet Union during cold war, its end led to Francis Fukyama clamming the "End of History" as liberalism as an ideology won. However soon, this absoluteness was challenged by rising Asian states, Islamic fundamentalism seen in 9/11 terror attacks and resurgence of Russia and China.

Democracy which is often considered the best political system is challenged by statesmen like Lee Kuan Yow who called it a "Western Obsession". Even during the inter-war period, whatever fascists like Hitler did was absolutely justified from their perspective but roundly condemned by the international community.

The current globalisation face is deeply contended for its impact – some argue that it has led to "Plutocracy" (Ramesh Thakur) some others like Jagdish Bhagwati cite declining poverty in China from 36% to 6% (1990-2016) as evidence of its virtues. Thus, subjectivity prevails here too.

But why then is absoluteness across spheres existing?

Gramsci, the contemporary of Mussolini, puts blame on hegemony or soft power which is manufactured by the elites in the society. The ad-industry is making human "One Dimensional Man". While consumerism and materialism is being projected as the absolute goals, it's leading to false consciousness.

Moreover, Human by nature is a social animal and tends to defend his long cultivated social beliefs.

Thus, the society in ancient Sparta glorified war even though peace/love are considered universal traits in modern world.

The reason for such absoluteness may lie in the pursuance of 'Power". There is a knowledge-power connection. Every theory is said for some purpose and by some person. So, Brahminical superiority was maintained via caste rigidity and even the Britishers maintained "White Man's Burden" theory to justify their rule over India.

But is the skepticism towards all that is absolute correct? All of us may agree on certain absolute principles such as empathy, love and peace. These are hard-wired in us from birth. Gandhiji considered non-violence as the "Absolute creed" for which he suspended the Non-cooperation movement post-Chauri-Chaura.

Similarly, human rights such as right to life, freedom of speech and equality are moral guarantees in most culture/political systems.

Absoluteness is rooted in scientific theories. Science tells about truth and false. We are all made of carbon, any doubts?

However, even the staunchest science theorist will agree that even science goes for constant revisions in postulations.

Newton's theory was revised by Galileo. Even the rebuked concept of black hole was defied with the Messier 87 photograph recently.

Now since, there is no absoluteness or minimal absoluteness, given the negative impacts (violence, conflicts, etc.) that we saw, how can individuals, society, nations come to terms with subjectivity. Is the term "Vasudhaiva Kutumbakam" totally elusive given the subjectivity in opinion and perspective?

The world need to accept the fact that subjectivity exists. Without accepting the issue, we won't be able to deal with it.

Once, there is widespread agreement on this 'fact that there's no absolute fact', there needs to be cultivation of toleration and acceptance of the other. Tolerance isn't weakness. It represents the strength of one's personality and openness to new ideas which enriches all cultures.

India is the 'guiding light' of the world as it has managed to accommodate diversity of unimaginable proportions under a single national identity.

Education institutions should profess 'value pluralism' i.e. acceptance of existence of equally right value which might seem conflictual. On the other hand, there also needs to be 'intolerance 'against evils such as violence, discrimination, hate, crimes etc.

Multi-culturists' idea need to be adopted by political system to solve the minority issue and refugee crisis. There needs to be more democratic sphere where people interact with each other and resolve conflicts. Only with exchange of ideas and more communication our societies/culture would flourish else even the romans saw their empire crumbling due to dogma.

Religion has taught of 'anekantavada' and "Middle Path" to avoid extreme to get harmony in society. Let's all unite by our acceptance of subjectivity rather than fight on the existence of absoluteness. The world of today presents equally truthful idea/values/ ideologies. We can all move together in the "search of truth" by accepting each other's perspectives and leaving behind dogmas.

The day then is not far when the utopianism of 'Vasudhaiva Kutumbakam' will convert into reality.

❑❑

6 People Decide Their Own Destiny, Fortunes are Made or Unmade by Humans

Jayant Nahata, IAS (AIR 56 CSE 2020)

The year was 1945...at the end of a gruesome world war, the international leaders decided to crave up the Korean peninsula along the 38th parallel. Though the two Koreas – North and South started from the same ravages and deprivations, the people of South Korea chose to alter their destiny forever! With massive investments in education, health, skilling, infrastructure and sheer dedication and will of ordinary men and women, the karma of the people finally showed fruit.

South Korea entered the club of "Asian Tigers" with 10% plus GDP growth rates for more than 30 years. It shrugged off poverty and ensured that South Koreans emerged as one of the most prosperous and technologically advanced countries in the world. Shifting to the north of the parallel, the misdeeds of authoritarian leaders and missed priorities have led to deprivation of basics like food and threatens nuclear showdown with USA.

Who says fortunes are pre-decided in heaven? Even the palm develops those fortune lines only because the palm is closed into a fist in the womb! Thus indicating that fortunes are made by Karmas and people chart their own destiny! But there's more to it that what meets the eye. Let's analyse how Karmas defines the fortunes good or bad. Whether there are exceptions to this generalisations? And how should we brace for the path ahead?

The phrase "what you sow, so shall you reap" beautifully and precisely captures the essence of Karma theory. Truly, the fruits of one's handwork and labour come one day or another. Thomas Alva Edison's untiring efforts and repeated failures, finally led him to the invention of the "light bulb"!

Karma is equally dangerous when put to negative use. The fortunes of Satyam Company evaporated with legal and ethical lapses on the part of its management. Similarly, one resorting to fatalistic thinking .i.e. everything is pre-decided more often than not see stagnation in their life or downturn. The lack of adaptation measures once brought the famed Harrapan Civilization to ruins with massive floods! History definitely has lessons to teach, but we can ignore it into our own peril!

The great philosophical thinker and realist, Machiavelli remarked that fortunes or bad luck can arrive to the doors of anyone, but it's only the prepared one who brave the storm. Luck is when preparation meets opportunity!

In 1999, the super cyclone in Odisha killed 12,000 people and damaged billions worth of property, but learning from it, the people and state did their "Karma" of establishing early warning systems, training state disaster response forces and developed protection infrastructure. Zoom to 2016, the cyclone Phailin with similar destructive potential caused just 40 odd casualties (although still unfortunate)!

One of the top "fortune 500" companies Amazon is the result of innovation and perseverance of its founder Jeff Bezos who braved the monopolistic giants like Walmart and charted his destiny to the top! Good karmas see a mixture of great handwork and perseverance guided by the values of altruism, compassion, love and integrity. It involves the ability to brave the daily failures and to literally chart way through mountains as the stories of Amazon, South Korea etc. demonstrate.

Bad Karmas can similarly upturn the fortunes. Ultra-nationalism and "Aryan theory of supremacy" led to Hitler's eventual defeat at the end of second world war. Napoleon's greed and dominating instincts caused him his biggest loss at Waterloo. Even during the Indian freedom struggle, the Britishers' wrongs and oppressions collided with Gandhi's truth and non-violent karma of satyagraha and saw the downfall of history's greatest imperial power!

Karma in the wrong direction can possibly evade the envisioned destiny. Trying to use outmoded technologies in agriculture and faulty policies such as skewed MSP (Minimum Support Price) literally led to "reaping what was sowed".

However, generalisations of sweeping return often hide more than they reveal. Despite human will certain structural factors may still prevent translations of Karma into destiny. In the case of women across the world, the social rule of patriarchy and male domination have shackled their growth story. Only a few likes of Sheryl Sandberg or Indira Nooyi have managed to create a place at the high tables of corporate world. Some holds true for politics where only 12 women leaders headed their countries in 20th century.

Similarly despite good karmas, such as adaption and rescue, millions lose their lives to disasters still! Super power rivalry led to proxy wars in disparate countries such as Cuba (Cuban Missile Crises of 1962) who were unwilling to get sucked up in militarisation.

But one may argue also that seemingly out of control factors like natural disasters or say biological parameters also lose their relevance in the face of grit and unbending attitude. Lionel Messi's short statures denied him bright prospects in football league but he crafted his destiny himself. He famously remarked – "after 17 years of hard work, I have now become an overnight success" – as he accepted his consecutive 'Ballon d'Or "Best Football Player" award!

Humanity will benefit if it takes cue from the essence of Bhagavad Gita which is "Nishkam Karma". As the Mahabharata's climactic battle was yet to start, Krishna asked the perplexed Arjun to "do his duty" without caring for the fruits.

Men and women should realise that only with efforts are the paths to prosperity and happiness created. There's no easy way out. The state should similarly do its "karma" of capacity building of its own population to brace for a fast changing word of 21st century. At the global level, nations should understand the collective future of humanity is linked. The efforts or Karma shouldn't breed exclusion and inequalities between west-east or global North-South, rather endeavour towards common good should be made. Let us all unite to realise our "tryst with destiny" using the power of Karma!

❑❑

7 Science is a Beautiful Gift To Humanity, We should not Distort it

Jayant Nahata, IAS (AIR 56 CSE 2020)

Yuval Noah Harari in his book "Sapiens" describes the brief history of human kind. Humans through the ages have advanced side by side as their scientific knowledge expanded. The discovery of "language" ushered in the "Cognitive Revolution"; "fire" discovered 1,00,000 years back kickstarted new mode of hunting and cooking finally leading to "agricultural Revolution"(1,00,000 years back). But the world was upturned with the ushering of "scientific revolution" from 15th century A.D. onwards!

From the printing to compass, the science of "mapping" (cartography) to spinning jenny and steam engines, (wo)mankind learnt to translate its scientific process into tangible technological developments. This opened up new trade routes, ushered communication revolution, kick- started Industrial Age while the 20th century internet made "Vasudhaiva Kutumbakam" a reality! Science definitely turned out as the most beautiful gift of humanity: it eased life, helped combat diseases via new age vaccines and put a serious dent on poverty and accelerated economic growth.

But a parallel script was being written. The man's inner devil, his greed and myopic view started to distort science. The same fire which lightened up cold caves was used to clear up vast tracts of jungles and destroy biodiversity. Ninety per cent of aboriginals and local species were wiped out within hundred years of Australia's discovery! Even today, the world looks on as the Brazilian Amazon is going up in flames!

"Now I am become death, the destroyer of the world"

J. Robert Oppenheimer uttered these famous lines taking a cue from Bhagavad Gita, on witnessing the destructive potential of his own creative genius – the atom bomb. His "atomic sciences" knowledge was misused and destroyed "Hiroshima" and "Nagasaki" flattering them to the ground. Even now, we witness the "nuclear umbrella" being used as a cover to wage "proxy wars" around the world especially with reference to Pakistan.

While on one hand, the medical sciences revolutionised healthcare such as global elimination of the dreaded "smallpox", its distortion is leading to anti-microbial resistance which is again threatening to push us back to pre-penicillin era! The advances in microbiology have created challenges such as designer babies and unregulated genetically modified crops which are headaches to policy-makers concerned about long term effects, equity and safety issues. The case of Jiankui who edited human germline is a befitting example!

On the farms, the agriculture science ushered green revolution and fulfilled food security to an extent but excessive fertilizers pesticide use and groundwater extraction again jeopardises and raise a spectre of "Malthusian population demise"

Not just the earth, the space is also witnessing new space weaponisation trends as the USA fired the first shots by ordering a "space force". Excessive space assets have already caused issues of space debris threatening the vital communication and remote sensing infrastructure.

The age of machines which propelled humans to our "golden era" of prosperity via the industrial revolution already raise fears of a "Frankenstein monster "with the arrival of artificial intelligence, deep learning, big data and internet of things. The "terminators" may well come to haunt humankind!

Serious legal and moral issues have come up. Concerns of privacy are heightened with Cambridge Analytic episode while the issues of cybersecurity are a new rage with attacks of Petya and WannaCry Ransomware! The internet which connects humans like "nerves in the brain" also has the capacity to bombard every node with fake news and radicalisation! Rise of ISIS recruitments in recent history, the Bulandshahar violençe were all facilitated by distortions of science of computers.

The Orwellian world is already coming to life with Chinese government using AI based mass surveillance to monitor Uyghurs. As Gandhiji warned of "Machines displacing Man", similarly the 4th industrial revolution threatens jobs as the OLO's future of work report points out.

However, the biggest existential threat which our "gift" of science has caused, is the ongoing climate change and global warming. The IPCC special report on "1.5° C warming" shows predictions of submerging coastlines, melting Hindukush, water insecurity and frequent extreme events like floods, and cyclones.

(Wo)Man's greed for more, ceaseless and endless desire for power, nationalistic jingoism have all contributed in the deadly cocktail that seems to go out of hand. As Charles Dickens eloquently put it "it was an age of wisdom and an age of foolishness" thus it's upon humans themselves to choose whether to exploit the beneficial effects of scientific knowledge or to misuse it towards our own impending doom!

In the age of globalised world, the challenges cannot be solved in silos. Science needs to be regulated towards useful purpose at a global level. Bodies like UN should formulate new rules to curb misuse. The Antarctic treaty can be a model as it promotes only research and sustainable use of resources.

But for the world to change, change has to start from within! Human's blessed with reason should grasp fully the consequences of their myopic view of science and its technological use. Learning to cooperate in peaceful uses of sciences can reap huge dividends as our past shows. We can make further advances in science to roll-back certain mistakes such as pollution of environment, weapons of mass destruction. Approaches such as ocean fertilization, sequestering carbon by geo-engineering can curb global warming. IAEA checks on nuclear plants and similarly surveillance on labs developing sensitive technologies like genetic therapy can significantly boost or safety and ensure inter-generational equity.

Finally, as Yuval Noah Harari also exclaims: humans with seemingly unlimited power facilitated by science have become "new age gods". But Gods who are unknown to the purpose of their scientific powers can wreak havoc. Let this 21st century be instead known by humanity's wisdom to channel their powers in pursuit of greater peace, harmony and happiness on our little planet!

❑❑

8 "To Be Beautiful, Life Doesn't Require To Be Big"

Jayant Nahata, IAS (AIR 56 CSE 2020)

As India celebrates the birth anniversary of its heroic freedom-fighter – the legendary Bhagat Singh in the coming month of September, his brief 24 years of life is a definite lesson that to be beautiful, life certainly doesn't require to be big. With his revolutionary struggles such as throwing bomb in the central assembly against repressive laws to his radical ideas of socialism, anti-casteism and anti-communalism, Bhagat Singh not only lived a great life but left a legacy to be cherished by Indians across the world till date.

On the other hand, Gandhiji although assassinated and dying unnaturally, was able to wage a protracted struggle based on truth and non-violence against British Colonialism. Certainly, long/big life of Gandhiji proved to be the greatest blessing for Indians. This raises the question whether even a small/short life can be beautiful? What is the meaning of beautiful or big life?

Beautiful life can entail wide connotations and multiple meanings. Furthermore, meanings and relative importance can vary from person to person, state or culture. For the tribes in Papua New Guinea, preserving their language and traditional ways of life may constitute a beautiful life. While for corporates in towering buildings of America, six figure salaries is all that's needed for a beautiful life!!

"Big" life, similarly, can mean a longer span of individual life or can imply fat pay-checks/income, luxury or to accomplish fame and respect. As the typical Ad line goes – "you have one life, make it BIG".

In the following essay, let's see whether and how life can be beautiful even in small settings limited circumstances! Whether long life may even be a "boon" adding to life struggle or if the opposite is true?

Further, we will see how a beautiful life can be led by all when (wo)man takes birth in this world, the "clock" of life-death cycle starts. As one socialises and comes to terms with societal hopes, country's problems and life's daily struggles, everyone, whether in high rises or slums strives to live a beautiful life in the future. Given the social-milieu, one tends to blur the distinction between "beautiful "and "big"– conflating the rich with happy or the rural/poor as living somewhat "lesser life". Nothing can be further from truth.

The lives of great men and women like the stated case of Bhagat Singh, makes it clear, that big life isn't a pre-requisite to a beautiful one. As Ambedkar said and proved with his own story – "life shouldn't be long, it should be great".

One should strive for value based, ethical life, a life of passionate stirring and courage/risk. The likes of Manjunath comprised their lives but not their ideals hence leaving behind a "beautiful "legacy for civil servants.

Contrarily, large/long life can even prove burdensome. Old age, quite literally, is painful for most and rich often live in constant fear of an impending robbery of their hard earned money.

The saying is not just applicable to individuals, but looked closely, seems to hold true across various facets of life.

The small community of Aristotle in Tamil Nadu exudes harmonious living while maintaining environment free of communalism often proves difficult due to tensions between two major communities/religions in India! Similarly the minority religion Jainism is also one of the most prosperous and educated community in India. This is possible due to the inherent dynamics of small groups which aid in cohesion, exchanges and building mutual trust.

Apart from small communities or religious, the tiny nation of Bhutan by holding the title of "the happiest nation" on earth, again shows how by isn't the criterion for beautiful!

Large groups often breed confusion, policy paralysis as had been the case of League of Nations needing consensus of all members for any collective security operations. Its failing was one of the major factors for World War-2 causing 20 million deaths and untold misery across the globe. Comparing it with the 5 membered (permanent members that is) UN Security Council, UNSC has definitely spearheaded a peaceful post-1945 world free of World War-3!

The current predicament of climate change facing mankind also has roots in the striving for "big" life. The Industrial Revolution of 18th century began with the promise of widespread prosperity but ended up threatening mankind's very existence as pointed out by numerous reports starting from Brundtland to IPCC.

Small life entails simplicity rather than complexity. Napoleon's ideal for laws was one that "comprehendable by a lay man and fits in the pocket".

The 40 odd central labour laws on top of 100s of state laws shackling India's employment and in turn the growth story, proves that policy-makers have yet to take a lesson from Napoleon preachings.

Outside the political-legal sphere, even in space, the norm has been to go small! ISRO with a small budget (₹ 10,000 crore) is a lean and mean body successfully dishing out series of successful proud-writing missions. Its Mangalyaan mission was in fact on a budget "smaller" than that for the Hollywood movie "Galaxy". Going small is actually a boon, as it forces innovation (suited to India's context), efficient operations and less wastage of public resources.

Even in the naxal infested red corridor, the success of Greyhounds (small elite commando battalions) of Andhra Pradesh shows small is an advantage even in strategic operations. The same was proven in Balakot and Uri surgical strike.

However, no generalisation should be made. It's imperative to point that even small can be bad and big can be beautiful! Small nations like Bhutan have often found themselves squeezed "like an egg between two boulders" of India and China as the recent Doklam crisis indicated. On the other hand, the "ASEAN Miracle" as foreign affairs experts term it shows how solidarity among small nations into a larger grouping can breed prosperity in economic and strategic security.

On an individual's life, the benefits of joint family such as love of siblings/cousins, values from elders etc. indicates that "big" life can be beautiful. Moreover, there are trends of personalities/famous stars to go for "cryo-preservation" in the hopes of being received when someday technology matures in the future. Thus, the craving for big life is nevertheless lodged deep inside humans!

So what is an ideal life which is beautiful? Big or small? Although mired in controversy, one should not value life in terms of length or wealth (bigness) alone, there's need for broad basing the concept of a beautiful life. This will definitely solve many of our society's challenges such as rising suicides and depression (even among rich) for those who struggle to make it big! The case of Bill Gates who despite making large empire (typical definition of beautiful life lived), is donating on "small" yet important causes such as $100 million for AIDS prevention in Africa or sanitation improvement in India. It shows satisfaction and happiness is earned in "meaningful life" rather than long one.

Our education should incorporate this lesson. The "Happiness Curriculum" in Delhi is already gaining positive feedback from parents who see their children more happier in their lives and desisting from the urge to go on 'social media' to portraying a "big/happy" life.

The State should similarly opt for sustainability in economic growth. This gains significance as the Industrial Revolution 4.0 has started to revolutionise economy but can entail a huge price on environment if not regulated properly.

Victor Franklin chronicling his experience, as prisoner in Nazi Concentration camps, in his book – "Man's search for Meaning" articulates that even in the greatest suffering, the (wo)man derives meaning in small hopes and wishes such as reuniting with his/her family or getting to savour a full meal. Beautiful thus doesn't require a big life to be lived!

❑❑

9 "In Today's World A Culture of Death is Gaining Supremacy Over a Culture of Life"

Abhishek Bharti, IPS (CSE 2017)

It was not very long ago that a body of 7 years old boy was washed ashore in Greece, which shook the conscience of the world, during Syrian crisis. But a tradition of inaction has resulted into a very similar problem on India's border with Myanmar, in the form of Rohingyas. Termed as the most persecuted minorities of the world, they beg for life to the world. These two instances are demonstrations of a "culture of death" that has taken over the world. It has resulted into sheer neglect towards value of a human life whereas a "Culture of life" is fast vaporizing.

Culture of life is engrained in the basic idea of humanity, where life of not only humans but even environmental life is valued and cherished. There are various factors contributing towards this culture of death such as mindless competition, envy, profit making attitude at any cost, inequalities in society and corruption. Various domains could be observed to demonstrate this.

International relations of the world are at a point that is explicitly following a culture of death. Wars for selfish gains in Afghanistan, Syria, Yemen, etc. have led to vast human rights violations like beheadings, sexual slaves etc. Refugee crisis arising out of it is the best illustration of new culture of death that has become a norm. Further, various autocratic nations of the world such as Saudi Arabia have extreme laws which have no regard for life. Borders between nations like India-Pakistan are testimony to barbarism where solder's heads are beheaded and played with. This culture of death is well documented in public domain.

Above mentioned issues have their genesis in politics and politicians, be it at national or international level. For example, despite call from human rights bodies and international organisations, death penalty is still practiced in India. It enforces a culture of death in ethics of the society. Further, politicians often resort to hate-speeches which lead to communal violence, tearing away last shred of culture of life. Regional politics, knowingly, gives fuel to the fire of xenophobia where people are targeted on the basis of race. Mass exodus of students of North-east from Bangalore is one such example. Persecution of labourers from Bihar in Maharashtra is another blot on culture of life.

Concept of life is an integral part of environment which is also not untouched by culture of death. Mindless pollution by developed and developing states is leading to inhabitable environment for all forms of life. An illustration of this is brutal destruction of Amazon rainforests for developmental activities. It has led to mass extinction of various species from the world. Construction of big dams not only effect local ecology but also displaces vast human population. Such is the onslaught of culture of death on environment that High Court of Uttarakhand in India had to give a living-status to two rivers i.e. Ganga and Yamuna, so that they could be saved. Voices of environmentalists and activists such as Medha Patkar fall on deaf years. They are minorities working towards culture of life. Paris climate deal was the game-changer towards final attempt at protection of life and humanity; even it is now stuck because of USA pulling out of it. Small island states will bear the brunt of such ignorance in the long run.

As stated earlier, this culture of death gets life from selfish nature of mankind, which is always focussed on economic domain. Neo-colonisation has appeared as a new form of exploitation which is used by developed countries to subjugate developing countries with money power. It has led to utter disregard to egalitarian culture of life and has led to widespread inequalities and lopsided development. Developed countries exploit resources of poor nations without any investment on health, education or human resource. It leads to a vicious circle of poverty-hunger-death, thus abiding by culture of death. High incidences of mortality rates are a testimony to this face. Growth of unorganised sector is another domain which is against values of human life. With no social security protection by the state, workers lead a life of agony, with even children employed in hazardous work. It leads to death of childhood in children and death of adulthood in young workers.

If observed closely, internal security challenges that India faces today are going towards path of culture of death. Uneven development, human rights violation and failure of state policies have pushed poor tribal population towards death by snatching away their lands. These areas have become breeding ground for Marxism and Maoism. These extreme groups believe in negotiations through death tolls. State, which is a mature partner in the dispute, seems to be neglecting nature of life and is engaged in continuous military operations against its own citizens. Further border areas of India have become a transit point for "trade of death" where drugs, women and children are bought, sold and smuggled illegally. Human piracy and sex rackets running in various parts of our country are worse than death itself.

Our national fabric, which was once based on humanism and reason, compassion for weaker sections and melting pot culture, is degrading fast. Communal riots are used to gain political mileages which are messengers of death. Further, social institutions such as family, religion, community etc. are moving away from tolerance and culture of life day by day. Vulnerable population such as disabled and elderly are left to fend for themselves. Younger working section is mindlessly chasing after money. Even family members are killed for money and property. Honour killings are another feature where even pure feeling of love is sacrificed at attack of death.

Thus, with focus on above mentioned onslaught of "culture of death" which is taking over "culture of life", new lease of life needs to be given to culture of life. International principles must be charted out which keep human rights and lives at top level. Proper enforcement and adherence of them will promote life. Mature political class must replace environment of hate, intolerance with inclusion and equality. State policies must try to promote the lowest and weakest sections of society which could be done by providing equal life chances. Environmental protection must be a top priority for all the nations because if our planet degrades further there will be no one to save humanity. Focus should be conservation of all flora and fauna. It requires intimate international collaboration.

Gandhian ethics are the best antidote for defeating this prevalent "culture of death" in today's world. The philosophy of "live and let live" along with "compassion for life" will give a new lease of life to the "culture of life".

❑❑

10

"Raise Your Voice, Not The Sea Level"

Abhishek Bharti, IPS (CSE 2017)

Last summer, India witnessed drought for second year in a row. Condition was such that in parts of north Telangana, Southern Odisha, eastern Maharashtra and parts of Uttar Pradesh – even drinking water was scarce, let alone water for agricultural purposes. Subsequent outcomes like farmer suicides have become a national concern today. Another case which is of relevance to this discussion is of recently concluded Rio Olympics in Brazil. An athlete after winning medal, standing on the podium, made an appeal to the world – to check global warming. He belonged to an island nation in central Pacific Ocean which is getting submerged due to rising sea level.

Although above 2 cases seem disconnected at first look – one of draught, other flood like situation because of ocean, but are very much connected because harsh weather conditions (like droughts, fires, floods) have become frequent because of climate change and resultant global warming.

Although a common perception among layman is that it's all result of sinister human actions, that too in recent past, is not completely true. Our planet is subjected to glacial cycles which take place on a time scale of millions of years. Ice age and warm age are consequent phenomenon. The epoch of geological time scale, where humanity is existing today i.e. Pleistocene era, is in warm cycle of earth. Although these cycles are very much natural and are triggered by natural causes but with the advent of humanity and recent advances in science and technology for the past 200 years, human have accelerated this cycle. Result is global warming and subsequently rising sea level because of melting of glaciers.

Various natural phenomenon and man-made reasons have led to a global climate change i.e. rise in average temperature of the earth measured on large time scale. Outcome of this is global warming.

Various facets of human activity in this regard could be discussed. The origin and tip-off point towards humanity's contribution was onset of industrial revolution in western nations (Europe) during mid-nineteenth century when large scale depletion of natural resources was undertaken. Steel plants, cement industries, automobiles etc. – all operating on fossil fuel based energy were pumping greenhouse gases in atmosphere. Greenhouse gases trap energy from sun, rising temperature of earth leading to global warming. It led to such damages that its effects are left even today. Even developing nations today depend on primarily fossil fuels for energy needs.

Sun's rays contain ultra-violet rays which are harmful to us and carry warming potential. These are filtered by ozone layer around earth. But because of use of Chlorofluorocarbons (CFC) which react with ozone and destroy it, a hole in ozone has occurred over Antarctica. These are discharged through their use in air conditioners, fire extinguishers etc.

One of the most potent greenhouse gas is carbon dioxide which is emitted heavily into the atmosphere by way of vehicular discharge, industries etc. Developed nations of today blame developing nations for increased emissions and vice versa. This blame-game never reaches to any constructive conclusion and humanity moves to dangers of warming.

Agriculture is one occupation which is practiced by majority in developing world. But because of lack of scientific practices and awareness, huge amounts of methane are released into the atmosphere which is also a very potent greenhouse gas. Mining activities and inundation of large parts due to dam construction are also contributing to methane release.

But human activity is not acting in isolation. Even certain natural phenomenon contributes to global warming.

Volcanoes emit plumes of hot gases from the earth's interior. They are a mix of various harmful gases which trap solar energy and raise temperature of earth. Water vapour constitutes 98% of greenhouse gases. It's presence in the atmosphere is mostly because of natural processes like transpiration, evaporation etc. Forest fires are also naturally caused (even some are human induced). They destroy hectares of forest releasing CO_2 in atmosphere.

Harmful effects of global warming and rising sea levels are around us – whether national or international level.

Various natural phenomenons that are related directly or indirectly to climate change and global warming are cyclones, foods, droughts, fires, increasing desertification etc. Worst affected because of these are island nations in between sea as well as coastal regions of all continents. Even a metre rise of sea level could wipe out many areas from world map along with wiping considerable amount of human population. Developing nations are worst hit who do not have resource to relocate and rehabilitate their vulnerable population. Recent cases of drought in central India and the resulting crisis was evidence of this. Japan is another country which faces the wrath of nature's fury where incidences of cyclones and earthquakes along with Tsunami have increased. They are related with disturbance in balance of nature. Similarly USA, Africa, Europe are also facing abnormal weather conditions in face of climate charge.

Solutions to this problem are not quick-fix but require long term vision. It requires immediate reduction in emission of greenhouse gases, no encroachment of coastal areas, adoption of non-conventional sources of energy (like solar, wind, ocean-wave etc.) which are renewable in nature and proper environmental impact assessment before taking up any development projects.

World has taken view of this grave problem and it has resulted in some commendable international collaboration right from Kyoto-protocol in 1997 to Paris climate conference in 2015. They are to reduce the emission of greenhouse gases in atmosphere. Other actions such as Montreal Protocol against ozone depleting substances have shown great promise. India has its own National action plan on climate change (NAPCC) to reduce harmful effects on environment.

Voices against global warming have been heard now and then in corridors of power but in recent past few decades they have gained momentum. Various environmental movements like Chipko movement have voices of villagers. Various NGOs like Green Peace India have been fighting tooth and nail for the rights of people affected by global climate change. Various celebrities like Leonardo DiCaprio have voiced their concerns and joined as ambassadors against climate change. Voices from civil society and media are always keeping decision makers on alert. These voices have led to better concerted action towards global warming.

Thus, no amount of facts and figures can deny that humanity itself is at risk today because of global warming. More voices need to join the crusade towards this cause so that these global concerns echo in every corner and street of world – whether rich or poor.

❑❑

11 Health is a Fundamental Right in India – Prospect and Challenges

Abhishek Jain, IAS (AIR 24 CSE 2019)

"Aarogyam Paramam Bhagyam Swasthyam Sarwaarth Saadhanam" (Health is the ultimate blessing it can help us achieve anything).

– Vedas

Muzaffarpur in Bihar was in news again. More than 150 children died there due to Acute Encephalitis Syndrome (AES). The malnourished children were already vulnerable to diseases. However, poorly managed and incapable public healthcare turned the disease into a tragic epidemic!!!

The incident here lays bare the horrific truth of how State pays the least value to human health in India. Therefore, there is an immediate need to make the State responsible by including right to health as a fundamental right in India.

In this essay, we will discuss what we mean by right to health. Then we will see as to why it needs to be made a fundamental right. Then we will look at the myriad of challenges in the way. Finally we will analyze the prospects of this idea and the path to achieve it. Let us begin.

Right to Health – A Holistic Right

When we talk about health, it does not just connote absence of diseases. Health as a right encompasses physical, mental, social and emotional well being of an individual. This can also be seen in ancient Indian texts of Charaka Samhita and Sushruta Samhita where health denotes overall wellness of an individual.

This right has indeed been envisaged by our Constitution under Directive Principles of State Policy. Article 47 says that the state shall strive to raise the level of nutrition and public health.

However, is making health merely a non-enforceable right enough? A big No. The problem here is that it does not make the state accountable for its failure to deliver health services, thus making it lack in attitude.

But, what difference will it make if health is made a fundamental right? The answer is – it will make all the difference!

A fundamental right will make it a constitutional obligation on the part of the state to guarantee health services to all the citizens. In case of denial, the citizens can seek judicial remedy. Thus, by making the state more accountable, it will force it to deliver results on ground.

Further, health has been recognized as a basic human right in the "Universal Declaration of Human Rights". Making it a part of fundamental rights will reinforce India's commitment to ensure universal healthcare.

However, it's easier said than done. There are bound to be a variety of challenges that we will face. Let us discuss some of them.

A Difficult Feat to Achieve

Firstly, it will require a constitutional amendment with a 2/3rd majority in both the Houses of the Parliament. But, this is also a relatively easier task. The real challenge will lie in actually delivering this right on the ground to all.

Our existing public health infrastructure is in shambles. We have only 1.3 hospital beds per 1,000 population! Out of these, 73% are in urban areas whereas 69% population resides in the villages.

Further, India spends only 1.15-1.5% of its GDP on healthcare which is shockingly low. With less than 1 doctor per 1,000 people, most of our rural and tribal population doesn't even have access to basic healthcare.

Going further, we have 38.4% stunting and 20% wasting. Poor sanitation and open defecation leads to faster spread of diseases in our slums and rural areas. Poor access to vaccination, exploitation by private sector and costly medicines further add to the enormous challenge.

Going even further, deep rooted patriarchy, casteism and communalism snatch away the dignity of an individual. This poorly affects the "social health".

Lastly, changing lifestyle, lack of physical exercise and rising stress levels take away the "emotional health" of an individual.

Clearly, we lack the capability at the moment to deliver this fundamental right. So, shall we not try at all? Are there ways to make it possible? Let us discuss.

The Prospects: We Need to Make it Happen

Yes, it's possible. The prospects of delivering health as a fundamental right will become brighter if certain steps are taken.

Firstly, the level of health expenditure needs to be raised to 2.5% of GDP as envisaged in the National Health Policy 2017. A bulk of it shall be spent on developing primary health infrastructure. We can follow the model of Mohalla Clinics by Delhi which provides free doctor, vaccination and medicine services to all.

Secondly, an All-India Health Services should be created on lines of IAS and IPS. This will ensure specialized and efficient health administration.

Thirdly, capacity building and technological upgradation of ASHA and Anganwadi workers shall be undertaken. This will lead to better delivery of mother and child care, immunization as well as nutrition.

Fourthly, behavioural change to improve social health of the marginalized sections is also a critical requirement. Campaigns like Beti Bachao Beti Padhao and promotion of inter-caste marriages and inter-religion marriages can help here.

Fifthly, promotion of AYUSH services and meditation to improve emotional health can also be taken up.

Lastly, a mechanism to enforce this right must be developed through a detailed policy. The actions that the courts can take in case of failure on part of the state should be listed out. This may involve compensation to the victim and strict actions against errant officials.

Winston Churchill said that "healthy citizens are the greatest assets any country can have". Thus, India needs to make strides towards enshrining health as a fundamental right. Despite many challenges, it is indeed possible and with the right steps, its prospects seem very high.

As Mohammad Ali said – "Some people want it to happen. Some wish it to happen. Others make it happen." We will definitely make it happen and only then we will achieve our goal of New India where Muzzaffarpur like incidents do not happen and the dream of "Sarve Bhavantu Sukhinah, Santu Niramaya" is actually materialized.

❑❑

12 Is Our Higher Education System Future Ready?

Abhishek Jain, IAS (AIR 24 CSE 2019)

Rahul is doing his graduation in mechanical engineering from a reputed college. His syllabus consists of things and technologies of the past like basic motor, conductor, etc.!!! His sole focus during his college days was to mug up the notes and pass the exams. Consequently, after graduation, he couldn't find any job because he lacked the necessarily skills to manage modern machines.

The problem is that there are millions of Rahuls in India who are unemployed because they are not "employable". This is because our higher education system as of now is not future ready.

In this essay, we will discuss what the future is going to be like i.e. what does it demands from our higher education system. Then we will analyze how, at present, our system is incapable of delivering the demands of the future. Finally, we will look at certain solutions to make ourselves future ready. Let us begin.

What Are the Future Demands?

We are on the verge of Industrial Revolution 4.0. It will be an era guided by newer technologies like Artificial Intelligence, Internet of Things and Data Analytics. Old skills will get redundant and the "degrees" of today will become a thing of the bygone era.

Similarly, rising complexities in industrial operations will demand specific functional skills, for example: there will not be "marketing managers" in future. But there will be" digital marketers", content creators, telemarketers, etc. Vocational education, thus, will become extremely important.

In the field of healthcare, digital technologies like telemedicine, robotic surgery and AI based diagnostics are the future. Thus, medical education of today needs to apprise students of it.

Tomorrow's agriculture will be guided by genetic engineering; AI based precision technologies, water smart technologies. Agriculture graduates need to be conversant with these future technologies.

Further, success in future will be guided by one's capacity to innovate and be creative. It, therefore, demands us to inculcate an innovative bent of mind among our students. They must be able to think out of the box and take risks if they have to succeed in the future.

Furthermore, future also poses grievous challenges to us like climate change, rising social tensions, wavering ethical compass and lust for power and money. The onus is on our universities to turn the students of today into better citizens of the future, citizens who are ethical and sensitive to the environment.

But are our colleges and universities ready for these future challenges? The answer is NO. Let us discuss.

We Are not Future Ready as Yet

Our colleges continue to teach outdated syllabus and are not apprised with the current or future realities. According to a recent survey, only 1.13% engineers in India have ability to handle future skills.

Further, there is a complete lack of R&D in our higher education. The funding is meagre and the infrastructure is in shambles. We file one of the lowest number of patents in the world. When the educator focuses only on rote learning and securing more marks, how can we expect any future oriented innovation coming out of this system?

The quality of teaching especially in state government universities is also a cause of worry. There is focus on theory but not on practical aspects.

Similarly, the level of internships and industrial trainings taken up by students to get hands on experience on jobs is very low.

Further, our universities do not focus on holistic development of a person. There is virtually no ethical training and no development of environmental sensitivity. This is dangerous, as Theodore Roosevelt has said – "To educate a person in the mind but not in morals is to educate a menace to society."

Therefore, if we want our higher education system to deliver the workforce of the future, certain important steps need to be taken. Let us discuss.

Miles To Go Before We Sleep

Firstly, there is an urgent need to grant full autonomy to our universities. This will enable them to update the syllabus regularly and offer multidimensional courses, e.g. KREA University has started offering choice of subjects to students to make "tailor-made degrees" like B.Tech in food science with marketing. Institute of Eminence (IoE) scheme which grants freedom is a good step and thus, must be expanded.

Secondly, higher funding in R&D must be made, especially by government. More industry-academia linkages and incubation centres must be set up to boost creative drive among students. This will help them develop capability to face future challenges.

Thirdly, centres of excellence in future technologies like block chain and AI must be set up. This will give practical training to students and give them a glimpse of what future holds for them.

Fourthly, teacher training should be undertaken so that our teachers are also future ready. They must "teach students how to think and not what to think".

Fifthly, our colleges must focus on holistic development of our students. To be able to face the future, we must learn from the past. Similarly, we can learn from the holistic way of teaching that was followed at ancient India's gurukuls. Thus, the students today must be made morally sensitive and made aware of their responsibilities to vote as a citizen, to conserve water, to respect women and to be inclusive.

Amartya Sen in his capability approach has said that true development comes by improving people's capacities. If India has to sustain its developmental path in future, we will have to usher in an "educational devolution". We have to bridge the gap between the existing capacities of our colleges and the demand of the future. Only then, our youngsters like Rahul will be able to succeed in future, because

"Yesterday is not ours to recover but tomorrow is ours to win or lose".

❑❑

13 Privacy in the Digital Era: Myths and Realities

Abhishek Jain, IAS (AIR 24 CSE 2019)

It was in 2013, shockwaves were sent across the world when Edward Snowden, an ex-CIA systems analyst revealed the grim realities of the surveillance programme of the US National Security Agency (NSA). The documents disclosed how NSA had tapped directly into the servers of Google and Facebook to keep a watch over the communications of millions of users worldwide!! Further, with a top secret court order, it had collected the telephone records of millions of users of Verizon!!!

These startling revelations busted the myths about privacy in this digital era and made the world face the astonishing realities. This calls for a close examination of the issue.

In this essay, we will discuss the meaning of privacy. Then we will try to bust the 3 most common myths associated with online privacy. Finally, we will look at the way forward as it should be.

Privacy means a state of not being observed and disturbed by others. It is the freedom from security and surveillance by others without consent. It refers to the right to determine whether, when, how and to whom one's personal information will be disclosed. With the emergence of the digital era, a lot of myths about privacy have emerged. Let us discuss them one by one.

Myth 1- Privacy is Not Important

A lot of people argue that when they do NOT have anything to hide, then why do they need privacy? It's of no use. However, this is a fallacy. As Edward Snowden said "saying that you don't care about privacy because you don't have anything to hide is in no way different that saying that you don't care about freedom of speech because you have nothing to say."

The reality is that privacy is a basic human right which is a part of Article 21- Right to life as laid down by the Supreme Court of India in the Puttaswamy Judgment. It allows an individual to maintain her autonomy, dignity and personal integrity.

Further, it is essential to keep alive freedom of speech and expression in a democracy. Imagine the government surveilling anyone who it thinks is opposing it and exploiting that personal information to ruin his reputation!! This will amount to muzzling of dissent and subversion of democracy.

In addition, privacy is essential to prevent cybercrimes like identity frauds and bank frauds e.g. terrorists misusing Aadhar data online to get fake SIM cards issued, cyber stalking and harassment and blackmailing of girls and women by accessing sensitive images on their mobile, etc.

Therefore, to water down privacy is a myth while to uphold it is a reality. Now, let us go on to the second myth associated with it.

Myth 2- Privacy is Not Really Threatened

Many argue that privacy is NOT really in danger as ample safeguards exist to protect it. Further, there is no use of anyone's personal information. However, this is again a myth. The reality is that our privacy is under a constant threat 24x7.

Several malwares like viruses and Trojans act as spyware. They track our data, replicate it and send it to the hackers for misuse.

Further, big data analytics and data mining have ensured that we are being tracked continuously online. Companies like Google, Facebook, Amazon, etc. "know" what we like, dislike, our political learning and even our sexual orientations! They easily use it to influence our behaviour through targeted ads. e.g. Cambridge Analytica used Facebook data of profile users and psychologically manipulated them through fake news and campaigns into voting for a particular candidate. It is alleged to have subverted Brexit vote and Bihar elections.

In addition, schemes like Aadhar in India have been alleged to be creating the scope of a "surveillance state" as well as involving privacy risks. According to Centre for Internet and Society, the Aadhar details with sensitive biometrics of 130 billion aadhar holders are available online.

Going further, our privacy is under threat from enemy states and terrorists who are now perpetrating cyber warfare and hacking our personal information e.g. Russian hackers influencing US Presidential elections. Thus, it is a myth to say that our privacy is secure. The reality is that it is NOT. Now, let us discuss the next myth.

Myth 3 – Privacy Cannot Be Secured In This Digital Era

Some people believe that due to the sheer expanse of internet, it is next to impossible to protect privacy. Further, they believe that to maintain national security, for criminal investigation and schemes like DBT privacy has to be violated. However, again, this is a myth. The reality is that privacy can be protected and secured.

Firstly, a personal data protection law on lines of General Data Protection Regulation (GDPR) in UK needs to be brought about. Such laws must provide for a rights based approach with complete user control over their information. In India, B. N. Srikrishna committee has suggested to establish an autonomous Data Protection Authority of India (DPI) to enforce such a law.

Secondly, the state and the companies must be made responsible for securing the information of citizens. Heavy penalties must be charged in case of breach of security or misuse of data.

Thirdly, use of technology like blockchain which involves decentralized, transparent and auditable database should be leveraged in schemes like Aadhar to protect privacy.

Fourthly, robust institutional framework like a cyber command of military to protect the country from external threats.

Finally, public education on ways to secure privacy is critical and should be made part of Digital India campaign. Simple steps like using an antivirus, not using public Wi-Fi, password protection, etc. can go a long way in securing our privacy. Thus, it is a myth that privacy can't be protected while the reality is that it can be.

To conclude, countries like India must lead the world and provide a model framework for protection of the privacy of its citizens. This should be the vision of "New India" we all envisage and will lead to SABKA SAATH SABKA VIKAS. We shall leave behind the myths about privacy in the past and join hands together to make privacy protection a reality because

"Yesterday is NOT ours to recover, but tomorrow is ours to win or loose."

❑❑

14 The End of Law is Not to Abolish or Restrain but to Preserve and Enlarge Freedom

Abhishek Jain, IAS (AIR 24 CSE 2019)

There is a lot of debate going around the proposed triple talaq law. Critics claim that it is abolitionary in nature and restricts freedom of minorities. However, they fail to understand that abolition of triple talaq is just a means. The real end is to preserve and enlarge the freedom of Muslim women. It is to liberate them from the clutches of a highly restrictive and patriarchal setup which condemns them to a status of second class citizen. Hence, the ultimate aim of the law is not to restrain, but to liberate.

When great philosophers like Rousseau and Hobbes studied how the concept of law itself was created by man, they were surprised that in the pre-historic times, when there were no laws, man was not at all free. Why so? Because he was in constant fear of being attacked by another man and thus was in hiding!!!

Thus, man who was selfish yet rational entered into a social contract with others. This way a system of law and state was created. They did restrict some activities like violence. But, they succeeded in creating a society where man was free: free from fear, free from to pursue his objectives and to grow and develop.

The same principle holds true in the contemporary times also. Let us examine it in detail.

The constitutional law in India guarantees tremendous freedom to the people. Fundamental rights in Part III of our constitution restrain the authority of the state. By doing so, they enlarge the freedom of citizens. From freedom of speech in Article 19 to freedom of religion in Article 25, this fundamental law of our land is a masterpiece of liberty.

Similarly, if we look at economic laws like Goods and Services Tax, it does impose certain restrictions on businesses. But its ultimate aim is to promote economic freedom through free and easy trade and country wide market access.

Further, there are several laws meant for good governance like IESA Act, RTI Act 2005 or Social Audit Law in Manipur. Such laws also have tremendously enlarged the scope of freedom by providing the "freedom to access information" as well as freedom to govern them.

Going further ahead, there are also various social laws which are passed by the state. In India, the laws that abolish sati, dowry, child marriage and untouchability. Such abolition has given social freedom to people at the bottom of the pyramid. Women and backward classes therefore, have gained freedom from discrimination and condemnation while having access to free and fair opportunity.

Looking at it from a global perspective, laws like General Data Protection Regulation (GDPR) in Europe significantly restrains information collection and sharing by online companies and websites. The end result is protection of citizen's privacy. This prevents creation of surveillance state where the state is like a "big brother who is always watching you". Thus, it boosts freedom of citizen and broadens liberty as highlighted by Supreme Court in Puttaswamy Judgment.

Till now, we have talked only about the man-made laws. But there is a greater law which is universal and much higher than any human law. It is the Natural Law or Moral Law. It says that every human being has right to freedom, fairness, equality and justice. Thus, freedom is inherent in the divine law also.

This reminds us of the time when Gandhiji was arrested by British during his Champaran campaign in 1917. He denied applying for bail in the court. He argued that though man-made law restricted his visit in Champaran but the higher moral law i.e. the law of his conscience made it his duty to help the poor. Thus, it sanctioned him with all the freedom to be compassionate towards others…Freedom in law is thus, like water in a river.

Therefore, we must understand that laws do put restrictions on us. But these are meant to provide us as much liberty as possible while restricting our right to infringe on anyone else's liberty. This is because "the liberty to swing my fist ends where your nose begins".

But, is it always the case? Can laws be misused or be meant to abolish or restrain? Yes. Let us discuss.

In several dictatorships or monarchies like North Korea law is used as a tool to instil fear and kill dissent among people. In India too, the end goal of certain laws like Sec 124 IPC, Sec 66 of IT Act (now repealed), porn ban, liquor ban etc. are just to abolish or restrain citizen's freedom.

But again, these are only a few exceptions to the wider system of law and state. The end goal of law was is to enlarge the freedom of all. Laws will have to use restrictions only as a means to a good end.

For us to become a more liberal society, we will have to ensure that the rule of law is firmly established, arbitrary powers are abolished and our institutions work independently and strongly. For this we as citizens will have to play an active role as the watchdog of law making process and for torch-bearers of dissent. Then, we will be able to realize, Gurudev Rabindranath Tagore's ideal society

"Where the mind is without fear and the head is held high."

□□

15 What Will it Take to Make Gender Equality the Norm, Not the Exception

Abhishek Jain, IAS (AIR 24 CSE 2019)

Meet Archana. She lives in a tribal village in Jharkhand. Her husband Arjun is a farmer. She started a self-help group comprising of 4 other village women to produce and sell their handicraft products. Her daughter, whom she had sent to Delhi to do B.Tech in computer science, has helped her set up an online website to market and sell. The women took a loan under MUDRA Yojana and began operations. Honestly, this was an exception for the orthodox villagers and Archana was frowned upon initially. But with her determination and support of Arjun, she kept working hard. Today her brand is a success and generates a very decent income for all the members. Looking at the rise in the standard of living of the families of Archana and others, the village women have began joining their SHG and are now supported by their families. What was an exception a few months ago, has become the norm today for the village. Thus, it will take a deep change in the mindset right from the grassroots level, handheld government support and success stories like that of Archana to lead the way towards empowerment of women and make gender equality a norm rather than an exception.

In this essay, we will examine the meaning of "gender quality" and its importance. Then we will look at the various challenges to it. Finally, we will discuss some solutions to it.

Gender Equality – Meaning and Importance

Gender equality refers to the equitable treatment of all genders- male, female and transgender in all aspects – economically, socially, politically, legally and ethically. It denotes an absence of discrimination on the basis of sex as propounded in Article 15 of our Constitution.

Gender equality is the cornerstone of basic human rights and our constitutional values. Harbouring it will provide tremendous boost to the overall development of our nation.

However, gender equality in India is a myth as reflected by 108th position out of 144 countries in the 2017 "Global Gender Gap Index". There are several challenges to gender equality in our nation.

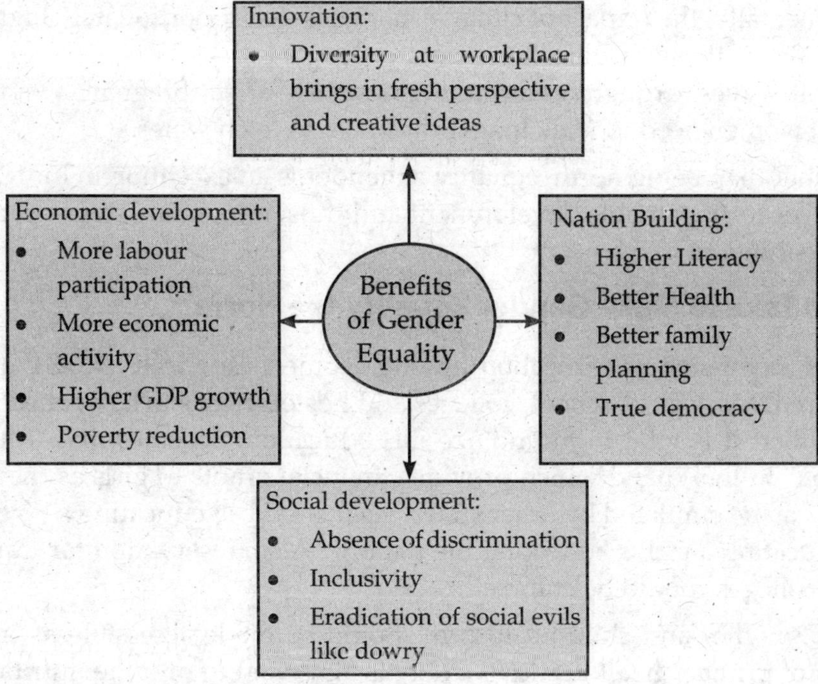

Gender Equality – An Exception in India

Economically, women constitute only 21.9% of the total workforce and most of them are engaged in unorganized sector. The figures are woefully low. Even at workplace, they face discrimination in payment, authority given and in promotions. As per "Monster Salary Index" by monster.com, women in India are paid an average 20% less than men.

Socially, women literacy in India is meagre 65% which is far below the global average of 79%. Poor nutritional support, early marriages and pregnancy takes a severe toll on women's health. High maternal mortality rate and acute anaemic are very common in India. Further, female feticide, dowry, several harassment at workplace, cyber stalking and bullying, rape, trafficking and forced prostitution make the claim of gender equality laughable in our nation.

Politico-Administratively, the representation of women and transgender in politics, civil services and judiciary is grievously low. A meagre 11.2% of Lok Sabha MP and 9% of total MLA are women. In the last 67 years of Supreme Court (up to 2017), only 6 women judges and no transgender judge has been appointed. The gender insensitivity of our institutions is thus evident.

Morally, women are not allowed to make life choices like choosing life partners (Hadiya Case), they are denied right to bodily integrity (marital rape), reproductive choices and lack of say in family decision making. Transgenders, on the other hand are considered untouchables and are forcefully excluded from the society.

Environmentally, the impact of climate change is disproportionately high on women. As per UN, 80% of those displaced by climate change induced disasters are women and children. Heat waves, drought and floods grievously affect pregnant women. As lakes dry up, rural women need to walk longer distances to fetch water.

Thus, rather than being norm, equality of gender is an exception in India. But it poses a severe danger to sustainable development and thus, immediate steps need to be taken to rectify the situation.

What Will It Take to Make Gender Equality the Norm?

Firstly, rapid expansion of education among women especially SC/ST and minority girls is required. More girls' school, colleges and hostels needs to be opened in backward districts. Further, it is vital to incentivize girl education. Schemes like "Mukhyamantri Laadli Yojana" in Jharkhand which provides financial grants to girls as they progress in school years can be emulated by other states. As it is said – "educating a boy is educating a person, educating a girl is educating the nation." Also, reservation for transgenders in schools and colleges should be enforced.

Secondly, mother and child healthcare should be made accessible by infrastructure upgradation of primary health centres. There is also need to provide nutritional support to girls, reproductive health awareness, access to quality sanitary pads and contraceptives in rural areas to improve the state of women health and family planning.

Thirdly, making women financially independent can be a great harbinger of gender equality. Skill development through vocational training to girls and transgender, preventing sexual harassment at workplace, providing technological, marketing and financial support to women and transgender entrepreneurs can dramatically improve their participation in workforce and reduce their dependency on family.

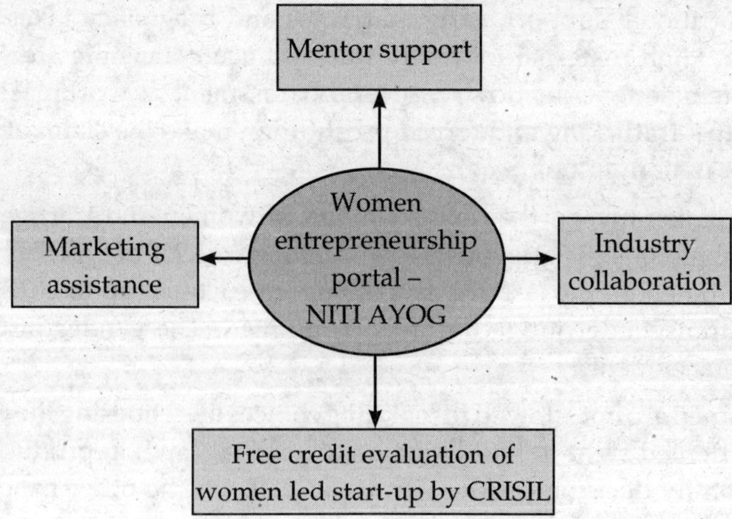

Fourthly, crackdown on female feticide and ostracisation of transgenders, self defence training, use of technology like GPS and alarm watch (e.g. Sonata Act Watch – sends alarm in case of emergency) and speedy trial in a sensitive environment has the potential to drastically curb gender specific crimes and make them an "exception" rather than the norm.

Fifthly, it is imperative to pass women reservation bill to reserve 1/3rd seats in Lok Sabha and state legislatures for women. Free coaching to girls and transgenders for civil services and judicial exams can be provided to improve their representation.

Sixthly, climate change adaptation and mitigation strategies with special focus on gender specific responses must be implemented. It is high time to provide more representation to women in climate change negotiation bodies, promote women led renewable energy start-ups and train women farmers in climate resilient agriculture.

Lastly, behavioural changes among the people can serve as the catalyst of gender equality. Campaigns like Beti Bachao Beti Padhao help fight gender stigmas. Community and religious leaders can also be involved to generate awareness about the importance of empowering all genders. Gender sensitive education can also be imparted in schools.

Though, we may be far away from making gender equality a norm in our country, yet, we are definitely making progress. I believe that our beautiful country with its great people will together lead the path to gender empowerment to achieve "SABKA SATH SABKA VIKAS" and realize the dream of "NEW INDIA". In the end, I am going to leave you with the excerpt of this beautiful poem by "Maya Angelou" which describes how women are fighting gender stereotypes and are overcoming them…I believe that gender equality will very soon be a norm in India as "women rise".

"You may write me down in history
With your bitter, twisted lies,
You may trod me in the very dirt
But still, like dust, I'll rise.

Does my sassiness upset you?
Why are you beset with gloom?
'Cause I walk like I've got oil wells
Pumping in my living room.

Just like moons and like suns,
With the certainty of tides,
Just like hopes springing high,
Still I'll rise..."

❑❑

16 Artificial Intelligence Has the Power to Make Human Intelligence Obsolete

Abhishek Saraf, IAS (AIR 8 CSE 2019)

Recently, Facebook witnessed what supra-human artificial intelligence (AI) would look like. Two of its AI algorithms developed a chat language of their own and started communicating – None of the researchers could figure it out. Struck by panic the team has no option but to turn the system off. But what if there was no off switch??

In another incident, Google's AI learnt over centuries worth of chess knowledge in a matter of four hours and started devising its own moves. Would Mr. V. Anand care to challenge such algo-Masters?

If we are to believe the warning of Tesla and Space X owner Mr. Elon Musk – We are actually summoning the demon with AI. These incidents show that AI clearly has the power to make human intelligence obsolete.

Much like anything else there are going to be benefits and loses of that. Humanity has to prepare so that challenges do not overwhelm it and benefits are shared collectively.

Man's desire for comfort led to development of machines to reduce physical labour. Now machines have been developed/developing fast that can even reduce intellectual labour. Artificial intelligence refers to such machines which exhibit intelligence of the characteristics of human – only artificially.

With such possibilities it is pertinent to wonder to what extent and in what sectors is human intelligence threatened by AI. As thing stand today – virtually every sector.

AI could replace human intelligence in farming as seen in AI-enabled precision agriculture farms of USA and Japan. AI-enabled identification of weeds and pests along with application of pesticides replaced human intelligence even at early stages of infection.

Manufacturing is seeing automation and rise of robots. These have precision and speed unmatched by humans. Construction sector is seeing AI assist engineers and architects both in design of as well as construction of buildings.

Not only blue collar jobs but white collar jobs are equally threatened. Alibaba CEO Jack Ma has predicted AI will be on the cover of time magazine by 2020 and work as CEO. Gartner's report predicts Indian IT Sector could lose 6.4 lakhs jobs by 2022 due to AI.

AI is fast intruding into share markets in the form of high frequency trading – must faster than what human brokers are capable of. Similarly, healthcare has seen AI-enabled diagnostics produce better cancer detection than oncologists. Remote surgeries assisted by AI are a reality.

Education could see AI teachers continuously assessing the understanding, learning pace of students and gearing pace of course as per the need, thus realising the idea of continuous comprehensive evaluation – which Indian teachers are yet to achieve.

Automated self driving cars, personal assistants like Siri (iphones), Cortana (Microsoft) and Google assistant where AI is replacing human company and agency.

Policing and crime control could see AI detecting signs of unrest and deployment of forces faster than human police. Facial recognition and lie-detection are yet another domain where AI is posed to exceed human intelligence. Not only local policing, but military could use AI for signature strikes by UAVs (unmanned aerial vehicles). Infiltration detection and border management using AI technology coupled with sensor based detection are the latest trend now. This all could surpass human surveillance. Trend analysis from big data to detect suspicious acts would put CCTNS, NATGRID of India to optimum use.

Research as well as policy making is increasing driven by big data and evidence base. Big data which seems incoherent to human eyes is AI's forte. Space research, climate change research and weather prediction from big data trend analysis is where AI has already surpassed human intelligence.

While AI is increasingly turning our intelligence to obsolescence, have there been comparable benefits?

Benefits have been seen in enhancing productively of human workers – who now use machines/robots instead of manual labour. This has shifted human labour to a higher skill level and economy to a higher growth path.

In service delivery AI could – if trained so – end biases inherent to humans and ensure progress to more inclusive society. AI could potentially help end human miseries like anti microbial resistance, climate change pest attacks, crop loss by timely action.

AI could also reduce wastage of inputs in manufacturing services etc. thus enhance efficiency of living. For e.g. AI driven cars would communicate with each other and reduce fuel loss due to braking. Timely action by foreseeing accidents would also save lives. Lives could also be saved by early detection of diseases and action.

However, this would not be without losses. Automation would cause loss of jobs. Feedstock of AI is data – and today collection of data causes lapses of privacy. It is thus pertinent to prepare for such challenges. Humanity needs to identify sectors where AI cannot replace humanity and up-skill in those sectors.

Alibaba CEO Jack Ma, in World Economic Forum identified them as intuition of humanity. Being data and logic driven AI can never be intuitive.

Areas of philosophy, compassion and development of ethics are where AI cannot surpass humans. Emotions are an inherent trait of humanity. Despite coding and data, humans are capable of wider range of emotions – AI will never make humanity obsolete.

Team work, sociability are yet another trait. Social cohesion is a trait which cannot be ingrained even in Sophia (Hanson computer's AI robot which got Saudi citizenship). Not only would these sectors give us an edge over AI but also develop us into a better society.

Similarly, while AI can replace human intelligence in search of legal precedents but AI cannot replace human intelligence in developing the idea of justice. The idea of justice is where the solution to AI challenges lies. We need to ensure gains of AI are equally distributed. The economic growth due to AI should be inclusive. National income due to AI should not go to the industry only. But the governments need to levy a 'technology tax' to provide for the welfare of those laid off.

Governments globally need to agree on a Geneva like convention to safeguard rights of all. Privacy should not be sacrificed at the altar of AI. Governments need to agree on non-military use of AI to ward-off another race of weaponization.

Governments needs to develop a code of conduct nationally too. Skilling of workforce and digital literacy for all should be the way ahead. Corporate as well as governments need to cooperate to regulate AI and its growth for a better sustained tomorrow.

Civil society organisations have also played a role. IT for change has been campaigning for inclusive growth by AI. Tech titans like Google, Microsoft, and scientists like Stephen Hawking have suggested ways to regulate AI.

On individual level one needs to prepare self for a tech enabled tomorrow. Just like any other technological revolution, so for AI has the potential to elevate humanity to a better future if used productivity so that we summon an angel not a demon.

❑❑

17 Is Data The New Oil?

Abhishek Saraf, IAS (AIR 8 CSE 2019)

Post-industrial revolution era of the last 200 years has seen economic growth on the back of machines fuelled by power of oil/coal or gas. This led to rapid economic growth and wide gaps between the industrialised countries and others. Today the global GDP has moved past $100 trillion. However the pre-eminence of oil/fossil fuels in economy is falling.

The industrialised countries of yesterday are becoming services dominated economies now. Knowledge economy today is being increasing fuelled by data. Ninety-five per cent of world's data was generated in the last 3 years. This has led economists to question, would data be the new propeller of global economy, would data be the new oil?

In this essay we shall explore the similarities and dissimilarities between data and oil. We shall see how data is something much bigger than oil – how it's potential for good and bad lies beyond oil. We shall conclude by looking at solutions to challenges and opportunities.

Oil/fossil fuels marked the turning point in global economic growth in the form of industrial revolution. It shifted the world from primary sector to manufacturing sector decisively. Those ahead were able to reap windfall advantages like the British. In 1100 India and China formed about 50% of world economy, by the end of 19th century they were reduced to a miniscule of <10%.

Similarly, data today is being used by the west to provide digital service globally. Consultancy, artificial intelligence, target market advertising based e-commerce, software services have propelled the growth from manufacturing led economy to service led one. This is shown by less than 10% share of manufacturing and over 75% share of services in U.S. economy. Rise of e-com billionaires is another example.

Oil changed the structure of global power. In the West it fuelled rise of capitalist countries, led to colonialism and imperialism. In Middle-East rise of countries like Saudi Arabia have changed global power equations and alliances. This has irreversibly altered global history. Wars have been fought for control over oil reserves e.g. Gulf War 1990s.

Similarly, data has shown the potential to change the direction of democracies as seen in recent 'Cambridge Analytica' incident. Moreover data is the fuel of artificial intelligence. As per the prophecy of Russian President Vladimir Putin – the country which owns the most powerful artificial intelligence will rule the world.

Discovery of oil led to global quest for oil and it continues even today. Chinese interventions in South China Sea, Vietnamese offshore projects, Arctic explorations, India's own offshore exploration, and global invasions like one of U.S. in Iraq were primarily to secure long term oil assets.

Similarly, data is being absorbed by global multinationals (MNCs), governments. Government projects like NATGRID, Aadhar, Chinese steps for data localisation, provision of free services in exchange for data by MNCs show global quest for data.

Oil has been sought by non-state actions, terrorists like ISIS to fund and fuel their war. Saudi wealth has been long known to have been used to fund Pakistan-sponsored terror in India.

Similarly, now data is being sold on dark web/deep web. This data pertains to ordinary people and is obtained by hacking of secure servers. Proceeds obtained can once again be used for terror funding.

Thus far we have seen the similarities between data and oil in economic, political and terror domains. Let's explore differences between data and oil.

Use of oil has caused global warming pollution. This has caused oil to be seen as dirty and a quest has been launched for alternative fuel. As per international energy by 2040, 40% of world's energy would be non-fossil fuel based. Hence oil is polluting, limited and replaceable by renewable energy. However, data is digital and non-polluting. Every human being, incident-metrological, geological, physical, chemical can be a source of data. Data is virtually limitless only limitation is our collection storage processing. Also, yet no replacement of data has been proposed.

Oil/fossil fuels are geographically dispersed and globally non-uniformly distributed. This makes access ownership uneven and unequal. However, every individual has potential to be source of data. Access is uneven only due to digital divide which is narrowing sharply. Further, legal frameworks can be designed to ensure access to be uniform to all. Cloud computing further eases access.

Oil fuelled innovation in industrial era. But that innovation was based on energy source, today even renewable energy can cause similar innovations. However, data has the potential to fuel innovations in our economy. This is seen in service sector start ups, new service delivery models. The very fact that 6/10 youth in India by 2035 could do jobs that have not been created shows the widest potential of data-driven innovation.

Oil does not lend itself to a direct role in governance. Only as an indirect foreign exchange resource can oil lead to wealth of a nation. However, data can be used eminently for data driven policy making based on evidence and feedback. This helps more citizen centric governance by targeted delivery of services.

Uses of oil are very limited – as a fuel and by-products. However, uses of data range far and wide from research, disaster prediction, management, policing, crime control, healthcare diseases burden surveillance and targeted supply of resources. Market decisions are now increasingly driven by use of customer preference data. Several banks use data for credit worth assessment. Consultancy sector, ecommerce is highly data driven.

Not only the uses and opportunities but threats due to abuse of data are much grave. True, that oil has been used to fund terror and caused wars. But data itself can be used as a weapon. For instance genomic data can be used for designing of pathogens to eliminate specific races, ethnicities etc. selectively. This could take terror to a whole new threat level.

Data can be used for surveillance as seen in PRISM Snowden leaks. This would be used to curb dissent, subvert democracy with utmost privacy and discreetness. Thus, posing greater threat to democracy than blatant authoritarian regimes like Stalin's Russia.

Further, incidents like Cambridge Analytica, social media echo-chamber would, coupled with psychological profiling, could attack the heart of democracy – without the voters even realising it – thus no chance to protest it either.

While trade in oil affects current account deficit explicitly, data highways pointing west don't show any explicit loss of forex. Only a deep analysis shows loss of service sector business opportunities.

Thus, we saw there are significant similarities and dissimilarities between oil and data. There are few challenges associated with data and significant opportunities too. Way ahead would be to prepare the masses to best exploit the opportunities and prepare for the challenges.

Preparation at global level would involve agreements between countries on the lines of Geneva Convention about legitimate reasons for sharing data – e.g. security, tax administration, justice delivery etc.

Democratic governance of global internet infrastructure could help use of data for the welfare of humanity – rather than cartelisation as seen in OPEC countries.

At national level countries need to come up with a legal framework to ensure privacy, strict laws on transparent framework for state surveillance as well as data protection. European general data protection rules, India's data protection bill are examples. EU–US Privacy Shield agreement could show harmonisation of global laws for cooperation.

Further, measures to ensure universal equitable digital access, digital sovereignty, net neutrality as well as uses/collection consent as well as right to be forgotten, data breach rights could help ensure data becomes oil for human welfare and world becomes a secure place to live in.

❑❑

18 Strengthening Healthcare System in India – Is Privatisation the Only Answer?

Abhishek Saraf, IAS (AIR 8 CSE 2019)

Welfare state of India aims to provide universal healthcare to its citizens. While not a reality yet, but public healthcare does aim at cheaper and quality primary, secondary, tertiary services. A chain of primary health centres to distinct hospitals has been set up. But was it not a failure of public healthcare when over 60 children died due to shortage of oxygen in Gorakhpur due to a seasonally recurring disease. How do we trust public healthcare when a man has to carry his pregnant wife in labour to a hospital on a bicycle?

Clearly private sector is needed. But on the other hand, Fortis Hospital in Delhi charged over ₹ 6 lakhs for dengue treatment for a girl who eventually could not even be saved. When such criminal breach of trust runs deep in private healthcare, can it be called on to strengthen healthcare exclusively in India?

In tug-of-war of shifting responsibilities – private or public, there is only one clear loser. The 6 crore Indians who fall below poverty line due to healthcare expenditure. Society as a whole suffers loss of productive human capital – the present as well as future-generations due to weakness of healthcare. Only a combination of both public and private sectors can strengthen the weak healthcare sector in India.

Healthcare in India suffers from several weaknesses. They range from quality of care and skill of professionals and their members, social security, out-of-pocket expenditure, accessibility and affordability of care. Sectoral neglect of mental and geriatric health and divides like rural and urban, rich and poor have posed serious challenges to healthcare in India. Few of these could be addressed by privatisation.

Privatisation would entail market based competitive delivery of healthcare like any other services – perform or perish scenario would compel hospitals to provide quality care. This can be seen in tertiary, super speciality care which has put Kerala on the map of global medical tourism.

Tertiary care by privatised healthcare institutions would alleviate government from fiscal burden. This becomes imperative, considering government spends meagre 1.5% of GDP on healthcare. Government could use services of private sector through 'Strategic purchase model' to fulfil any crucial needs.

Purchase of service by government could also be done for poor through insurance models like seen in National Health Protection Scheme – thus alleviating government from burden of direct delivery and ensuring quality care.

Moreover, a blooming private sector would attract the best human-power-doctors and allied staff. Private hospitals as training institutes under proper government regulation could help offset the current shortage – (1/1,676 as against 1 doctor per 1,000 people recommended by WHO).

Private sector would also be encouraged to reach out to the marginalised as seen in Pradhan Mantri Surakshit Matritva Yojana. In this scheme private practitioners voluntary render consultation services to pregnant women every month. Further, CSR initiatives could help channel profits for public welfare. Newly emerging social enterprises in healthcare are the future of this sector.

Looking ahead private sector globally has taken lead in pharmaceutical research. Research in both pharmacy and overall healthcare would get a boost by massive participation of private hospitals.

Further, private sector would also help breach rural urban divide through initiatives like telemedicine, e-hospitals, Indian Academy of Paediatrics Health phone and digital diagnostics thus, strengthening healthcare in India. However, having analysed the benefits of privatisation it is only prudent that we look at pitfalls.

Textual precedents show a pragmatic approach is needed. Market dominated healthcare model would exclude those who cannot pay. Private sector would have no profit-incentive to invest in either rural healthcare or primary healthcare. In a country where 80% of poor live in rural areas, can we really risk that?

Solution can be found in NHPS/RSBY model. Precedents show that presence of moral hazard, over-charging, information asymmetry could lead to exploitation of patients to their exclusion. Collusive corruption with insurance partners could lead to wastage of resources.

In a country where 60% of healthcare expenditure is out-of-pocket, can sole reliance on private sector be the key? Cases like MAX hospital overcharging, unnecessary procedures, insurance frauds hardly inspire confidence.

Further, in our society several eminently treatable diseases like leprosy, mental health disorders are subject to stigma. Stigma causes abandoning of the patients by their family. Can private sector cater to those unfortunate individuals whose right to life and dignity has been risked to verge of denial. Similar is the case of old age problems of senior citizens. Would it not eliminate the accessibility of healthcare to them?

Moreover, several reports like Global Burden of Diseases have shown how private sector in India fails at mandatorily reporting of diseases like TB, AIDS. With no active in interest in long term health of society would private sector invest in healthcare and rehabilitation of drug addicts? Initiatives like family planning, organ donation and blood donation would hardly attract private attention.

Profit motive often blinds the market players to unethical practices. This is seen in kickbacks in medical sector for prescription of costly drugs in place of generics. Clinical trials are another domain where active involvement of government is necessary. Empathetic delivery of healthcare would suffer when healthcare becomes a business.

Thus, clearly a combination of private and public sector is needed as both have their strengths and their weakness. The strengths of the private sector has been discussed earlier. The weaknesses could be solved by active involvement of government thus necessitating public healthcare.

National health policy directs the government to spend 2.5% of GDP to healthcare. Focus of government should be on primary healthcare. Strategic purchase along with NHPS from empanelled hospitals in competition with public tertiary hospitals could ensure cheap, inclusive and quality healthcare for the last man.

Further, regulation by government in terms of education, ethics, and curriculum could be done through reform of Medical Council of India. Active involvement of all stakeholders would be the key here – leading to minimum government intervention and maximum governance.

Price regulation could be achieved through Pharma Sahi Dam Application as well as initiatives like Drug Price Control Order. Frequent revisions of National list of essential medicines along with trade margin rationalisation, voluntary licensing could achieve affordability and accessibility in Pharma sector. Generics could be promoted under Jan Aushadi Scheme. Quality could be maintained by mandatory bioequivalence studies. Health being state subject – here cooperation of state and central regulators is necessary.

Moreover apart from wholesome sectoral interventions could help government initiatives like early childhood care under ICDS, National Health Mission – rural and urban could help BPL – children and adults. Poor performance on IMR, MMR could be improved by schemes like PMMSY, PMMYY.

Moreover, initiatives like mission Indradhanush could help reduce incidence of diseases. Government involvement is necessary to promote vector-borne disease control programmes. Healthcare of adolescents through SAATHIYA, family planning by Prerna could lead to welfare of present and future generation. This has to be an exclusive responsibility of public sector.

Most importantly, government intervention could help end knowledge asymmetry between patients and private healthcare providers through 'my hospital' initiatives. Grievance redressal is a role of government as well.

Beyond all this, there is a need for interventions that would reduce the need for hospitalisation itself. Government needs to focus on 'Swachh Bharat Abhiyan', National

Nutrition Mission, Sanitation and Clean Drinking Water. This could reduce incidence of communicable diseases and loss of immunity.

Focus has to be on preventive healthcare, AYUSH system as well as health and wellness for a sustainable happy living. Focus on nutrition security along with food security would help realise the right to health for all. This would relieve us of the challenge of stunting, wasting and underweight children.

Several global models like that of Cuba, Vietnam or UK, domestically models of Maharashtra and Tamil Nadu are available. Most of them emphasize of role of public and private together playing on each other's strengths. Several NGOs have taken lead like – Arogya Netram, Health for India have done some excellent work. They need to be promoted.

With joint efforts via public-private-people partnership we can realise the dream of universal healthcare in the welfare state of India. A robust healthcare sector would lead to security of mind in healthy body to a progressive nation on path to sustained rapid inclusive growth.

❑❑

19 Diversity in India, Does it Better or Fetter the Economic Growth

Ankush Kothari, (AIR 429 CSE 2019)

A 1932 classic dystopian novel, 'Brave New World' by Huxley talks about a society where no class or social differences exists. Everyone is cloned by the state to make population homogenous, brain washed to prevent any diversity thus to provide as labour for economic growth, with no questions asked. However, it only backfires as even Darwin has advocated need of diversity for better growth and adaptability.

Above context brings in the debate regarding multi-diverse country like India whether its diversity is assisting or hindering the economic growth. In this essay, we shall analyze both the aspects carefully.

India has been hailed as a land of diversity. Mukhya Upanishads talks about the concept of 'Unity in Diversity'. India has seen ages, various explorers and travellers coming to the peninsula to observe, cherish and learn from its diverse nature.

India is diverse in linguistic, religious, ethnic, geographical, territorial, economic, social aspects. National diversity has led to a mosaic model adopted by us, which welcomes and supports various groups, thoughts and practices. Indian democracy is the biggest example of accommodating and integrating its diversity.

At an international level, the diversity has boosted economic growth by promoting innovation, varied thoughts of inquisitive nature and inventions. Examples of Sir Abdul Kalam, Homi Bhabha, V. Sarabhai etc. are before us. TISCO (by Tatas) set up the base for economic growth of India.

At societal level, diversity helps us in growing economy in a multi-faceted way. Women provide for eco-feminism, basis of care economy and designing better policies that are sensitive to public. Transgenders in army and police, elders sharing their wisdom and children as the future of tomorrow can shape the destiny of Nation.

Geographically, diversity has helped in tourism. India's diversity ranges from Himalayas to peninsula, deserts to seas etc. This has led to a better economy as it helps in forex earnings. Also, GI tag in various parts as Tirupati Laddus, Benaras Sarees etc. helps in better economic growth.

Tribals provide for very crucial and valuable medication and traditional knowledge. Linguistic diversity has been documented to provide the basis for academic research. For example, Sanskrit is a scientific language is used in statistical models and computing.

Diversity not just in these, but in agriculture (crop diversification), industries etc. can boost our exports and increase India's competitiveness globally. A young workforce, skillfully and diversely trained can supply into various roles from architecture to handicrafts making.

Territorial diversity has immensely contributed to economy and security of the nation. Gorkhas provide for one of the largest and finest segment of Indian army. It is said that, if a man is not afraid of dying, he is either lying or is a Gorkha. Various sports person from north-east like Mary Kom, Baichung Bhutia have raised India's prestige.

Diversity in politics provides for constitutional safeguards to minorities and vulnerable, diverse groups that aim at protecting, developing and achieving their full potential in contributing to the Nation (Fundamental Duty). Rajya Sabha is an excellent example of giving representation to the diverse voices in the development of country.

Even at global level, diversity brings immense gain for India as it enhances its soft power (Yoga, Bollywood, culture, tourism etc.) and Indian diaspora, the largest in the world, provides valuable remittances to India ($80b alone in 2018). Clearly, diversity has helped in better economic growth.

However, all that shines is not gold; diversity in a way has also fettered economic growth in several ways, one simple example would be the invasion and colonialism of India by foreign powers as Indian subcontinent was too diverse to be united against exploiters. Africa is another case in point.

Religious diversity in India has often led to rise in communal conflicts, riots and clashes. One dark and major event in history of India would be partition of 1947 which not only shook us morally and politically but also economically as resource rich (Baluchistan) and fertile Indus floodplains went to Pakistan.

Linguistic diversity led to clashes several times, starting from 1953, Vishal Andhra movement to the Punjabi Suba demand to recent GTA issue in West Bengal over imposition of Bengali language are few cases.

Diversity has also compromised economic growth by giving rise to 'sons of soil' doctrine, movements for separation as Khalistan, Nagalim etc. came to picture. Even the complex diversity in Jammu and Kashmir over Ladakhis (Buddhists), Kashmiri Pandits (Hindus) and Muslims in the valley led to the bifurcation of state into two Union Territories.

Article 35A had impeded economic growth, investment in J&K over 70 years and after abrogation too, internet shutdowns has caused a non-conducive environment. Tackling diversity in a way that it can see better economic growth is yet to be seen in J&K.

Other issues associated with diversity are Dalit lynching, intolerance that puts a ban over creative experiences that are considered as a threat to Indian diversity. It degrades India's credit rating and leads to human rights issues which in turn affect confidence of investors.

Migration and minority rights have always been at the forefront of development debate in terms of inclusive growth. Recent exodus of migrants originating from UP and Bihar from Gujarat and Maharashtra affects labour availability. Minority protection and development has always been a contentious issue for India.

Development-Displacement debate in case of tribals has affected various projects related to dams, mining and industries. As a result of stalled projects and delayed land or environmental clearances has affected ease of doing business and caused a rise in NPAs.

If diversity has fettered economic growth in some aspects then the solution for better economic growth too lies in diversity. Inclusive growth, regional development and respecting federal features of the constitution provide the way out for faster, sustainable growth.

Para diplomacy can help in the cause. It means empowering states to attract investments by establishing diplomatic relations, without Centre's help. It can help in tapping investment for smart city projects, solve river water disputes and lead to reducing disparities.

It can also be used as a tool for diplomacy. Soft power is enhanced via diversity. Indians in Canadian Parliament, UK, etc. provide opportunity for better partners.

Therefore, by effectively utilizing India's diversity by providing decentralization, autonomy of funds, functions and functionaries, India can very well be on the path of becoming USD 5 trillion economy. There is a need for constructive debates in Parliament by diverse parties and promotion to free thoughts, ideas and expression.

India as the land of non-violence, tolerance, truth, compassion embodied by Mahavira and Buddha, can become a global superpower by leveraging its diversity and ensuring inclusive growth. Better economics is often reflected in better policies shaped by grassroot and participatory democracy. Diversity thus can better economic growth via e-governance and inclusion (spatial, financial, and digital).

❑❑

20 Evolution of India's Foreign Policy: Continuity and Changes

Ankush Kothari, (AIR 429 CSE 2019)

'Ultimately foreign policy is the outcome of economic policy and till India properly waives her economic policy, her foreign policy will rather be vague'

– J.L. Nehru (Constituent Assembly 1947)

A nation's foreign policy is shaped by several factors like economic, geopolitical, strategic interests etc. but the most important factor is the National interest above all (Machiavellian Doctrine). India's foreign policy has been to several phases of change yet has maintained its connectivity in several spheres. Aspects of strategic autonomy, territorial interest and universal values of peace and freedom are always respected and cherished by India.

Since ancient times, India has maintained ties with foreign rulers. Indus Valley civilization had links (though less political, more economic) with contemporary civilizations of Mesopotamia, Armenian etc. for trade and commerce. Ashoka sent Dhamma officials for preaching values of peace and non-violence. Chola kept strong navy to advance their interests, Alauddin Khilji and Mohammad bin Tughlaq prevented Mongols from entering into India.

However, the Britishers succeeded in capturing the 'Golden Bird' of the time. They also evolved their own version of foreign policy for their petty interests. Dreaded by Afghans, ring-fence policy of Hashing, policy of proud reserve by Lytton or forward policy of Auckland, their foreign policy maintained the elements of change and continuity. It was only post-independence that independent India could evolve its own foreign policy. In this essay, we shall examine various phases in the evolution of India's foreign policy.

Phase-I: Ideological Period of India's Foreign Policy: [1947-1962]

India's foreign policy just after the independence was marked by strong sense of Nationalism continuing from the freedom struggle. The focus was more on improving the domestic situation of illiteracy, agriculture, etc. In the international affairs, we went with the continuing principles of M.K. Gandhi which led us to come with NAM and panchsheel.

Though India was offered a few opportunities to enter the world geopolitics and being the world's largest democracy, chance to spread her ideals institutionally. Mediation in the Korean peninsula and UNSC seat (1955) to name a few. These were the examples reflecting India's importance in the global arena.

However, the ideological approach didn't bear much fruits as we offered the UNSC seat to China instead of keeping it for ourselves. The implications of this are much visible today when we are fighting tooth and nail to get the permanent stature in UNSC and China is blocking our candidature. Panchsheel's failure resulted into 1962 war as we accepted Tibet as a part of China instead of voicing against it and it ended the buffer. Also, decision to take Kashmir issue to UN proved disastrous as it made a bilateral issue an international one.

Thus, the failure of ideological approach, overlooking the defence sector, lack of tilt towards any superpower (NAM) and allowing China to grow steadily yet assertively resulted finally in defeat in 1962 war which broke the chains of ideological dreams and forced India to adopt a pragmatic approach under the new PM.

Phase II: The Period of Pragmatism (1962-1991)

The hangover of phase I of India's foreign policy and back to back 2 wars in 3 years resulted in boiling domestic situation. Famines of 1965, 1966 made it worse and India had to turn towards US under humiliating PL-480 program for food grains. However, India had already begun to take pragmatic steps by now, in the evolution of her foreign policy.

Enhanced focus on Defence sector led to India's victory in 1965 war against Pakistan. Going a step further, India became instrumental in the creation of Bangladesh from East Pakistan which clearly showed India's changing foreign policy from passive to an active Nation. Though, it maintained continuity by not following any bloc in the Cold war and remained with NAM, the new outlook was certainly pragmatic.

A change came with US's Nixon-Kiesinger policy of 'tilt towards Pakistan' and it openly supported Pakistan too, in the 1971 war. India with the help of Soviet, resisted this but clearly realized that to protect its national interests, it must come into the select league of countries. Hence, 1974 Pokhran test made India 1st non P-5 country to try nuclear capabilities. India also started interfering in other neighbouring countries' domestic issues like preventing the coup in Maldives 1988 (India was asked to intervene) and LTTE issue in Sri Lanka (proved disastrous).

Increasing role in foreign affairs, failure of Sri Lanka domestic affairs intervention, all time low with US relations etc. coupled with the perils of being a close economy led to 1991 economic crisis. Long pending reforms, balance of payment crisis, foreign exchange all time low, shortage of food supply, export pessimism and license raj leading to deadlock in domestic growth of industries, made several political-economists ask the question: Does the Elephant Dance?

Phase III: Economic Diplomacy at The Forefront of Foreign Policy (1991-today); [continuing with other changes too]

'No power on Earth can stop an idea whose time has come' [Victor Hugs] this was quoted by Dr. Manmohan Singh while introducing India's New Economic policy based on liberalization, privatization and globalization. The Elephant had to dance as it became inevitable with the 1991 BoP crisis, collapse of Soviet Union and changing geopolitics and geo-economics.

India as the founder member of WTO, thrusts the need of economic changes vital to shape the foreign policy. India established formal diplomatic relations with Israel, joined various trade blocs: ASEAN, G20, Indian Ocean Region also became pivotal to India's growth and diplomacy.

However, there was a change in world's equation with bi-polar world reducing to uni-polar only to re-emerge as multi-polar. Pakistan acquired nuclear power capabilities and other nations also tried to test their nuclear weapons. India's national security interests pushed her to do test nuclear weapons in Pokhran-II (1998) as she is surrounded by two hostile neighbours. This received condemnation from the world and many countries like Australia, Japan etc. cut the diplomatic ties and stopped ODA (Development Assistance).

Thus, along with economic diplomacy of being an open economy, India adopted another outlook in its foreign policy (not a separate phase though, as economic diplomacy still continues today), i.e. of de-hyphenation. This brought India closer to US, while maintaining ties with Russia, then, resulting in the Civil Nuclear Agreement (123) in 2005.

De-hyphenated foreign policy can be seen in India managing its foreign relations diplomatically with both Israel and Palestine at the same time, Israel and Iran, Iran and Saudi Arabia, and most importantly with US and Russia. India's stand on Palestine and didn't accepting Jerusalem as Israel's capital (despite US did) reflects India's active as well as assertive foreign policy. Space diplomacy is a major part of it.

Continuity in India's foreign policy can also be seen with continuing to vouch for peace, non-violence, extending diplomatic and economic support to least developed countries, fighting against violation of Human Rights etc. It has continuously pressed for CCIT in UN and called for a global fight against terrorism. Its stance on NPT and CBT remains same of being discriminatory and thus, is unwilling to sign even today, as it calls for no-first use and universal rid of nuclear weapons instead of dividing world into 'haves' and 'have not'.

India's stand on respecting sovereignty, territorial integrity and strategic autonomy is seen on its Kashmir stand. It has voiced against China suspicious Belt and Road initiative and till date has not joined it as it undermine India's sovereignty and territorial integrity. In the South China Sea issue, it has maintained that rules based order should be followed for a free, open, prosperous Pacific with freedom of navigation and over flight. Act east and look west policy are elements of India's role in foreign affairs.

India's increasing global dominance can be seen in the US recent National Security strategy by Pentagon, where it has accepted India as the net security provider in Indo-Pacific region (renamed from Asia Pacific to highlight India's role). Groupings like QUAD, SCO and BRICS show as well as present India an opportunity to emerge as a global power.

However, certain challenges persist. With abstaining to vote on UN resolution on Libya and Syria, silence on Myanmar's persecution of Rohingyas and Israel's atrocities in Palestine and Saudi Arabia's Yemen episode reflects India's passiveness in foreign affairs in bit to maintain everybody happy. To emerge as a global player in geopolitics and keeping its continuity with Gandhian ideals of being a champion of human rights, India must address it to enhance its 'Smart Power'.

Still, India's foreign policy has shown a substantive change as she is a potential candidate for UNSC. Her stand on environmental sustainability is in line with 'politics with principles'. Also, there has been total continuity in neighbourhood policy as first and the most important. Non-reciprocity and mutual respect dominates everything.

Thus, India's foreign policy has evolved as per the time and has helped India in becoming a major player in the international affairs, managing its international relations in conformity to its National Interests. As Nehru quoted,"The art of foreign affairs lies in finding what is most advantageous for the country".

❑❑

21 Gender Equality: Myth or Reality

Ashutosh Dwivedi, IAS (AIR 70 CSE 2017)

"Where women are worshipped, there the Gods dwell."

- The Rig Veda

These high ideals are the hallmark of status of women in Indian society but the actual ground situation seems patchy and this gives rise to the debate whether gender equality is a myth or reality.

The society is characterized by many dichotomies and status of women presents a classic case of such dichotomy, where even from ancient time, we see existence of multiple standards.

During Vedic times, on the one hand we see women like Apala, Lopamudra who have written verses in Vedas and on the other hand, we find terms "Gahapati", which clearly denotes the male head of household. "The Pati Manusmriti", during first millennium showed that women's position further deteriorated.

If we take a look at mythological epics and treat them as depicting the situation of society, and not for their mythological value, we see existence of both gender equality and inequality – on one hand we have Shurpanakha, a lady bold enough to ask for the hand of Rama in marriage, while on the other hand we have Sita, who got abandoned by her husband for no fault of hers and even after going through the test of so-called purity. And this has to be underlined that we are talking about the Queen of the kingdom, let alone the common women! During medieval times also gender equality appeared to be a myth because of almost complete social ostracization in the form of Purdah and simultaneously we have example of Razia Sultan who became the ruler, even though that was not "because of" social conditions rather "in spite of" the social condition.

In present day modern world, the difference has become even starker, and the pace of divergence between myth and reality is even higher, as the overall social situation are characterised by high dynamism.

The dream of gender equality appears to be realty when we acknowledge that India has already have a female Head of state and Head of government a feat not yet obtained by the perceived advanced country like United States of America.

Increasing participation of women in public arena, breaking of glass ceiling by women like Indira Nooyi, Chanda Kochar, closing gender gap as shown by improvement in Indian's raking in World Economic Forum's gender gap index from 109th to 87th; all shows that there is some semblance of gender equality.

The days when women were struggling to be inducted in armed forces appear to be past us when we see that not only women are accepted in combat roles, but also a woman is today responsible for the defence of the country as Defence Minister.

For the first times the cabinet committee on security have two women in the form of Defence Minister and External Affairs Minister.

Globally also, things appear to be improving on gender front as gradually the participation of women is increasing and that too at all levels. It was a woman, Angela Merkel towards whom the whole world was looking at during the Syrian refugee crisis.

But the debate of equality being a myth or reality riles up once we start digging deeper. A constant increase in rise of crime against women in public sphere shows that though women are taking to public sphere, but they are constantly are at threat as a section of society cannot yet accept women as equal.

News of rapes and sexual assault have become so common that victims appear to be mere statistics, and the fact that in 90% of incidents, the perpetrators are known to women shows the gory reality behind the so-called civilised society.

The participation of women in paid jobs appears to be increasing but the female labour force participation rate of mere 15% in urban areas and 25% in rural areas shows that there is still a long way to go. Just pose it with the gender pay of 27%, and the myth of gender equality appears shattering.

If we go to deeper layers of the debate and try to find out why this inequality persists, we come across social structures, economic situations and historical constructs which help in perpetuating gender inequality.

The social set-up of a patriarchal society imposes multiple barriers and does not let women reach their true potential though, patriarchy is justified on the basis of biological factors like brain laterization, higher muscle to fat ration in men but gender is essential a social construct, otherwise why in households cooking is the work of female, where it is unpaid, while in hotels and restaurants, where cooking is paid employment, we see that most chef are male?

The conscious segregation of women from paid work and non recognition of the care economy dominated by women, gives rise to economic situation, where women are left with no social security and they become dependent on male and thus create gender inequality.

It is not that our policy makers are unaware of these problems and also multiple efforts are on towards converting the myth of gender equality into reality.

Our constitution, not only recognises the concept of equality enshrined in Articles 15, 16 and many other places, but also goes beyond equality and prescribes for favourable treatment to women and children as an exception to the principle of equality.

Various legislation like Harassment of Women at Workplace Act 2014, tries to make workplace a safer place for women, so as to increase their participation.

Recent Amendment in Maternity Benefits Act grants 26 weeks of paid maternity leave, which goes beyond the 120 standard of 14 week.

Programmes like Beti Bachao Beti Padhao, selfie with daughter, Sukanya Samriddhi are aimed at not only umpiring situation of girls, but also changing the perception of people towards girl child which goes at grassroot of gender equality remaining as a myth in our society.

Schemes like Nai Roshni, Mahila Shakti Kendra ,induction of mahila police volunteer (in Haryana Police), reservation of women in government service by Bihar government are focussed on empowering women.

The judiciary has been at the forefront of the mission of gender equality right from issuing Vishaka Guidelines in 1997 in absence of any law to protect women at workplace, and this time has been reinforced by banning instant triple talaq recently.

All these initiatives have their own positives and negatives but one turning needs to be understood that gender inequality is a social problems, and hence solution also lies in the society. Laws and state intervention will not be much beneficial in absence of social transformation e.g. in spite of having anti-dowry law since more than 50 years, dowry is still rampant because it has social acceptance, in spite of being illegal.

Transformation is needed at the level of society, community, family and individual level to accept gender equality as the norm.

Children need to be gender sensitised from school only, so that they turn into a responsible and sensitive citizen.

Youth need to be reminded of the value of respecting girls and accepting them as equals. In control of social menace like dowry, it is the youth who have to take the lead.

Changes are needed from grassroot level and at the level of social thinking then only we will be able to convert gender equality into a reality.

The Need of Debate

Regarding gender equality being a myth or reality itself shows the level of equality in society. The need of the hour is to move beyond the debate of gender equality and focus on women achieving their true potential and we should not be surprised if they even surpass the men, as this is their true potential, which they will certainly realise.

❑❑

22 Cashless Economy – Challenges and Opportunities

Lavish Ordiya, IAS (AIR 18 CSE 2019)

Today morning, I woke up to the doorbell ring of milkman, only to realize I only had a ₹ 2,000 note but needed to pay ₹ 34. He happily accepted payment on Paytm. On my way to office; I stopped at a stall for tea and breakfast and paid him on PhonePe, and to my surprise a cashback of ₹ 12 on ₹ 55 transaction.

I need not stop to buy any ticket for the metro train to my office, as the metro smart card provides seamless travel across the city and I can recharge it online just like a mobile topup. As I reached my office, I got an SMS of the salary being credited to my bank account, as it was the last day of the month. I quickly transferred ₹ 15,000 to my parents using BHIM-UPI within 10 seconds. We have surely come a long way towards a cashless economy.

Starting from the barter system of economic transactions, to terracotta seals of Harappa, silver and gold coins of Harrapan civilizations, the beautifully inscribed gold coins of Gupta times to silver tankas of Iltutmish and Rupee introduced by Britishers to the BHIM of Government of India and even further cryptocurrency, the economy of transactions have gone through various phases to culminate into cashless economy of today.

A cashless economy can be simply put as an economy where most or all the financial transactions and exchanges take place without any physical exchange of currency or money.

It may involve the use of plastic cards like ATM/ credit cards, digital wallets or a direct bank account transfer. Banking system has a critical role to play in the entire chain as they form both the ultimate source and destination of the money exchanged. Cashless economy requires a seamless integration of all the units of economy like individuals business government etc. through banking channels.

Recent steps taken by government of India like Pradhan Mantri Jan Dhan Yojana, Small and Payment Bank, Direct Benefit Transfer, Demonetization, GST etc. have all given a significant push to the country towards digital economy.

The transition of the country towards a cashless, paperless economy presents both new opportunities and challenges.

The opportunities and benefits of cashless economy are multifaceted and for starting from the very obvious benefits of requirements of lesser bank branches, lesser ATMs and less staff resulting in savings and lesser cost of printing money and minting coins. It is also a safer option providing hassle free option of shopping, transacting without need to carry a bundle of cash in pockets.

The social benefits of this move are rather much bigger. The cashless economy has promoted financial inclusion within the country including access to credit, insurance etc. to all sections of the society including farmers, women, poor etc.

The Kisan Credit Card, insurance cover on Rupay Debit Card etc. are examples. This will not only result in reduced inequalities, but also reduced corruption and leakages through use of direct benefit transfer.

Further, the economy of the country benefits from the money multiplier effect resulting from increased circulation of money. The central Banks's monetary policy transmission will tend to be more effective in controlling inflation. This will help achieve the much needed formalization of Indian Economy.

The benefits also include lesser tax evasion & black money generation. This will ultimately also help control illegal criminal activities like smuggling, terrorism, money laundering and transaction strengthening the country's security.

In the political sphere it may be used to improve funding transparency of political parties, thus reducing use of money and muscle power in elections, crony capitalism & criminal politician businessman nexus. The peripheral benefits include reduction of prices of real estate, private education etc.

However, with new opportunity comes new challenges and needs for newer solutions and approaches.

In our country with less than 25% digital literacy and divide between rural and urban areas, the push towards digital economy seems to be rather forceful than natural. The case of death of Jharkhand girl due to hunger on not linking Aadhar Card to Ration Card loudly tells the reality. The digitally unaware rural people become easy targets of the fraudsters who extract details of their cards/accounts easily over phone.

Further, low penetration of banks in rural areas and hinterland, lack of internet connectivity and digital infrastructure poses yet another challenge.

Unavailability of applications in vernacular languages makes it difficult for a common man to use such tools easily.

In our society, several practices tend to be deeply associated with money and its physical form. For instance, among Muslims, depositing in a bank to earn interest is a sin. Use of coins on occasions of marriage, donations in temples etc. is yet another example.

The increasing cases of cybercrimes pose serious threat to the credibility of cashless transactions. UN International Telecommunications union has classified India as the fifth most vulnerable country in cyber safety. The recent cases of siphoning of funds from Banks of Baroda is a cause of concern.

Strategically, most of the payment gateway companies like Visa, Master Card etc. are located outside India and carry a huge amount of data and information about Indian consumers, posing serious data sovereignty and privacy concerns.

The possibility of misuse of data for kidnapping, extortions etc. cannot be ruled out.

Further it seems the use of cashless economy has further eased the job of terrorists and criminals who have been using it extensively for raising funds, financing arms and attacks. The emerging use of cryptocurrency has become a worry globally.

New challenges present new opportunities. Despite the problems, there are ways to work around and solve them through dedicated, focused and collaborated efforts. First and foremost, efforts towards digital literacy of the citizens through schemes like Digital Saksharta Abhiyan need to be promoted. Digital Infrastructure creation under schemes like Bharatnet, USOF need a renewed focus & funds. A strong legal framework at national level must be prepared in addition to amendments to IT Act 2000, in line with new developments.

Incentives to use cashless payment mechanisms through cashbacks, discounts are much appreciated. The recent limits on cash withdrawals in Union Budget 2019-20 will ensure elimination of black and informal market. Recommendation of Justice B. N. Srikrishna committee and RBI on data localization should be considered after multi-stake holder consultation with companies, Banks and international Bodies. International collaborations like UNESCO's Internet governance forum must be further explored to come up with global legislature to control money laundering, terrorist financing data breaches and control etc. through cashless medium.

In our goal towards moving to a $5 trillion economy by 2026, we must take structural reforms like cashless economy to accelerate our economic growth and inclusive development of all in the society.

❑❑

23 Daughters of India – Their Strength, Their Plights and Their Achievements!

Nikhil Rakhecha, IAS (AIR 197 CSE 2018)

"Women constitute half of world's population, perform two third of its work hours, received one tenth of its income and owns less than one hundredth of its property" says UN report published in the backdrop of international decade of women (1980s) plights of women in India are even worse. Deep rooted patriarchal social structure of our society governs entire life cycle continuum of neglect, abuse, discrimination and inequality in women's life.

Struggle in women's life starts even before she's born. Preference for male child turns fatal for them. Widespread incidences of sex selective abortions are prevalent in modern Indian society. If she manage to survive this ordeal, neglect and abuse that she had to face throughout her life makes her sad about why she even survived at first place. Neglect starts from denying right nutritious food to even basic elementary education, childhood is meant to be enjoyed only by male child in Indian society. As culture demands girl child needs to take care of household chores and take care of younger siblings. Only after doing this job, she could join her brother in leisure activities.

This discrimination increases with passing age. She's made to choose non-technical career, if she even allowed to complete schooling. As girl child is treated as financial burden by most parent only to be married of as early as possible thereby wasting least resources on her upbringing and career even in marriage least voice is given to her in choosing her life partner.

With marriage new journey of exploitation and abuse starts in the form of domestic violence. And culture prescribes any kind of protest to such acts. It places husband in ranking of god for women, thereby prescribes multiply tolerating any kind of treatment. Her whole universe revolve around husband, who also becomes her source of identity and status. Economically as well she is completely dependent upon her male counterpart.

If some brave, ambitious manage to get paid employment she had to face whole new array of hardship. First, there will be no sharing of domestic work even when women is involved in paid employment outside. Secondly she will be discriminated at work place too. Unequal salary for equal work, involvement is limited to low paying, low status jobs. Even in formal organisation, glass ceiling exists which prohibits mobility of women to higher echelons. And not to mention abuse and harassment she might face at work place and in journey to and from office. Devoid of access to formal credit, she could not even start her own business. And she could be asked to sacrifice her whole career for family irrespective of her ambitions and goals.

But very few managed to get such exposure to economic activity, as female labour force participation in country is less than 21%, rest keep themselves busy serving needs of family. Even doing this would not be an issue, had their sacrifice received due recognition. But they are made to work round the clock, deprived of any appreciation and say in domestic decision making.

Failure to deliver male child would bring loads of abuse from family members and society. And death of husband would make inauspicious and blameworthy. Society ostracizes widows and leaves them to die in neglect and penury.

Compel this gender with disability and life would be hell for her. And so is the case with one belonging to lowest caste/class. Society exploits them with great impurity and backlash. Devoid of any political voice, their grievances are hardly paid heed to.

Through Panchayati Raj Institutes tried to give some political power, at very few places it had effectively empowered women. Representation in Lok Sabha is as small as 12%.

Even after such precarious scenario, in conducive environment and loads of challenges many women have left their mark in society. Political sphere being most visible one houses many charismatic women leaders. Mamata Banerjee, Vasundhara Raje Scindia, Sushma Swaraj are some such leaders. Even at grassroot level, many women Sarpanch are fighting against patriarchal culture and have managed to exercise independent authority.

In economic sphere through few to name are leading some of the largest organizations. Arundhati Bhattacharya, Indra Nooyi, Kiran Mazumdar Shaw. Some had to run away from country to escape from discrimination and pursue one's dream Chanda Zaveri being one such business women. Being forced to marry at young age and denied higher education she escaped to US and soon established multimillion dollar biotech firm.

Recent Olympics game result have depicted power of such resolve of daughters of our country. P.V. Sindhu, Sakshi Malik bagged silver medals for our country. In earlier world championship Mary Kom had brought many gold medals for country. Sania Mirza features among topmost tennis players of the world.

There are many other, recognised, unrecognised, appreciated and unappreciated women who'd brought glory to our country. Many are working selflessly and fighting against social injustice to make our society a better place to live for future generation. Women of Garhwal region started Chipko Movement which not only prevented deforestation and degradation of environment but also inspired numerous future movements to save our environment.

Our countries daughter also had distinct role in freedom struggle. Picketing liquor shops to burning foreign clothes, spreading Swaraj's message to marching in rallies of Satyagraha women had contributed significantly in our fight against foreign rule. Sarojini Naidu, Annie Besant, Rani Gaidinliu are few such leaders. Some even took revolutionary path which was considered male bastion to secure independence for country. Veena Das, Pritilata Waddedar assassinated many British officials.

Through women movements they had ensured that they get equal recognition in the eyes of law and discrimination become punishable offence. Ending inhumane social practice such as Sati to gaining right to remarry for widows, securing right to education to reservation in local bodies, these movements are easing access to public sphere for women.

New feminist movements have kept gender justice and equality debate alive. Through numerous Acts such as Hindu Succession Marriage cut age old discriminations have been curbed. Domestic Violence Act, prevention of Sexual Violence Act, Public Place Act, PCPNDT Act are culmination of relentless fight of women to end abuse and violence against them.

But the fight and achievements have not reached to its rightful place yet. Women are far behind their potential. Patriarchal mind-set is yet visible coherently in most places. Change could not be brought only by government. Everyone has to understand necessity for such change first.

Recent McKinsey report had noted that India could develop at double pace if we bring gender parity at work place. Even Swami Vivekananda had said that if society is to survive it cannot afford to neglect other half of its population such as bird cannot fly on only one wing. The historical injustice should be done away by promoting participation of women in public sphere by provision of reservation in state assemblies and parliament. Schemes such as Beti Bachao, Beti Padhao should be implemented on mission mode.

Sense of security too have larger role in ensuring participation of women. Cohesive environment should be created at workplace. Gender disparity had been prime reason for our laggard growth. As 21st century is seen as Asia's century, we too can achieve our rightful place on the world but only if we shed our patriarchal attitude.

❑❑

Diversity in India: Does it Better or Fetter the Economic Growth?

Nikhil Rakhecha, IAS (AIR 197 CSE 2018)

With every 50 km, dialect and culture changes in India. It is home to nearly all major religions of the world. There exist more than 1,700 dialects and 250+ languages in the country. Unique culture and language was a major criterion for division of vision into numerous states. With the history of invasions, influence of foreign culture is clearly visible on domestic art and architecture.

Being the most diverse country in the world, many predicted that India would be balkanised into hundred Indias. Many attribute slow economic progress of country to diversity of race, religion, caste, language, ethnicity etc. In this essay, we shall discuss whether this diversity is better or fetter economic growth.

Diversity: Bettering the Economic Growth

Incredible India campaign of tourism ministry projects India as must visit destination. Unique culture and tradition of India has historically driven travellers and tourists from throughout the world.

Foreign tourists as well as new middle class out of their curiosity and willingness to experience culture take to tourism. From Naturopathy and classical dances in South India to hospitality of Rajasthan and Gujarat, from world heritage sites to pilgrimage all attract these tourists. Tourism contributes nearly 10% to India's GDP and one of the largest employees in service sector.

Diversity is also reflected in cuisine, clothes and culture. Revival of interest in trying out what is called tradition has led to demand of such traditional products. Hotels providing traditional foods (Rajasthani thali, Manipuri fishes etc.) to handicrafts and jewellery all contributes to business opportunities. Handicrafts are also one of the important element of country's export basket.

Unique culture associated with particular region creates feeling of regionalism. This is positive sense compels individual to work towards progress and betterment of region. Thus fuels competitive federalism. As tapped by NITI Aayog, states are competing with each other to attract investment and transform their state into business friendly (Momentum Jharkhand, Dynamic Gujarat etc.)

Tribal and ethnic diversity which is largely untapped has huge economic potential. Traditional knowledge of tribals if patented could earn huge royalty for country. Recent case of Turmeric is one such example.

Diversity of culture is well trapped through geographic indication. Unique products of the region are heavily rewarded in domestic as well as international market. Mangoes from Ratnagiri to Roshogulla from West Bengal are exquisite examples of such products.

This diversity is also reflected in art and architecture. Madhubani painting from Bihar to Warli painting of Maharashtra. Similarly, temples of South India to music of North India, all are contributing to economy through tourism, business opportunity and employment.

Diversity could also be seen in geographic terms. India has vast coastline (7,500 km), lofty mountains (Himalayas), huge forest reserve (Western Ghats). Nearly all kind of geographical features are present in the country. And thus vital minerals such as iron, coal as well new energy resource such as methanol and shale gas. All these heavily contribute to economy.

Coming back to cultural diversity, Indian diaspora is most widely spread. With diversity of religion and tradition it has constructed a good brand with respect to the nation. Thus enhancing soft power as well as creating a market for Indian exports. Projection of India as tolerant and accommodative has helped to create goodwill which in turn results in more investment in the country.

Diversity: Fettering Economic Growth

Despite plethora of economic dividends brought about by diversity, it also accused of slowing down and at times reversing economic growth.

Starting with regionalism, which is strongly visible many a times works antithetical to economic interest of nation. For instance reservation of jobs for locals in Karnataka or son of soil movement in Mumbai. This restricts free movement of labour. Thus cost of labour rises for companies and it becomes uncompetitive.

Religious diversity when politicized creates communal conflict. Communal riots reverses the economic progress of region drastically. Precisely this insecure climate is restricting growth of J&K and other communally sensitive areas.

Similar conflict is also seen in case of ethnic diversity. Tribes of North Eastern region are perennially at loggerheads with each other by the Meitei-Naga-Kuki of Manipur to Bodos of Assam. All such conflicts creates unfavourable atmosphere for industries to develop.

On similar footing tribal conflict of Central India, guided by Naxalism against the state prevent any infrastructural development of the region. Diverse level of development among tribes prevented government efforts to be streamlined in even areas resulting into relative deprivation and associated conflicts.

Caste based diversity has also worked antithetically to economic growth. Occupational restrictions have prevented deserving from 'lower' caste to take up jobs. Prevalence of undignified jobs due to concepts of purity pollution prevents reaping of demographic dividend.

Such caste based stigmatisation spills over business as well as educational choices. It restricts the mobility of individual and confine them to unproductive areas of economy.

Caste and religious doctrine also comes into way of women while taking up paid labour outside their household. As depicted by Human development index while adjusting to gender inequality India loses significant GDP growth to such discrimination.

Linguistic diversity also hinders economic expansion. Globalisation meets with linguistic barrier and so numerous new technologies. Digital divide across language prevents adoption of such transformatory tool. This also puts barrier in movement of labour. Thus, they remain disguisely unemployed locally. Reservation of jobs on the lines of language is another instance of language creating barrier in economic growth.

Similarly religious diversity is spilling over economic sphere. Recent case of zomato over cancellation of order by customer on communal lines. Religious diversities creates atmosphere of suspicion and divide business as well as customer on communal lines. Recent cases of vigilantism has also affected numerous profession.

Harnessing Diversity for Economic Growth

Diversity in itself is not antithetical to economic growth. It actually creates potential to be harnessed for growth.

However vested interest and politicization of diversity makes it lag on economic growth. Many a times communal violence or ethnic conflicts are used to settle economic rivalry vested interest prevent economic development of minority ghetto.

This is essential to break away from stereotypes and uncover vested interests.

Start could be made from shaping our political attitude. Discarding leaders who use religion to garner votes. Appeasement politics should be boycotted.

Diverse language, tradition and customs should be preserved and promoted. TKDL portal under science ministry should be revived and patent for tribal knowledge should be filed. Through various tribal mela and portals such as Tribal hat marketing access be provided to reap economic benefit of such diversity.

Regionalism dialogue should be given a positive outlook. It is natural for individual to be aroused by regional issue and identify oneself with it. Thus through competitive federalism and equality of opportunity overall growth of nation should be aspired. Balanced development should be taken up to reduce deprivation concentrated across religious or regional lines.

Affirmative action for vulnerable sections spread across religion, caste etc. should be taken up. Recommendations of Xaxa Committee, Sachar Committee should be taken up for implementation.

Diversity is not bane but boon in this rapidly homogenizing world. It has huge social and psychological impacts which help in economic growth of country with ancient philosophy of 'Vasudhaiva Kutumbakam' we shall embrace and promote our diversity.

❑❑

25 Ecological Consideration Need Not Hamper Development

Abhisek Oswal, IRS [(IT) AIR 154 CSE 2019]

Students remember that nature bestowed us with abundant riches. In return all it asks for is its co-existence with development. If humanity has to progress ecology and development have to co-exist or the latter gets eliminated. Ecology is not a hurdle but a facilitator in the developmental process.

With this Professor Sharma concluded his developmental economic class. But he said ecology facilitates development and is not a hurdle. This view of his left me confused. With rapid population growth, urbanisation, demands for food, job, shelter how can ecology facilitate development? I approached Professor Sharma for the enlightenment.

Me: Good Afternoon Professor (I wished him)

Professor (sitting beneath the tree in campus garden): Good Afternoon.

Me: Professor I have some doubt to be clarified regarding toady's class. How can ecology facilitate development?

Professor: (Asking me to sit down) what do you see around? Tress, lush green grass Don't you feel a little relaxed sitting beneath this trees, isn't the temperature a bit cooler here? Doesn't nature add up to the beauty of our campus?

Me: yes sir, I do agree with you.

Professor: see you got the answer for your question Nature and ecological consideration have led to aesthetical development of our campus. Also the micro climate it provides adds upto our productivity.

Me: (I said) wow! I never looked in this way. But sir always consideration of ecosystem stalls development?

I have read that major cause for the development projects getting stalled is due to no environmental clearance. This have led to piling up of non-performing assets. The banking sector have been reeling in ICU like condition. The credit flow for Capital expenditure have stopped. This have completely halted new investment, creation of jobs and slowed economic growth.

On one hand we are facing the demography bulge by adding 8 new children per minute. On the other hand we are short of land for agricultural expansion, urbanisation industries don't come up on time due to shortage of land.

We cannot expand into forest areas because of legal compulsion to pursue them. The increasing presence on land and its resources could not be eased with exploitation of ecological resources. Haven't too much ecological consideration led to laggard development?

Professor: when individual society and ecology are in harmony then it is true development. The problem of the world is since nature don't tax for the resources it offers, it haven't got the due attention. History says tragedy of commons have led to tragedy of mankind. Let me explain what happens when nature is not considered in process of development.

Indus valley citizens were nature worshippers. The worshippers took no time to turn into exploiters and what happened next is an open secret. Human intellectual progress is traced since the age of machines .i.e. industrial revolution. But today that revolution led to climate change evolution and is currently threatening the entire humanity.

Our own green revolution started with aim to acquire food security and self-sufficiency. But the unintended outcomes are enormous. Right from groundwater depletion in Punjab, Haryana to land degradation in the same region.

Our steps to develop agriculture without considering the agro-climate condition of the geography, substituting traditional crops with water guzzling ones have plagues the entire agriculture economy, making it unsustainable.

Reorganisation of states marked a new era in Indian federalism. But the political development did not considered ecological voices. This resulted in inter-state water disputes across the country. Iron, coal and many natural minerals were mined or rather I would say exploited in an unsustainable way. Resulted are eviction of traditional dwellers, decertification of land.

Bloodshed for water in Tamil Nadu or even south Africa or Bogota is this the model of development? You know one of the hidden reason for the Arab Spring was not considering the ecological assets?

Me: Yes I remember that due to overexploitation of oil, land degradation, eviction and drought led to food insecurity. This was one of the major cause of Arab spring.

Professor: Yes you are absolutely correct!

We have encroached into jungle which eventually leads to fragmentation, cut enough trees than ecosystem could hear, realise enough obnoxious gases than atmosphere carrying capacity. All this in the name of development led to air pollution, contamination of water, soil, man animal conflict.

You know, on average 56 humans are being killed by shark attacks, but 1,500+ sharks for pleasure. Who is the real predator?

Our ecologically isolated development have hampered our social development, poor being the worst hit groundwater pollution, lack of sanitation have resulted in undernutrition. Loss of livelihood due to droughts and rural districts have led to forced migration into urban areas. Here too they fight with slums dwelling, unorganised working, poor health and income.

On one hand, we have the green jungles and on the other we have grown concrete ones. The cities which are called economical workhouse gets stalled with a little bit of down pour you may have heard about Chennai floods, Kerala floods. The nature paid back humans in its own coin.

Marshlands which acted as natural super sponge have been completely encroaches. The lopsided development have left with event of floods in monsoon and drought in summer. You may be well aware with recent events on banks of Yamuna. The event aims for spiritual development at the cost of ecosystem and the result is total destruction of Yamuna flood plains which will have impact on future generation. Ecology only plays foul when human begins it.

Me: I have clearly understood the importance of ecological consideration in development. But isn't it too late to undo the changes? Have we awakened yet?

Professor: Gandhiji said "Our future depends on our present actions" the global community has woken up right since 1970's when we set 'limitss to our growth'. Economic growth was overshadowed by economic development, which was in turn overtaken by sustainable development.

From Montreal protocol to Paris Climate deal across the international community have been standing in solidarity to support the adoption of sustainable practices. Ecological consideration have allowed the men and nature be in harmony since ages.

Have you heard about qanat system?

Me: no sir, I haven't!

Professor: It is a desert irrigation system practised in Iran since 2000 B.C. and even today supports the Persian community to carry out their livelihood. Watershed management in Hivere Bazar and Ralegaon Siddhi have changed the life of the rural folks. Our own desert development program, afforestation mission is aiming towards as sustainable living. Harnessing solar energy has led to generation of clean electricity and also availed new employment opportunity.

Climate smart agriculture, organic farming is aiming to produce more with less without affecting the local biodiversity. Urban forestry is part of all greenfield cities, you know that in spite of tsunami waves sinking the Pichavaram coast, there was no loss of life. Mangroves acted as barriers, defending the villages from the waves.

From agriculture to disaster management, ecological consideration have become imperative.

Me: I can now imagine the value of ecosystem and ecological services. Thank you for enlightening me sir.

Professor: It was my duty to ensure you intellectual development.

Ecology consideration supplements our economic, social, environment development and not supplant it. Nature gives maximum towards human progress and in return asks nothing. It is our duty to make it an indivisible part of our life. We have to co-exist with ecology, ecosystem and nature if we have to exist, ignoring the former will only result in our eternal exit.

❑❑

26 Education is the Antidote to Poverty

Amrit Jain, IPS (AIR 96 CSE 2020)

Ramgopal is a rickshaw puller from Delhi. He migrated along with his family from Bihar. Laxman, his 21 year old son also accompanies his father to support the family. The family is barely able to meet their ends. One day while pulling the rickshaw near Old Rajendra Nagar which touches Karol Bagh, Laxman dreams about becoming an IAS. Two years later, he clears the exam with flying colours and rescues his own family from a poverty trap.

India inherited a poverty rate of 75% in 1951. The largest absolute number of poors are still a scar in India's growth story. United Nations has defined poverty as inability to meet the most basic ends. Rising to this challenge, the international poverty elimination has been made SDG-1.

The statistics of poverty present a grim picture. But what it fails is to present a roadmap for its elimination. The historical experience of the world points towards education as the panacea. This essay evaluates the necessity and sufficiency of education as an antidote to poverty.

HOW EDUCATION IS AN ANTIDOTE TO THE EPIDEMIC OF POVERTY

Before prescribing an antidote, we will first diagnose the problem. Is poverty a recent phenomenon? If not, how poverty in today's world differs from that of earlier times? What does education bring to the picture, which other solutions don't?

Poverty is not a recent phenomenon. It existed even when man was foragers. However poverty exists in many forms in modern times. There is an additional component of relative poverty which finds its origins in the Industrial Revolution. Moreover, today's poverty has expanded itself from socio-economic domain to cultural, ethical and psychological spheres. To support the above hypothesis, lets look at 2016 Oxfam Report. The top 8 richest individuals of the world have more than 50% of world's wealth. In such a scenario, even a millionaire might feel poor to such economic giants!

Now the role of education in poverty alleviation becomes easier to explain. Modern education system includes modern science, liberal arts, latest technological courses etc. All of them are high in demand. But this does not alleviate the abject poverty and the gruesome future of a poor.

Just in the case of Laxman, education at an individual level increases the financial stability. Our present Minister of Women and Child Development Smt. Smriti Irani has built her future from the ashes of future through education.

Former President A.P.J. Abdul Kalam used to sell newspapers. The quest of knowledge and " fire in his wings" took him above the levels of deprivation.

There is no doubt that the purpose of economic sufficiency served by education gets a long way in eradicating poverty of a nation. The graph which follows this paragraph paints India's experience in this regard. Moreover, the very first Asian country to follow modern education and industry (Japan), rose to become a major power in the world.

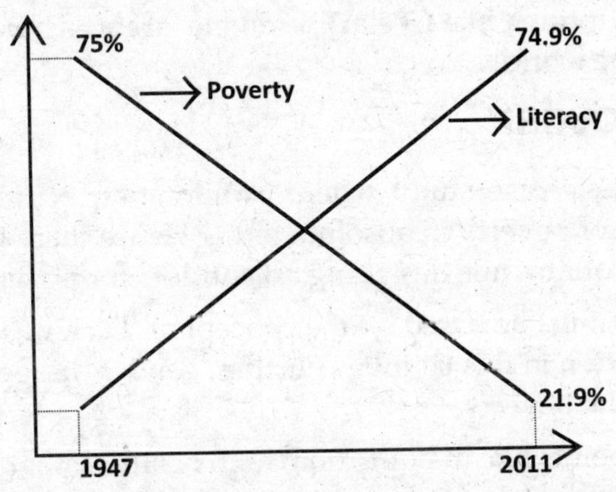

India's Journey to Glory

B.R. Ambedkar who was himself a victim of socio-economic poverty warned the Constituent Assembly in his concluding speech. He said "we are entering into a life of contradiction. We have given one person, one vote, one value in political sphere, however we fail to provide one person, one value in social sphere".

The social poverty manifests itself in the form of social injustice meted out to marginalized sections. Caste equations still hold strong in rural India and every months we read about many manual scavengers dying.

Education in this context will not only enlighten the dominant castes but also empower the lower castes people. The Affirmative Action taken by Indian state has improved the situation somewhat.

The more widespread social poverty has been the global disempowerment of women. UN Report 1980 found out that "even after being half in number, women did 2/3rd of work, received 1/10th of wages and only held 1/100th of the world's assets".

The role of education has improved this scenario NITI Aayog in its last report mentioned that all women related indicators have been improving with improvement in education.

One of the biggest factors of poverty in India is the menace of overpopulation. The educational campaigns of last two decades regarding family planning has started showing results and Total Fertility Rate (TFR) will stabilize soon.

The much anticipated environment vs. Development debate has a context of environmental poverty attached to it. Millions in world are getting displaced not only because of developmental activities, but also because of climate change.

Education in this respect can not only bring in the concept of Environment Impact Assessment but also can help better relocate and rehabilitate the affected ones.

Education has played immense role in eradicating the ethical poverty since ages. The ancient legendary scriptures like Geeta, Quran etc. are much needed to guide the value based education in the world.

IS EDUCATION ENOUGH?

India has been a classic case study where proliferation of modern education has far outpaced eradication of poverty in absolute terms Hence there is surely much more that we must take into account while designing an antidote for poverty.

Formal education must be based on the concept of 'Earning while Learning'. It's time to bring a skill revolution in this country. Further, gender disaggregation of data sets can help us better target the poverty.

Many other flashpoints like malnutrition, high health expenditure, water crisis, safety of women etc. play a pivotal role in increasing economic productivity of people. This must also be put into antidote. Further, the idea of economic circle of power (Gandhiji), Idea of Radical Humanism (M.N. Roy) and the ideals of Sarvodaya and Antyodaya point towards the same thing.

Empowering Direct Democracy at rural level is highly effective antidote. The successful example of Hiware Bazar which not only empowered people but also modernized village and rejuvenated the environment.

As a last antidote, we must avoid the blind pursuit of crude capitalism which not only accentuates inequality but also ignores human dignity.

A unique index of how much one has taken and how much one has returned to the society must be designed. This will foster a sense of trusteeship in rich and satisfaction in poor.

History has taught us that poverty anywhere is a threat to prosperity everywhere. Education being the major component, an antidote to poverty must be developed so that IAS Officers like Laxman who rose above poverty can lift millions out of it by good work.

❑❑

27 The Higher We Are Placed, The More Humbly We Should Walk

Himanshu Kaushik, IAS (CSE 2017)

"With great power comes greater responsibility". One who is at the top of hierarchy, one who enjoys power is a source of inspiration for many. He is seen as an ideal; hence his responsibility towards society increases. Though each should have virtue of humility yet, humility is the most important aspect of a leader. He cannot have high headedness and sense of arrogance and prejudice. It is true that power corrupts and absolute power corrupts absolutely. Hence, to remain humble, one must avoid ignorance. He should make knowledge a real virtue. An ignorant, corrupt leader makes the society regressive. The importance of real knowledge was recognized by ancient philosophers like Plato who wanted a "Philosopher King". A king who has access to real knowledge and who does not consider materialistic world as reality.

In modern times, inequality and prejudice are on rise. Those enjoying power must empathies with powerless common citizens. We see the emergence of power centres in several spheres of society, starting from the first institution of family to the level of International Affairs.

In a family which is the first institution of social interaction, the head of family is a power centre. He is a father figure, economically independent, experienced and usually commands respect. It is his role to guide the family. His actions determine the level of unity and integrity in the family. Disagreements are bound to occur in a family, majorly due to "generation gap". If the head of family is not accommodating, intolerant towards contrasting view, it will drastically reduce the integrity and unity of family. His own respect would reduce. Each and every child expects support from his family head, but if his family head is not open, tolerant then the child is bound to suffer. Family head should take tough decisions when required but only for genuine reasons and for greater good.

A society becomes the second institution after family where power is enjoyed by a certain section. In an egalitarian society, such a section looks after welfare of all other sections. However, in a diverse society like ours, power is enjoyed by few which lead to exploitation of others. Caste system presents the most suitable example where prejudices and discrimination against weaker sections exist, leading to years of subjugation which further affects the unity and integrity of society. In such a system, members from upper caste limit the opportunity provided to weaker sections. They are not even allowed to visit temples. This system reflects the level of arrogance and apathy towards weaker sections.

When it comes to Nation, the Prime Minister or the President is usually the one enjoying power supported by other ministers. As Chanakya said, a leader should not be corrupt and selfish. He should not be lazy, arrogant and heartless.

We have plenty of examples of arrogant leaders not caring about citizens, going on a killing spree, putting whole humanity into danger. The dominating ideologies of Nazism and Fascism led the humanity into a World War. Arrogance about being in power perpetuates such violence and mass killing. Fortunately, in India, we did not experience such brutality after Independence. However, those who are in power continue to exploit the weak.

The banning of red beacons by the Government are some steps taken to reduce VIP culture prevalent in the society. It is said about India that we are freer than we were before Independence, yet not that free which our forefathers hoped for.

Similarly, in case of International Affairs, the basic idea has been to dominate since ancient times. The respect to rights of humans has not been there. Old colonial powers traded slaves for their benefits, exploited them, annexed countries, exploited natural resources to sustain industrial revolution. All this was done without any regard for welfare of other humans who were probably different in culture, tradition, race and religion. In modern times, everyone wants to establish itself as hegemony, first it was UK, then US. The rise of superpowers is not without bloodshed. US became a superpower after dropping Atom Bombs over Japan, such blatant disregard for humans arises from ignorance. It can be argued that a superpower needs to dominate to maintain world order, but using smaller nation as a means to achieve own goals is not good.

The disregard shown to environment has already resulted into world wide environment issues like climate change, Ozone hole etc. Economic superpowers are running away from their responsibility and putting the burden on underdeveloped and poor nations to mitigate climate change.

Human beings can be less cruel and more appreciative of other species. Our activities are harming them such as death of Corel reefs. Those in power need to think and realize the importance of humility, brotherhood to respect dissenting views, to respect nature and its resources.

A humble leader can bring about a change in his centre of influence A father who teaches his child to respect women can start a change to remove patriarchy. A social reformer like Raja Ram Mohan Roy can bring a change into Ethics of Society, ending the evil practice of Sati. A national leader can ensure welfare of all; he can create on an egalitarian society. Environmental issues can be mitigated if leaders start respecting the resources we are left with. As Barack Obama once said, we do not inherit the nature and its resources from ancestors, we borrow if from our future generation.

A world where peace prevails can be achieved if human rights are ensured in every policy decision. It is up to the man to decide whether he wants to live a happy life or a life in greed and need.

Those enjoying power needs to realize that it's not your position; it is your conduct that makes your superior. Hence, one should always be a guiding light rather than a source of darkness.

❑❑

28 Poverty Anywhere is a Threat to Prosperity Everywhere

Himanshu Jain, IAS (AIR 4 CSE 2019)

Governments across the world have become welfare oriented with their primary goal to uplift millions of poor people out of poverty. Even at the international stage, the Millennium Development goals and now the Sustainable Development goals are directed to eliminate poverty and provide basic minimum to all. Also, Indian Constitution in the form of fundamental rights, fundamental duties and directive principles of state policy seeks to ensure basic rights to all and prevention of concentration of wealth. Thus poverty is something big. What is poverty?

Poverty means lack of opportunities. The inability of people to have what is considered necessary for survival. But there is no one definition of poverty. It has been changing over spatial and temporal zones. Over the years, societies have advanced, what was earlier considered luxury may now be called a necessity. The definition of poverty changes owning to a number of factors like level of economic development in the country, advancement of technology, availability of resources, social structure, etc. So, when in the past owning a concrete house was considered a luxury, now it has become a necessity. In the recent times, when owning a mobile phone was a luxury, it has become a necessity now. Similarly, over spatial/geographical areas across the world, one standard of life may be considered as rich in one society and poor in another, for example: social security in USA is an essential requirement but similar insurance in Africa may be luxury thing. Thus, societies can be relatively rich and relatively poor. But when people are unable to meet basic requirements of survival, food, clothing and shelter that is absolute poverty. It can be dangerous. Absolute poverty is manifested in many forms:

Hunger and Malnutrition: Poverty means lack of resources to feed the hungry. Thus, poor tend to be malnourished.

Disease: Poor people live in unhygienic societal conditions which make them vulnerable and prone to diseases, more to communicable diseases.

Lack of Education and Skills: Poor people do not get adequate schooling, hence they lack proper knowledge and awareness which may be necessary in day to day living.

Fear: Fear and lack of confidence are two major forms in which poor people exhibit their helplessness. Poor tend to lack confidence to claim what is their own.

No Hope: Poor tend to lose hope for a better life since they get used to it.

Thus, a vicious cycle of poverty sets in where people over generations go through similar treatments at the hands of those who are rich or who have power.

Consequences of poverty are:

Discrimination and lack of aspirations result from chronic poverty. Overtime, the feeling of non-inclusiveness gains weight. Then expresses itself to the world in diverse ways. The prosperous cannot be peaceful without prosperity of the poor. This threat to peace has been persistent over the history and has expressed itself several times. Be it the 'Kalyug of the 4th or 5th century, where poor and caste discriminated people revolted against the Brahmin order. Or be it communalism by Marx which grew as retaliation to the oppression of the poor working class by the capitalist. This struggle is still on in the form of larger struggle in United Nations, where poor and third world nations are demanding fair share in the organizations which are dominated by rich, developed nations. Thus, long term poverty can have grave consequences to the peace of all. Examples of poverty leading to destruction of prosperity are present in the present world.

Left wing extremism in India developed as a consequence of lack of opportunities and poverty. These people came in contact with an ideology and turned to violent means to claim resources. Thus, this is a fine example of poverty anywhere is a threat to prosperity everywhere. As it has put on hold the growth story of a number of states like Jharkhand, Odisha to name a few.

Similarly, it is poverty which pushes the Kashmiri youth towards stone pelting. This is due to lack of resources that people protest in violent ways.

Outside India, in neighbouring countries of India poverty in Pakistan has made it to fall into Chinese trap. Pakistan is now a full-fledged state destroying the prosperity of adjacent regions.

In West Asia, concentration of wealth in few hands has made it prone to external interventions and has turned it into a war torn country/region.

Apart from these, there are people who become poor due to special circumstances for example climatic refugees people who will have to leave their lands due to rising sea level and migrate to safer places. The Rohingyas who are a result of state-led ethnic cleansing. These people eventually will have to be accommodated otherwise they can pose grave danger to the prosperity.

Thus, we observe that poverty in one region halts the growth of other regions and if not treated in time it may regress the process of development, for example terrorism leading to loss of men, material and money. Or the left wing extremism, occupying a lot of resources which could be utilized for developmental processes.

Societies across have realized these dangers and therefore growth strategies are made with focus on inclusion. Inclusion in the form of their participation in the growth process and their claims of benefits of growth. Indian strategy of inclusion is aptly manifested in government policy. Various schemes like PM Jan Dhan Yojana, PM Mudra Yojana, PM Suraksha Bima Yojana, etc. have their primary focus on inclusion, be it financial inclusion or inclusion in the supply chain. With the newly launched PM Jan Arogya, government aims to include poor into the health infrastructure of the country.

Also the universal focus on SDGs like no hunger, no poverty, good health, are all directed to uplift the societies from life of poverty to life of prosperity.

But eradication of poverty requires funding. Funding has to come from within the society. Therefore, rich have to realize that their prosperity depends upon the prosperity of all. They should voluntarily make efforts for the upliftment of downtrodden. Otherwise the truth is – Poverty anywhere is a threat to prosperity everywhere.

Even Mahatma Gandhi has said that

Real freedom will come when all the people are brought out of poverty.

❑❑

29 Consumerism Kills Culture with Overproduction and Heightened Sense of Need Established by the Marketing

Himanshu Kaushik, IAS (CSE 2017)

In Delhi, a capital city with a population of around 12 million, there are 9 million vehicles running on roads. Fifteen million mobile phone connections are currently active. Perhaps Gandhiji was right when he said there is no limit of greed. Philosophers and Reformers like Gandhi wanted world to be a big family, however what we have today is a big market. World is facing overproduction of oil, steel, food especially grains etc. which points out towards the materialistic basis on which our world is built.

The rise of industrial production led to colonization of third world for resources which gave rise to ideology of mass production i.e. capitalism. Capitalism which further needed Globalization for markets created a single market for whole world and hence the phenomenon of consumerism arrived. Multinational companies began expanding their operation to multiple countries, continents bringing with them the dominant ideology of consumerism where irrespective of need, one will purchase the product for-his greed.

These MNCs further led to decline in power of third world countries and also diminishing power of governments. These MNCs now form the so called "deep state" and influence major policy decisions. Consumerism brought with itself many evils like decline of institution of welfare state, joint families. It led to increase in inequality, skewed development, and serious environmental concerns like climate change. The original culture got diminished and the dominant culture of consumerism prevailed. Consumerism has affected all aspects of a society. Wars have been fought for markets and resources. Countries which refused to fall in line faced economic sanctions and had to face issues of food shortages.

It is often said that consumerism gave people no choice. It was not a voluntary adoption but a forced ideology.

In third world countries like India society was based on ancient norms, Buddhist and Hindu Philosophy of self restraint gave priority to spiritual well being over material well-being. When country failed to adopt the mass production methods shortage of food was seen and hence modern science and technology was promoted. The need for oil and demand of products forced us to open our market. Globalization become inevitable and so is the transformation of society.

Society became materialistic and profit making became the main goal. The institution of family and marriage also got influenced. We got to see the rise of nuclear families where not more than two generation lives together. Earlier concept of joint families became less popular among masses as focus shifted on jobs from agriculture. Large scale migration was seen to urban areas leading to urbanization. The immediate fallout was the older people living alone in villages. Hence, change in need brought a change in society which further changed the culture.

Individual became more materialistic, profit seeking and selfish. In quest for greed, he started ignoring relations. He become self-centered and it further lead to deterioration in the institution of marriage leading to increased divorces, concept of live-in relations etc.

Individual is competing for status and he is overburdened with greed, leading to increased cases of suicides, depression and other mental issues.

The effects of consumerism are evident in the choices we make in our attire, our food, language, religion. Earlier, the Indian attire of Kurta, Pajama, Dhoti, was common but now majority prefers Jeans. In our food habits, junk foods and packaged food is dominating. McDonaldization is evident where food giants offer same food with same taste at different stores throughout the country. Languages also become a hybrid mixed with English. In India, we popularly refer it to "Hinglish". It was the need to adapt English language in order to communicate with others in a Big Market i.e. World. Music and Movies also got influenced, Hollywood Movies are being watched throughout the world and are even more popular than domestic movies. Walmartization is another process which is taking place, which involves a supermarket culture where multiple products are sold in a single shop under a single roof. One is always tempted to purchase irrespective of his need.

The products from other counters began flooding the domestic markets. These often degraded the health however, medicines too were provided through this open market. Hence, individual became a part of the chain of demand and supply. These health concerns also leads to rise in non communicable diseases like diabetes, cancers etc. The changing food habits also required change in cropping patterns. New technologies are being introduced for mass production like use of high yielding variety of seeds, GM Crops, Mechanical Irrigation etc.

To gain maximum profit, each country joined the bandwagon of mass production. Countries like China, Saudi Arabia are facing mass production in sectors like Oil, Steel, and Cement and are exporting products to other countries at cheaper rates leading to gradual decline in domestic production. Dumping of goods is a rising challenge and even world trade organization is not accommodating for third world countries.

The worst affect of consumerism is seen on Environment. Mass production of crops, irregular and indiscriminate usage of groundwater, pollution by industries, change in cropping patterns, rise of barren lands, deforestation, decrease in biodiversity all leads to degradation of environment and leads towards problems like global warming, ozone depletion, environmental hazards etc. Exploitation became the new norm and rich countries became richer by exploiting resources from poor countries.

Consumerism, though, have resulted into certain positives like uniting the world by improving communication, improving the life of millions, providing geographically irregular terrains with food security. Yet, it cannot be continued to go on forever. Sustainable development keeping in mind the requirement of future generation, and using as per our need is the way ahead.

Time has come to go back to the philosophy which Gautama Buddha preached of self sufficiency, finding joy and peace through societal gains not through material gains. The preservation of culture is also essential as it is our heritage. A world which is based on unity of diversity is always better than one based on unity of uniformity. It is up to us now to realize the need and differentiate it from greed. It would however be like lighting a matchstick in a hurricane and trying to sustain the flame. Yet, it is only humans that can sustain the flame and give everyone a better Earth to live.

❑❑

30 Fighting Corruption is Not Just Good Governance But Also Self-Defence and Patriotism

Himanshu Kaushik, IAS (CSE 2017)

Corruption has been prevalent in Indian Society since ancient times. Chanakya, the great ancient scholar wrote extensively on the issue of corruption. He recognized corruption as the root cause of downfall of any empire. He emphasized on a rule based society where corrupt should be effectively punished and should not be let off at any cost. However, Indian society did not see much reform. Father of nation M.K. Gandhi promoted simple living based on needs and not acting on greed. Even Rajiv Gandhi famously held that only a small portion of government provided benefit reaches common man, rest is collected by corrupts.

In recent Transparency International Report, India was among the worst countries in terms of corruption.

As evident, corruption is still a major cause of concern in Indian society. It affects us at all levels be it individual or societal. The image of India in global politics is not good in terms of transparency. Developmental Deficit which is a feature of Indian society is partially due to corruption.

These are also a trust deficit in common people that state has not done enough for their welfare. The "Sab Chalta Hai" approach reflects the cultural aspect of corruption where it is a new normal for a person to do corrupt practices, or to face corruption. There is ignorance towards corruption which needs to ends as corruption affects everyone in the society. Fighting against corruption is actually a self-defence as it is equivalent to fighting for our rights. However, in order to root out corruption, its manifestations at different levels need to be tackled.

Corruption at individual level occurs when an individual takes decisions for his own gains overlooking the interest of others and society. It devoids the individual of compassion, empathy and sense of responsibility towards society. Corruption is like a black hole which has no end. It will keep on increasing the greed. Individual who is exercising power must have a strong moral fiber to avoid the gains from corruption. It is said that power corrupts and absolute power corrupts absolutely. Hence, it is important for individuals to stay focused on their goal of working for welfare rather than personal gains.

It is also the responsibility of citizens to not offer bribe in lien of services, to not go for shortcuts but follow official procedure. It is also the duty of citizens to vote for honest leaders and vote out corrupt candidates from politics. As Gandhiji said, Be the change you want to see in the world. Hence transformation starts from self. An honest citizen when achieves a position of power should work for the welfare, should not follow others in pursuit of personal gains. It is required to tackle corruption at individual level first. Change can only take place from base.

Corruption in the society is evident from the fact that it is abnormal for a government department to work without corruption. It has become a cultural phenomenon where general ignorance towards corruption has made it a new normal. Bribes are common and people think it is a part of the system. The morality of individuals promoting corruption has significantly affected the ethics of our society.

Corruption is leading to exploitation of the weaker sections of the society. They are not represented in proportion to population. They are still being exploited and due to corruption, they are denied their basic rights. Corruption is an evil in a just society and perpetuates other forms of evil like violence, intolerance in the society.

Corruption in spheres like sports, religion has led to various issues like lack of opportunities for sports, use of drugs and performance enhancers, commercialization of religion where institutions demand money by hitting at religious beliefs. Corruption has led to environmental issues as projects are being cleared by government departments which will greatly affect and degrade the environment without proper Environmental Impact Assessment. The infamous Coal Allocation Scan overlooked environmental concerns in many coal blocks.

Corruption has badly affected India's image in global politics. India is seen as a country with an inefficient corrupt system of bureaucracy. Lee Kuan Yew, father of Singapore analyzed what India lacked which stopped it from becoming a superpower. He could only find out the reason to be corruption. China implemented its policies with transparency and control and hence succeeded. Hence, he held that unless India reforms its society, system and get rid of corruption, it will be impossible for her to be a superpower.

The multiparty democracy where there is a greater role of regional parties has also led to policy paralysis and corruption. Economic Inequality, Developmental Deficit, Slow Service Delivery, Judicial Pendency can all be improved if corruption is tackled. Fighting corruption is perceived as self defence as corruption affects everyone. It is not a process limited to an individual. As evident, it spreads in a society and perpetrates other forms of evil. Corruption is an antithesis to democracy and hence, it preaches inequalities, injustice and selfishness. If one does not speak up against injustice done to poor, he is bound to suffer injustice at later stage.

Patriotism is not only about rising for National Anthem and respecting National Symbols. It is about fighting against the evils prevalent in society and it is necessary to fight corruption. Corruption is actually defeating the idea of selfless service. It is defeating the idea of India given by our freedom fighters.

Government in order to empower citizens and deal with the issue of corruption has enacted laws like Prevention of Corruption Act provided Citizen Charter and actively pushing for Digital delivery of services through Digitization. These methods are necessary and use of Information and Communication Technology is bound to reduce corruption. However, these efforts are not enough as much needs to be done to bring societal changes. Laws are useless unless implemented well and supported by society.

Activism is needed to fight ignorance towards corruption. Recently, there has been a ray of hope as seen in various Anti corruption moments like Anna Hazare's India Against corruption. It linked the idea of fighting corruption with patriotism and hence got massive support. Government brought the much needed Lokpal Bill in response but is still in Lok Sabha due to delayed implementation. These social movements are necessary in order achieve a fair, efficient and just society. Transparency will fetch India greater goods and has the potential to bring millions of poor out of poverty.

India is at crossroads where it can be a superpower or it can remain a third world country. The choice is ours to decide. It is wise to recall Plato who held that Sparta lost to Athens because of corruption. He gave us the importance of real knowledge which enables us to differentiate between greed and necessities. The time is right to recollect the values and work for a fair, just and transparent Nation.

❑❑

31 Yesterday's Score Does Not Win You Game Today

Himanshu Kaushik, IAS (CSE 2017)

The only thing that is constant in this world is change. Nothing is permanent. It is a new day everyday and each day requires a new approach. Everything is relevant to its time. Yesterday's score does not win you game today as what was relevant yesterday may not be relevant today. Hence, it is about doing what is required today. The only thing worth remembering about past is the experience that teaches us to improve and improvise. Self-realization of mistakes is essential to improve. There is no need to stay in the past as it only draws one back. It is good to let go off the past and embrace the present.

History teaches us that overconfidence and living in past glory has led to downfall of many empires and individuals. It brings a sense of comfort and ignorance and ultimately downfall. It is not good to be a prisoner of history. Japan during Second World War faced crushing defeat as it lived in the past glory of defeating Russian empire. Even India was invaded several times by foreign invaders as India chose ignorance over action. It is also not good to over glorify past and avoid modernization. Reforms are needed to stay relevant at both individual and societal level.

At Individual Level, one needs to be rational in his approach. One should not be drawn to the past as it leads to stagnation of growth in personal skills. The past should remind us about our mistakes and it is present which gives us a chance to improve. Achievements in the past do provide a sense of pride but they also preach over confidence and complacency. It is up to the individual to deal with it. He can choose to be complacent or chose to introspect to improve.

If one is preparing for exams the studies before the exam will help, not after that. Hence, respecting the time is important. Time is crucial and does not stop for anyone. A parent avoiding his child and not caring enough is bound to suffer in future when he would not be having opportunity to improve the moral fiber of his child later on. Similarly, it is seen that children do not care enough for their parents in old age and then regrets it when they themselves become old. Similarly, having a past which promoted exploitation and glorifying it is not good. An old mindset never leads to progressive life. People with prejudices in mind face prejudice themselves at a later stage. Hence, it is true what goes around, comes around.

In sports, each day is a new day. Recently, world's fastest man Usain Bolt lost in his favourite event of 100 m sprint despite of being the world champion since past 8 years. This shows no one can take his position for granted. One needs to perform each day to win.

Former PM Atal Bihari Vajpayee called General Elections early in 2004 and suffered an unexpected defeat that too when his previous government gained majority comfortably. Hence, it is necessary to acknowledge the present challenges and fight them and one should have the capability to recognize his limits. Our actions should be limited by the time. Present time may require new approach and should be adopted.

Similarly, at Societal Level a progressive society is one that is reformative and welcoming to modern beliefs and changes. In societies where old beliefs are still prevalent and not in line with modern ideas tend to be exploitative to certain sections. Sati System which was considered a custom in Indian Society was stopped when society acknowledged it to be exploitative. Yet, there are other social evils like casteism, female infanticide, patriarchy which are still prevalent and can only be removed if society accepts modern ideas and is keen on reforms.

Modern times require modern approaches and glorification of past needs to be stopped. Glorification of culture often leads to promotion of exploitative exercises which further subjugates weaker sections and makes them vulnerable towards crime.

Patriarchy which has led to subjugation of women both in family and society needs to be tackled by adopting modern ideas of gender equality and gender empowerment. Issues like feminization of poverty, feminization of labour can be tackled if women are made equal participants in policy framing and decision making. For all this, reforms should be welcomed, and exploitative practices need to be discouraged.

Our Education System needs complete overhaul as it is promoting rote learning and not promoting scientific temper. This could be seen in less innovation and production capacity in Indian Manufacturing Industries.

India, in order to gain its rightful place in world, needs to rise above the glories of past in which it was a golden sparrow and needs to introspect what needs to be done about the pertinent issues like poverty, malnutrition, unemployment and casteism. Over dependence on cultural pride and nationalism can further lead to neglect of structural changes required in the administration of country.

The modern ideas of Human Rights, Secularism, Gender Rights, Tribal Rights, Equality etc. needs to be adopted fully by the society and country by way of reforms.

Reluctance towards modern technology needs to be avoided. Hence, it is good to embrace modernity and leave contradictions of history behind.

□□

32 In An Age of Digitalisation, Data is the New Oil

Nikhil Rakhecha, IAS (AIR 197 CSE 2018)

Third industrial revolution guided by computer technology ushered in new age i.e. digital age. Nearly 2 billion people around the world are actively using internet. In India itself there are 700 million mobile phone users. Having online presence has become prerequisite for successful business. Governments all over the world are striving to harness e-governance models. We are all surrounded by smart phones to smart homes. In this rapidly digitising world, basic fuel running these plethora of application is DATA.

Recently world's biggest social media corporation Facebook was scrutinized by US Congress over misuse of this data. This incidence brought forward the extreme potential data could have. Thus many equate data to oil.

Oil has been instrumental in driving our economics. From transport to industry oil has been fuel running it. Similarly data has become basic ingredient. Data about costumer, their choices-preference, purchasing habits have become essential for business to chart out their marketing strategy. Advertisement which pops up on our screen precisely what we were searching for, are noting but customized using data.

Not just for business but for governments too data is new oil. In age of evidence based policy making, governments are collecting data for tailoring its plans to ensure efficiency.

Education sector could be taken as an example. UNICEF in partnership with HRD ministry created gender gap map. It represented girl students having poor levels of learning outcomes in select pockets of country. Now using this data specialized intervention is being done through remedial classes to bridge the gap.

Similarly recently formulated aspirational district program of NITI Aayog was formulated using data on various development parameters shown as literacy, income level, health standards etc. Without data government historically been intervening through one size fits all approach.

Data facilitate much needed customization in highly individualizing world. It allows for precision in intervention and thus improves its efficiency. Data allows to understand need and demand of products/services. Thus, it helps to undertake targeted intervention.

It also assist in monitoring the progress of such interventions. We have numerous ranking such as human development index, human index etc. formulated using data.

Analogy of data with oil thus holds time for its worth and utility in almost all spheres of life. Like oil it is also most essential for the economy.

We have million dollar companies offering their services for free (Facebook, twitter, google). However, they are harnessing rich data from our activities online. Thus, emerging as data aggregating platforms.

Just like gulf countries have monopoly in oil production, these social media giants have acquired similar distinction. They collect millions of bytes of data every day and sale it to third party or use to improve its own service.

As oil has to be mined and refined before its use, raw data too cannot be utilized. Thus, we need big data analytical tools which could make sense out turns voluminous data being generated every day. Raw data is transformed into patterns and fed into system for business process re-engineering.

So just like oil data has become expensive. Though it is available with many activities, not everyone is equipped to process it. So the expensive technology and well trained human resource to process data makes it expensive.

To contrast oil, developing countries are net exporter of data (raw). Companies in developed world use this raw material to capture markets of third world. Not just business, but foreign policies of these countries are data driven.

This brings our attention to few other shortcomings associated with new oil just like conventional. Scarcity of oil creates inflationary pressure on economics. Similarly this monopoly and inequitable access to meaningful data makes it scarce resources.

Oil extraction has environmental fallouts. Similarly data mining has negative repercussion at personal level. Privacy, an integral part of right to life with dignity is compromised in this digitalizing world. Recent incident of Cambridge Analytical is evidence of this threat.

However, data goes beyond the potential of oil. Latter, once used gets exhausted however data is used, reused, returned and restructured. There's no limit on use of data. Same data could be used by different agencies by extracting what is relevant to their domain of operation.

Countries like India have to realize the potential of this new resource. We were deprived of natural resource like oil. Thus, our economy depended on input of such resources.

However, huge young population programs like 'Digital India', 'Smart Cities' rising penetration of mobile technology to remotest corners will generate massive data. Budget

2019 also announced mission on internet of things (cyber physical system). All these connected devices would communicate billions of bits continuously.

This data advantage could help us even replace old oil. Mapping of renewable energy potential throughout the country, smart grids to enhance efficiency of power use, data driven mobility to reduce fuel consumption, smart energy efficient housing etc. could reduce demand of old oil.

To achieve success in harnessing this new resource transformation alteration have to be carried out. First step would be to generate and capture data. Digitize services wherever possible (land digitization, direct benefit transfer), extensive use of Aadhar to map data usage.

Next step would be to standardized data collection, aggregation and sharing methods. Plethora of data is already available, but in discrete format. Thus, cannot be put to analysis. Develop common data standard throughout the country and facilitate data sharing.

Availability of standard data would then be processed using sophisticated big data analytics tool. As recently CAG and economic survey has shown how data could be used in policy making, government should utilize the processed data to tailor its interventions to suit local needs and plug leakages.

Throughout this process there is a need to have strong data protection regime. Recently B.M. Srikrishna Committee has suggested Data Protection Bill. This could be enacted to prevent misuse of data and create institutionalized mechanism to address grievances upon breach of data privacy.

Soon the world would move towards fourth industrial revolution guided by robotics and artificial intelligence. Facilitators of earlier revolutions were steam engine, electricity and internet respectively. Now this upcoming revolutions would be fuelled by new oil i.e. data. Artificial intelligence would be acquired through learning and processing of data.

Potential of automation in fields of agriculture, manufacturing and service would also be facilitated by data. In India, the IT back offices of world is already at advantageous position to reap benefits of this new oil. Appropriate intervention has to be done to sustain and harness this new oil.

❑❑

33 India is Yet to Celebrate its Diversities

Abhisek Oswal, IRS [(IT) AIR 154 CSE 2019]

It was a bright morning of 15th August. The national flag was flying high, the atmosphere was filled with patriotic vibes, 'Mille Sur Mera Tumhara' playing in the background. Our team was particularly excited as we were taking part in annual debate.

The topic for the debate was 'India is yet to celebrate its diversities'. Debates are sign of a healthy democracy. They let us analyse, give various opinions and views and broaden our perspective. Rules were simple, two teams – Team Patriot and Team Progressive will get 15 minutes each to keep their views and results will be announced at the end of the debate.

Team progressive – Our diversities are half celebrated.

Historically we have been a plural society. But the plurality came with biasness. The society from Vedic ages have been patriarchal and conservative. Women played subservient role in shaping the society. Our sacred texts commented women as 'selfish and wicked'.

The plague of caste system was legacy of our history. Chandelas were socially ostracised. Slavery and force labour exploited and marginalised the weaker section. The description of caste hierarchy with shudra belonging to 'feets' is self-deplorable. How can we celebrate our historical legacy with such unjustice?

Geographically we occupy 2.4% of global land, possess 7,500 kilometres of coastline. But don't you think the focus on development have been geographically skewed? On one hand we have strengthen our western arm industrially, economically. But on the other hand, the eastern part of the country is neglected. The skewed focus undermine our geographical diversity.

Politically, we say we are the world's largest democracy. But the largest democracy of the world is plagued by communal and caste based politics. The state of governance is infected by corruption. The government of the people, by the people is not been able to fulfil the promise.

Money power in elections questioned the efficiency of results of 'free and fair' process. Women representation have been dismal. We celebrate our regional representation in upper and lower house. But have the representation been equitable? Favouritism and ideological dominance have eroded our political diversity.

Demographically, nearly half of our population consist of women. But they constitute only 26% of labour force. Our laws have been archaic and gender biased. Inspite of democratic and cultural progress women are subjected to sexual violence, female foeticide. The dichotomy of our society is we worship them as 'Shakti' and even burn them for dowry.

We probed in our syncretic culture. But every other day we hear of fight between communities in name of religion and caste. Couples are burnt alive for dishonouring their caste values. Justice nowadays are met on road, rather than in courts. With all such events how can we celebrate our cultural diversity?

Economically, agriculture has been our backbone. But backbone is now being weakened. The neglect of the agriculture sector has led for farmer suicides, faced migration. Gandhi said 'India lives in its villages'. But today the same villages are being left behind in development process.

This has only deplored the rural dwellers to forcefully migrate for better living and basic amenities. Oxfam reports says 1% of top Indians owned 73% of resources with crony capitalism how can we celebrate our economical diversity?

Environment has been part and parcel of our life. Rishis used to stay in forest. A sustainable Indian life was connected to preservation of nature. But today we have crossed all our limits and bounds in exploiting nature and its resources.

Our rivers are getting polluted with every passing day. Forest have been cut indiscriminately and forest dwellers have been evicted forcefully. The neglect of our nature, environment and ecology have broken the syncretic connect with it and question today our environmental diversity?

At global front we have an image of a responsible power, a tolerant and vibrant nation. But also some of our acts have been criticized in terms of intervention in other nation's affair. Our historical hospitality and humanitarian approach to refugees have been questioned today by our discriminatory treatment towards 'Rohingyas' or fellow 'African student'.

Tolerance was the core pillar on which our plural society was built. But pluralistic diversity is being questioned today. Growing communal disharmony, dictation on what to eat, what to wear and what to watch have threatened our creative and intuitive rights of expression. Linguistic and dominant cultural enforcement have questioned our secular diversity.

The audience were awe-struck with the views put forward by Team Progressive and Team Patriots took stage to defend India's diversity.

Team Patriot – Indian diversity is being celebrated from ages.

Historically, though caste and untouchability was an unintended outcome but we should never forget that our cultural legacy with syncretic tolerant society was also an off-shoot of our past. India has been the land of sufis and saints. A land where world's largest two major religion- Buddhism and Jainism were born and Islam thrived and flourished.

We are also land of the mother Sita and also Rani Laxmi Bai. Women have played equally important role to shape our history. Purans may be criticized for being biased, but they show the way for living a fulfilled life.

Our is a land of Nizamuddin Auliya and Guru Nanak both being served and worshipped cutting across religion domains. Our festivals are themselves epitome of our diversity in celebration.

Geographically, we are divided by mountains, rivers, valleys and hills. But each state region have its own uniqueness in terms of food habits, cultural practices, economical life and most importantly we are able to co-operate and co-exist with such diversity since ages.

Politically, our constitution by itself is exemplification of diverse, plural and secular value. When matured democracies of West hesitated to give universal adult franchise, we set an example by doing so right since our independence.

Our free and fair electoral process have been a Steller example for democracies world over. The 73rd and 74th constitutional amendments exemplify our commitment to empower women. Our constitutional institutions always stand for the rights of weaker sections. Free speech, constructive criticism and dissent have been a marked celebration of our political diversity.

'I shall not agree with your view, but

I shall defend your right to say so'

Socially, we are a syncretic, vibrant nation which enmasses 7 different major religions, 3 major races, thousands of different languages and dialects. We are the land where Kabir preached gospel of religious harmony, where Gandhi stood against all odds for Harijans and government is standing up for Divyanjans.

Our policy of reservation have politically and economically weaker section women are provided level playing field in all spheres to realise their true potential social justice for an inclusive and participative society have been our goal. Tribals are ensured their culture is protected, backwards are empowered for social advancement. The co-existence and collaboration in all sphere of development from gender justice to human rights showcases our social diversity.

Environmentally, we Indian have always been close to nature and celebrated its beauty and diversity. From Chipko Movement to Narmada Bachao our love for our ecology is time tested. Nature has been part and parcel of our daily life and its conservation is our duty. Namami gange was not just a mission to clean the river put an emotional appeal. Sikkim has a practice of having fraternal ties with trees. Isn't it showcase our celebration of environmental diversity?

'Vasudhaiva Kutumbakam' is our motto is international sphere. We have always supported and even been forefront in humanitarian assistant. Our Panchsheel is followed across the world for global rule based order. Our soft power ensures economical human and cultural development across borders. We supported Tibetans from Chinese prosecution, help to liberate Bangladesh yet ensured and strives for global peace.

Economically, we have undone historical biasedness. Women labour face participation is bound to increase with breaking of glass ceiling, education and skills. 'Jai Jawan and Jai Kisan' shows our commitment towards agriculture and farmer right from times of independence to green revolution and till today with aim to double farmers income.

Tolerance, as said was and is a core pillar of our plural democracy. Our country is a land where 130 crore people exists cutting across regions, religions and linguistic backgrounds. But with a common identity of being Indian which is above all ideological and political identities. The idea of India is not defined by sporadic communal tensions, but on solidarity to stand with each other amidst differences. Tolerance, secular, and progressive values are indeed celebrations of our diversities.

With this both teams had finished presenting their views and it was the time for results. Audience were amazed with views from both sides, appreciating every single opinion. The judges came out with analysis and results.

Both the team have presented and substantial their view on one hand. Team Patriot who showcases our historical legacy and tolerant society, and on other side Team Progressive highlighted the current situation which plague our society.

True that these are issues with the current societal norms, growing intolerance gender biasness and marginalisation of weaker section. But also our unity amidst so much diversities, upholding the principle of democracy for more than 7 decades, have strengthened our secular fabric.

On one side we have a world where there is bloodshed within religion, politically sponsored ideological dominance, growing protectionism and inequality. On the other we have our own country where 130 crore citizens stands together for each other's rights, social justice and freedom to express. In the long journey towards mature society from a nation-state towards nation we have and are bound to face hiccups of communalism, biasness. But our resilience have only strengthen the plural fabric and enabled us to celebrate our diversity through dissent, debate and discussion.

What new India needs today are the patriots with progressive thoughts and actions. The winner in the whole debate is Indian values, Indian tolerance and democracy and overall Team India.

❑❑

34 India's Focus Shift from SAARC to BIMSTEC is Strategic but Underused

Abhisek Oswal, IRS [(IT) AIR 154 CSE 2019]

In 300 BCE the Indian philosopher Chanakya in his world renowned theories on state politics – "The Arthashastra" talked about the principle of 'Beri - Sandhi'. In 15th century AD Machiavelli elaborated it as enemy's enemy is my friend.

This diplomatic philosophy was applicable since the era of colonisation to cold war. Thus India's strategic shift from SAARC to BIMSTEC is based on the greater 'Rajamandala' predicted by Chanakya for his own geostrategic and economic interest.

Recent invitation to BIMSTEC leaders for the oath- taking ceremony of the new Government and (previous invitees where SAARC leaders) itself validates the strategic importance of the grouping. But why this shift from SAARC to the Eastern and for Eastern neighbours? Is this the signal that SAARC is no more relevant? Is this a strategic ploy to isolate Pakistan in South Asian region and internationally at large? Or there are other strategic weightage?

SAARC was formed to integrate politically, economically and culturally the disintegrated region in the world. The region with quarter of the world's population hosting some of the world's fastest growing economies aimed to share mutual benefits of development didn't move as per expectations.

The obstructionist nature of the neighbour Pakistan is to blame for SAARC's state. The multilateral regional forum was stalled because of the bilateral rivalries. The disinterest between the neighbours was clearly seen when Pakistan was suspicious about India's gift of South Asia Satellite to SAARC members.

Neither the previous treaties like SAFTA have reaped intended benefits, nor are the issues on counter terrorism, trans-regional motor vehicle agreement moving ahead. Apart from Pakistan, rest of the members have time and again criticized India for its 'Big Brother' attitude.

The gains achieved by SAARC are minimal. But BIMSTEC, on the other hand, gives India an opportunity to pick the low hanging fruit of economic political and cultural integration.

The strategic shift goes well with India's Act East Policy. The geographic mix of the BIMSTEC with SAARC minus Pakistan plus Thailand and Myanmar who are also the members of Asia gives India opportunity to pursue beyond neighbourhood policy.

Historically, this region had close economic and cultural links with India. Chola's trade boost to south East Asia is well known. Bangladesh hails India for its support in the 1971 liberation war. Nepal and India since time imemorial enjoy 'roti-beti ka rishta'.

Geographically, the region is the bridge between India and South East Asia. India since two decades has been trying to strengthen economic relations with the Asian tigers, boost trade and BIMSTEC is sure to play a complementary role in this. Moreover the region forms a part of the larger Indian Ocean region which India is trying to capitalise upon. Thus, the focus shift to BIMSTEC is imperative in Indian diplomacy.

Politically, the BIMSTEC grouping is a stable one. The countries enjoy good support of the Indian government. 'Hilsa diplomacy', 'Buddhism diplomacy' have added new vigour to regional integration process.

The Indian cultural and soft power is more than visible in BIMSTEC. Once the Thailand's ambassador said- 'It is difficult to point out where India starts and Thailand ends'. He said this after watching a drama based on the epic Mahabharata. Yoga, Buddhism, Bengali culture gives India commendable hold in this regional forum culturally.

Economically the region is progressing faster than SAAARC. The trade between the regions have increased ten folds in just one decade. Also, the region also faces similar economic challenges of poverty, malnutrition, climate change and natural disaster. This gives the forum an immense scope to formulate, co-operate and coordinate on the common issues and achieve sustainable development goals.

But above all the top priority while increasing integration in BIMSTEC, is the development of north-eastern region of the country. The region is the link between mainland India and BIMSTEC countries. But it also the most under developed, least integrated and ethnically most sensitive region of country.

The BIMSTEC grouping could turn-around the fortunes of the north-east by thrust on transportation for transformation of north-east. The security scenario can be enhanced with co-operation and joint operations. This was evident when Indian army along Myanmar performed surgical strike on (NSCN-CK) leaders. Thus north-east is to immensely gain from thus strategic shift.

Inspite of all feel good factors the advantages of BIMSTEC are strategically underused. For instance, though there is immense political will to give thrust, there is regional asymmetry with India being the largest and fastest growing economy.

Most of the promises, commitments have remained only on papers or are work in progress for instance, the Kaladan multimodal project have been looming in delays for the last 12 years. The ambitious Asian highway have been confined to papers.

The region also faces bilateral hurdles for examples Bhutan's no to BBIN transport project, the Teesta water sharing argument between India and Bangladesh and the recently cropping up issue of Rohingyas refugees from Myanmar. The political stability also depends on the present regime. For illustration India- Bangladesh enjoy cordial relation when Awami league is in power.

The grouping also doesn't hesitate to use China card to caution India. This is frequently done by Nepal to warn India. Also, the region barring India is crashing under China's cheque book diplomacy. The recently released report by Ministry of Foreign Affairs shows drastic reduction in fund allocation to BIMSTEC countries. A new threat of Islamic radicalisation has also engulfed the BIMSTEC forum.

The diplomatic and bureaucratic hurdles with complexity of regional polity stalls the regional progress. Another angle which inhibits and undermines the region's growth is negative para-diplomacy. The state of west Bengal has not been co-operative on Teesta water sharing issue. Tamil Nadu still criticises Srilanka for war crimes on tamilians during the liberation war with LTTE.

BIMSTEC is more than often seen as a substitute to SAARC. But the truth is neither one can be a substitute to another. It is rightly said 'you can change your friends, but you cannot change your neighbours'. The strategic shift to BIMSTEC can gain new momentum with political will, faster implementation of projects, regular meets and briefing and by confidence building mechanisms.

But at the same time, SAARC has its own utility and cannot be left alone. It holds its own significance in turn of geostrategic and security complexities. BIMSTEC compliments SAARC at best and can become a new forum to bestow peace, economic prosperity and regional stability. The priority should be on culture-commerce and connectivity with an all-new vigour and keeping in mind the Gujral doctrine of non- reciprocity while implementing the new 'Rajamandala' with BIMSTEC.

❑❑

35 New India in the Pursuit of Excellence

Mudit Jain, IRS (AIR 173 CSE 2017)

It has been 70 years since India became an Independent democratic country. Long ordeal with colonial rule left a poverty ridden, precocious India marred by challenges like feudal agrarian nature, casteism, communalism etc.

The India of old carries a monkey on its back in the form of baggage like socio-economic-political-environmental and so on challenges. To turn the tide in its favour, new India was marked by paradigm shifts in various spheres is moving towards India of dreams and pursuit of excellence is important part of the process.

Excellence as per Dr. Kalam can lead to an India ahead of all other nations. What is needed is that all individuals preach and practice excellence. Let us see with various dimensions where in New India in pursuit of excellence is moving to rectify its old baggage, starting with sociological.

Pursuit of excellence in sociological paradigms is seen in measures for emancipation of women where in women themselves are torch bearers of empowerment, gender equality, reducing crimes against women etc.

The youth today is excelling in fields of sports, business, and societal transformation, becoming champions of change like casteism, communalism, corruption etc. This is reflected in improving rankings of India in corruption perception Index.

All this has led to focus on reducing inequalities (SDG-8) and excellence in economic sphere.

Excellence in economy will improve trickle down if it is inclusive and concerns with even the last man standing in the last row.

Reduction in hunger, poverty, economic inequalities etc. require excellence in fields like skill India, digital India and make in India so that inclusive and productive jobs are created for one and all. Ease of doing business is another fact of India's pursuit of excellence.

The sphere of economic excellence has taken upon itself to transform, clean and energize India by economic reforms like GST, demonetization, solving NPA crisis etc. which will increase India's potential to harness demographic dividend.

This takes us to another sphere, the political aspect of new India and its pursuit of excellence.

Reduction or weeding out corruption, finding solution for criminalization of politics, electoral reforms, improving parliament's functioning, eradicating the bug of terror and bad bureaucracy are age old issues.

Pursuit of excellence in political sphere is manifesting in competitive federalism, cooperative federalism, minimum government and maximum governance, centricity of citizens in governance by e-governance, participatory governance etc. so that solutions to age old issues are found out sooner. This will create an ethical framework embedded in fabrics of transparency, rule of law and integrity to improve overall environment of new India.

Let us now analyze new India and its pursuit of excellence with respect to environment.

Climate Change, global warming, disturbances in life on land and life in water have affected mankind in general and marginalized in particular.

New India's efforts to excel in environmental sustainability are seen in recognition of principle of stewardship and trusteeship by New India in form of INDCs, Paris deal, and pledge to build sustainable cities and responsible consumption and production (SDG).

This is reflected in Swachh Bharat Campaign which recently celebrated ODF week and "Swachta He Seva" campaign including Indian cricket team in the pursuit to excel by reaching out to youth. This reflects in improvement of sanitation to 62% of India from 38% in 2014.

New India's pursuit for excellence will remain incomplete if it does not address the psychological growth of its drivers.

The global happiness Index ranked India at 122nd rank. This marks the proof of increasing depressing and suicides in society.

New India's pursuit to excellence here is seen in national health policy and mental health policy which focus on wellness, rehabilitation within families and societies along with decriminalization of suicide.

This is also reflected in utilitarian approach of inclusive growth taking divyangjan together, transgender and other vulnerable sections of society so that India excels as a whole and not just a part.

Other areas where India's excellence drive is evident are fields of education, innovation, industrialization, infrastructure creation etc. so that India sheds it's precious society tag as discussed by economic survey.

This excellence pursuit reflects in India's global partnership for enhancing development, peace and justice in other countries as well.

Example of this can be seen with respect to new India's positive role in Afghanistan and Africa on one hand and free-open-peaceful-Indian-Pacific ocean on other.

New India's changed paradigms haven't been able to counter poverty or casteism. It has so far not found out sustainable solution to issue of declining jobs and increasing inequalities in society. This has also been a laggard as far as countering corruption and terror is concerned. Environmental challenges are no different.

But this is not because failure of idea of new India's pursuit of excellence but because these are deep rooted problems. New India's drive towards maturity by solving these core issues is possible only by pursuit of excellence as it will make solution sustainable and long term.

"Sankalp Se Siddhi" or New India is not just a pledge or a paradigm shift. It is an idea or vision toward building an India of tomorrow. It is a revolution to make this century not only Asian century but also India's century.

Excellence forms core part of new India. Again, as Dr. Kalam said, a nation can excel only if its citizens excel individually and in society. New India's pursuit to excellence is a novel idea that needs to be nourished, nurtured and taken care of by one and all. Excellence is like a tiger that new India is destined to ride. Disembarking is not a possibility and staying on it is worth the challenges.

❑❑

36 Women Empowerment: The Need of the Hour is to Move Beyond Emotive Posturing

Mudit Jain, IRS (AIR 173 CSE 2017)

Character of a society is a function of many inter-twiddled aspects. Women represent one such keystone in the arch of societal architecture and hence have importance no less than other genders. But largely they have been reduced to a 'vulnerable' section. It is not that nothing has been done for women empowerment, but what matters is the way it is done.

Historical injustices against women have their roots in a patriarchal society. Pre-independence era saw many social reformers like Raja Ram Mohan Roy, Ishwar Chandra Vidyasagar etc. all grappled with social evils like sati, widow's stigmatization, girl child issues etc. The reforms were driven on sense of true justice but by a small section of Indian society.

Post independence the basis of women empowerment was derived largely from glorification of the past in name of social reformers, with women examples being very few. This failed to provide women with real participation in their own empowerment and strengthened the emotive posturing of the gender. By giving women "status of goddess", a false sense of empowerment got deeply embedded in society.

This gave vent to hypocrisy which is reflected till date in form of failed measures and policies. The reforms remained superficial and unsustainable because they failed to embed feeling of justice, respect and honour for women.

Let us analyze how the measures taken till date faltered at various ends including socio-economic-political and psychological.

The emotive posturing of women hardly helped their social status and their issues. Indian women have one of the poorest health indicators in the world with 56% being anaemic, having one of the lowest longevity in not only Asia but lower than few African nations too.

Sex ratio is paltry low at 940 while child sex ratio has decreased from 976 in 1951 to 914 in 2011 census. All those numbers have their roots in early marriages of women, average age being 21.8 years only. This causes denial of reproductive rights, domestic abuse, and higher level of maternal mortality rate (212) and consequential poor infant mortality rates (44) as per census 2011.

Focusing on just interplay of words gives false sense of participation leading to poor inclusivity, gender inequality (India placed at 135th position in IHDI). Society has failed to not to commodify women which has affected them psychologically so much that it has given way to internalization of crime. This is manifested in poor implementation of various Anti-Rape, Anti-Abuse, Criminal Law Amendment Acts etc.

Emotive posturing of women has led to myth that goes against their ability to be part of economic growth of nation and hence caused genderization of labour. Hence schemes remain aloof from ground realities and perpetuate poor participation in decision making, low to no economic rights. This leads to perpetual ineffectiveness in countering lack of women empowerment, domestic abuse, male chauvinism and other ill practices.

Political participation perhaps represents meagre emotive posturing of women in the best possible manner. The long awaited "grant" of 33% representation in Parliament has remained on papers with representation for women languishing around 11%. It is true that right to vote was given to Indian women far more 'generously' than even western nations, but it remains to be seen how many women we vote to parliament.

This has led to poor orientation to women's issues, grievance redressal and even day-to-day sufferings.

All these limitations have hurt women psychologically more than anything else. "Women move shoulder to shoulder with men" is been said for decades. But this is way far from truth. Emotive posturing has not been able to change societal mindset, has not led to societal sensitization and raised questions like redistribution vs. participation, growth vs. sustainable and inclusive development including women, entitlement vs. favour etc.

Hence it is well clear that there is a need to change the way women empowerment is looked into. But does it call for complete overhaul? What should be done to ensure that women empowerment is not just a namesake? Perhaps the answers to these questions lie in addressing basic issues leading to cyclic degeneration of status of women.

Lets us see what steps can be taken for a sustainable women empowerment which is beyond mere promises and addresses ground realities.

Societal sensitization has been long talked about. The recent "He for She" campaign is a bright step forward to change patriarchal nature of society to a just one.

The vicious cycle of women abuse needs to be countered right from homes. Parents need to realize that they have important role in imparting value education particularly to male and instil confidence in girl child. Various governmental education schemes like Sarva Siksha Abhyan, Right To Education etc. need to be focusing at practical implementation of value education via change in curriculum, teacher sensitization etc.

This will embed a girl's right to education in social fabric of country and not look at it as a favour. This will provide real participation of girls in economic and social growth having positive externalities on nutrition, health, delayed marriages, reproductive rights etc.

An educated girl child would have an empowered adolescence and hence will be aware of her entitlements and rights including socio-economic-political. This will allow women empowerment to be internalized within women making it sustainable and driven by an "invisible hand". This has been shown by a UN report which says that even 7 years education delays marriage age, reduces MMR, IMR, malnourishment in women and children etc.

This applied and pragmatic approach towards phase containment of problems at levels of girl child would provide for female participation in formal work sectors, while currently 90% women workforce is restricted to informal sectors. Hence next step that logically follows is skill development of women, vocational trainings etc. It is not that these are not done now, but need is to streamline the policies on sound basis and truly implement them. For example, recently framed policies like 'Skill India', 'Make In India', 'Digital India', 'Swachh Bharat' etc. should have dedicated departments and focus on women involvement for their real participation and empowerment.

This will have positive effects like make women self dependent, increase their financial autonomy, increase their say in decision making in family and prevent domestic abuse.

If all goes well then this will itself help women empowerment and make it a virtuous cycle leading to empowered old age where by they will be aware of their entitlements, live a dignified life ahead without need to be dependent on their children. Such a path to women empowerment will create positive external linkages in form of more and more women joining hands for self empowerment, with more and more males realizing their role as facilitators towards the cause. But is the demand too much? Do these logically interlinked sceneries really work? Let us find the answers.

Western nations, even the lesser developed Latin American nations and eastern European nations after offer not only hope but many examples.

Feminist movements in USA largely began with demand of voting rights but culminated with participation at all levels. Today they represent themselves as one of the most empowered society with high gross enrollment rations in primary and higher education for both genders. This is hence an example of how investing in girl education really leads to an inclusive society.

Latvia, though not known to be an economic powerhouse, has done well to achieve highest sex ratio in the world at 1187 females per thousand males. This is because of governmental policies and women empowerment and present example to India on how to streamline and implement anti-child sex detection and illegal abortion laws like pre conception and pre natal detection techniques (PCPNDT).

Long denied reproductive rights to women in Ireland were recently changed. This was possible only by moving beyond emotive posturing of women and achieves real empowerment for women.

Other example from across the world are effective rights in Bangladesh by focusing on girl education and economic linkages and general end of hypocrisy bringing parity of thoughts, evolving emotive posturing into real empowerment.

Hence it can be well seen that limiting women empowerment to emotive posturing has not worked well and moving beyond that is way ahead as shown by other nations. It is important that the Indian society realizes that there is a definite fault in its women empowerment programs. Now it depends completely on us that we take logical steps forward or be like an ostrich and dig our heads in sand to be in a false sense of being a part of completely empowered society, which is definitely non-existent in India as of now.

❑❑

37 Courage to Accept and Dedication to Improve Are Two Keys to Success

Namrata Jain, IAS (AIR 12 CSE 2018)

In the late 1960s, when Sri Lal Bahadur Shastri was assigned with the Railways' Ministry portfolio where he took the job with zeal and determination. But unfortunately, he resigned following a major train accident as he felt moral responsibility which killed 140 people in post-Independence era. Hence, under his Prime Ministership, he made it a point to prevent train mishaps.

The above anecdote is a mere depiction of what constitutes 'success-code'. Inter-linking the ingredients, only when an individual/community/society or an entire civilization has the courage to acknowledge the misdoing and promise to improve on it, the standard of living as well as the moral fiber stays at a pedestal.

This simple yet value-centric "success-code" is not a child's play. It requires years of evolution and maturity to achieve stability. For instance, in the political scenario the birth of a nation may happen in silos but its rise or fall is absolutely dependent on the ingredients of the "success-code". Case I, involves democracies where natural rights are respected and adhered. They are at times penned down in a holy document – Constitution. Case II, is generally the reactionary states, where the sword is mightier than the pen. Thus, Case I is more likely to sustain than the latter and helps in installing constitutional propriety.

Taking a look at the economy section, the current Indian government by acknowledging the impending slowdown is a positive sign in a negative space, which in turn has made its ministries to burn the midnight oil and identify and take on targeted measures to prevent a cyclical slowdown.

The "success-code" has crept into the cultural aspect of the society as well. Recently Justin Trudean, the Prime Minister of Canada issued an apology for being insensitive and racist when he was in college. Thus, just by accepting the wrong he committed couple of years back has brought happiness to millions in the community.

The corporate sector breathes onto the "success-code" but it is recent century's doing. This is also credited to the fact that the consumer has become an important, aware stakeholder thus treating him as an important player in the process. The recent recalling of the Johnson and Johnson faults him implants is a sign towards knowing the mistake and rectifying the same. Same goes with how Apple made it a definite point to replace all its 2015 Macbook Pro batteries so as to prevent damages.

Drawing connections from the above, the boom in technology advances banks on the "success-code" for its existence. A very apt parallel in this regard are the industrial revolutions. James Watt to Sam Pitroda to Klaus Schwab had the will-power to break and make a better future, as centuries pass by. In the age of self-driven cars and robots as housekeepers, it becomes very crucial for the makers to own up if something goes south and keep on improving to fight in the cut-throat marker scenario. Examples would include the ever changing bitcoin technologies, internet of things etc.

Philosophical school of thoughts has been society centric and dynamic in itself. The forever debate between classical-Keynesians-Monetarists and the non-versions of the same have served its due purpose. For instance, classical like Adam Smith flourished till great depression of 1929. Post that a new set of people like Sir J.M. Keynes brought to the light new reasons. But the former school survived by Fredrick Hayek rectified the past mistakes and now such names recipients of the highest praise.

The current reversal of the section 377 in India which denied the identity to the LGBTQ+ (lesbian, gay, bisexual, transgender, queer) community is a shining example of how bold reforms come through only when the Supreme Court of India came to terms with the archaic provisions and did everything in its capacity to improve.

The much needed heed that is being paid to the environment is appreciated and at the same time, is essential. The renewal of Kyoto Protocol into Paris Agreement (2015) and a push to the renewable sections like India-France's commendable partnership in the International Solar Alliance is a point in the direction that years and years of abuse of the environment through means like exploiting non-renewable need to come to an end, so as to achieve sustainable development. At the national level, the Indian government has installed a new ministry - Jal Shakti ministry. By doing this, it reconciles with the fact that India is a water-stressed nation and if urgent steps aren't taken it will become a water scarce nation by 2045. It is visible in statistics in the 1950s, annual water availability was near 5000bcm and currently it has dropped to a miserable 1700bcm. Thus, by starting a Jan Andolan to save water it will prevent such a situation where:

"Our great grandparents saw water in lakes and ponds Our parents saw water in packaged water bottles and Our children (hopefully not) see water in mini-capsule."

The "success-code" has the capacity to influence an individual's lifestyle. Post 1991 India has faced a surge in lifestyle diseases like obesity, diabetics etc. Thus, the current Disease Burden Initiative report shows a horrifying truth that two extremes – malnutrition and obesity are underlying major health risk factors. Thus, by accepting the glory truth, various initiatives like National Nutrition Mission, Poshan Maah, Yoga etc. are taken up to meet targets. Via this, a societal acceptance and a behavioral change among individuals motivate them to befit.

The dynamics in the International perspective is also served by the "success-code". Ireland, being a strict Catholic norms following country, where abortion is considered a sin, came up with the 'Savita Law', after the death of an Indian origin Dentist Savita where she was denied abortion despite of her precarious circumstances. In another incident, the Bishop of Canterbury (UK) got highly emotional at the Jallianwala Bagh massacre and apologized for the shameless act of his ancestor. Thus, diplomacy, preferably soft is tested and approved by the "success-code".

The "success-code" has been there for quite some time. It has taken different forms but the essence of it – the ingredients have been refined with every incident. Citing from the Indian experience, to begin with, the Vedic age, a highly intellectual society but stratified in varnas was overhauled in the 6th century BC, with Buddha and Mahavir taking the centre-stage. Similarly, they tried to improve the socio-cultural status of women-indicating the gender-bias and domination of patriarchy. It took several ages and kingdoms to accept and rectify the oppression. Jumping to the Independence struggle, capable leaders like M.K. Gandhi, Nehruji, Patel, etc. realized the importance to promoting social integration by fostering societies that are stable and safe would be the real freedom. Thus, during salt satyagraha, leaders like Sarojni Naidu, Kamla Chhatopadhya, etc. took the centre stage. During post-Independence era, recent verdicts like the Sabarlimala Temple have shown the determination to achieve a gender neutral society.

Thus, by depicting the diverse nature of the "success-code" the formula remains the same but the journey to accomplish the same involves sweat, revolution, courage, determination and staying true to one's ethics. Thus summing it up to be a "process" just how Rome was not built in a day, the "success-code" is an ever-evolving process with the intricate details of courage and determination.

❑❑

38 Economy is Losing Out on the Potential of Women

Namrata Jain, IAS (AIR 12 CSE 2018)

Recently, an Indian woman was appointed as the Chief Financial Officer (CFO) of IMF. Until recently, the Commerce Minister of our country and the chairperson of the largest state-owned lender SBI were women. Global conglomerates like PEPSICO and BIOCON are headed by Indian women. While we celebrate all these facts, at the same time the recently released employment data of the country revealed a declining female Labour force participation ration (from approximately 36% in 2012 to 26% in 2017-18).

This entire hullabaloo regarding these figures naturally raises questions – why the women's role is so important in the economy and what are the reasons we are not able to harness this potential. In the following essay, we will try to answer these questions and look out for possible solutions.

Women constitute one-half of the population of any country and therefore one half of the potential workforce. Their non-involvement in labour market means we are already foregoing half of the country's human resource. World Bank estimates that better inclusion of women in workforce will improve its economic growth rate by at least 1.5 percentage points if 50% of its women join the workforce.

Also, women are mainly responsible for purchase decisions at home. That means, consumption patterns in the economy are heavily influenced by women. Having women in marketing and higher management will allow companies to better understand this consumer segment and better cater to it.

Women also are generally more pre-disposed to care for education and health needs of the family. Empowered women with better awareness and access will lead to a more skilled and healthy future workforce.

All this establishes the importance women hold in the economy of any country. However, despite this, countries around the world and India in particular, have been unable to tap into this potential of women.

The foremost reason for this has been the low HDR of women in India. Both educationally and health-wise, women lag behind their male counterparts. Census 2011 shows that while male literacy in India is more than 70%, female literacy is close to 60%. This becomes even more glaring in rural areas.

These differences can largely be boiled down to societal attitudes towards women. Women are considered 'paraya dhan' who would be married off to another household and therefore, investing in their education is considered wasteful.

Also, after marriage, since their role is that of a primary caregiver, they are seldom allowed to work outside. Another issue is that the jobs available for women are restricted. Women are not considered eligible for many jobs and are therefore confined to jobs like nursing, apparel industry in the formal sector and as domestic helps in the informal sector.

Even upon entering jobs, there is an informal glass ceiling where high quality, top jobs are restricted for men since there is a high attrition rate among women once they are married and/or have children.

Apart from this, the work environment is often not conducive for women. For security purposes, women are unable to work late night shifts and there is a high prevalence of sexual harassment at workplace recently highlighted through the #Metoo movement.

Companies also find it burdensome and economically unviable to provide for maternity benefits like maternity leaves and daycare facilities like crèches as made mandatory under the recent Maternity Benefits Act.

For all these reasons, it has been difficult to improve the female participation in labour force. While these problems are structural and also societal, various steps can be taken to improve the situation right from the childhood days.

Improving education levels comes first. In this regard, promoting education as is being done through Beti Bachao Beti Padhao and Sukanya Samriddhi accounts, to effect behavioural change, can be complemented with focus on financial literacy and skill up gradation/acquisition in latest technologies.

Self employment is the greatest source of empowerment. In this regard, promoting financial inclusion through women self help groups and startups through MUDRA loans are being done. Besides, women-centric incubators can be established as well.

Making it easier for women to work in formal sector would entail providing paternity leaves along with maternity benefits, promoting flexi-work hours and work from home for women and making it mandatory to provide cab services.

Improving work environment through appointment of independent women directors, mandatory and effective Internal Complaints Committee to report workplace abuses and checking of glass ceilings through equal pay for equal work law enforcement would go a long way.

At the same time, it needs to be emphasized that all these measures will only come to reality when societal attitudes towards women change and companies are made to understand the economic and cultural benefits women bring to their organizations.

Only when this is realized, will we have truly tapped and utilized the potential of women in our economy. Then we would not need to count women achievers on our figures tips as every household would then have produced a daughter equally capable as a son.

❑❑

39 The Greater the Difficulty, the More Glory in Surmounting it

Namrata Jain, IAS (AIR 12 CSE 2018)

The world remembers the heroes. Heroes are those who despite innumerable difficulties have come out at the top. An everyday achievement where the odds were not set against us does not seem like an achievement at all.

Even our mythological stories tell us so. Although it was the Crown Prince Arjun who was known as the greatest archer in the world, people still remember the poor and exploited Eklavya who surmounting his Guru's reluctance, learned the art from afar in a forest. The fact that he had to pay the price of his disobedience with his thumb, adds to the charm of the hero that was Eklavya.

Why is it that his difficulties were the reason of his glory? What does glory entail? And do only difficulties result in glory? Are everyday tasks not praiseworthy? These will be the questions we will try to answer in the following essay.

Glory means worldwide appreciation. A child is appreciated by parents when she performs well in a test. When the child performs consistently well, she would be congratulated but after a point of time, everyone will come to expect that the child is naturally capable and her achievements will become a normal phenomenon.

However, if a child with poor track record suddenly performs well in a test one day and also beats the child who consistently performs well, thus will not only result in appreciation from her parents but also the teacher would proudly present her example to the whole class to learn from.

This points to a very important reason why greater the difficulties, greater is the glory. While the same feat when achieved by a normal person does not become the talk of the town, when achieved by an underdog invites everyone's praise. The reason is HOPE and a positive example for anyone who is struggling in life.

This is the reason because of which people like the Phogat sisters became a role model for girls in Haryana in wrestling. If they can overcome gender biases in a predominantly patriarchal society and that too in a sport known for men, we can also fight societal perceptions.

Another reason why greater difficulties result in greater glory is that it broadens the frontiers of human potential. We find satisfaction and pleasure that humans have yet again conquered a new milestone.

The landing of the first astronauts on moon in 1969 was one such feat. Humans were able to not only go past the Earth's gravitational force but also enter moon's atmosphere and step on a new celestial object. That is why we see a constant race among nations on who could go farthest and first in space.

Even at an individual level, overcoming nature imposed restrictions makes for a splendid display of human power. The more unachievable the goal, the more pride we feel.

That is why, the 'firsts' are always remembered. The first man to climb the Mt. Everest is praiseworthy himself, but the first woman to do so becomes extra special. And this is why Bachendri Pal will always be remembered. She did not only surmount the harsh terrains of the mountain, but being a woman, she displayed that women are no less than men.

This brings us to the question why everyday tasks cannot be glorified. Do they not give us HOPE, are they not a reflection of human persistence and motivation and do they not hone our skills?

The simple answer to this is that the tasks which have now became mundane were also once new and achieving them the first time invited similar glory. Now since they have been already achieved, human beings naturally curious have moved onto new arenas.

The charm is in the new, yet unconquerable and hence more difficult by those who have traditionally been marginalized. In overcoming these physical, natural and societal restraints lies the source of glory. These obstacles excite the human mind to see how one overcomes them.

Therein lays the essence of human development and progress so far. Glory is the fruit for our hard work and courage. And therefore, the greater the difficulty, the more glory in surmounting it.

❑❑

40 Expect the Best, Prepare for the Worst, Capitalise on What Comes

Pradeep Kumar Dwivedi, IAS (AIR 74 CSE 2018)

Expectation, preparation and capitalisation are three wheels of a cycle called life. Every day we expect something to happen, we prepare for something which we have planned for future, and we try to avail the opportunities that are present at the moment. These three words however philosophical or distant from each other may seem, are binded by a common thread called story of success. Every single example of success and every single example of inspirational life has gone through all these steps of expecting, preparing and capitalizing thereon.

Now the question before us is what to expect? What to prepare for and what to do at the moment because 'present' is what we have got right now, future is yet to come and past has already gone. Expectation signifies hope – hoping for something that we desire, that which we want to see in the society around us and the world around us.

Hope is a magical word which has done wonders since ages. Hope brings positive energy which in turn gives us belief on our strengths. Without hoping for desired result, it's almost impossible to proceed. Hope for better future is what makes a student study hard, hope for bringing medals to country is what makes an Olympian devote his entire time to practice. If somebody loses hope about some task, depression and detachment is bound to follow.

Hope is what inspires us to begin working towards our dream. Like Plato said 'WELL BEGUN is HALF DONE'. India would not have become a free nation if our freedom fighters didn't hope for a country without foreign rule. America would have still struggled with citizenship rights of black population if great Abraham Lincoln did not hope for an equal and just society.

Indian paralympic gold medal winner Deepa Malik lost both her legs in a traumatic accident. Yet she is a passionate motorcyclist, athlete and an inspiration for millions. In her felicitation ceremony, she emphasised that losing something or everything does not count unless you lose hope. Hope will make to regain everything with renewed vigour and energy.

Apart from expectation, another important wheel is preparation. Before going into the multiple aspects of preparation, it is necessary to understand why preparation is necessary, and how much we should prepare?

Expectation, although, provides positive energy, yet harsh realities of life are to be faced and to tackle these harsh realities effectively, we need to prepare. Preparation is about assessing the risks and difficulties and planning for them in advance.

Napoleon once famously said "Every battle is first won in the mind" which means that every battle requires a planning, assessing the worst possible scenario and, with our limited resources, approaching that scenario with our best shot. All the great people who succeeded have endlessly prepared for the worst case scenario.

Mo Farah, the long distance runner of England, fell on the track while running during Olympics, it looked like all his preparations, endless hard work will go in vain, but he won the race. That is the magic of preparing for worst case scenario.

Mohammad Ali once said that "I don't fear a person who practices a thousand punches per day but at the boxer who practices one punch thousands times" because the perfection that comes with preparation is ultimate and glory is bound to come.

Inspite of all the expectations and preparations, all that we have in our hand is the present, the opportunities that we have in present demand their best utilisation and here comes the role of the art of 'capitalisation'. Capitalisation simply means expecting best results out of everything that we have without whining and whimpering about what we don't have.

Capitalisation requires the attitudes of accepting challenges as an opportunity. However difficult the situation may look, it is accompanied by inherent opportunities and those who identify these opportunities wrapped in cover of difficulty are bound to excel, are bound to be the inspiration to many.

In a scene of 'CHAK DE INDIA' a Hindi movie, coach Kabir Khan is not worried by the girls of his team uniting against him because he smells an opportunity in this process. He uses this incident for building the attitude of unity and team spirit among girls. He takes this newly born unity forward and translates it into a world cup winning team, a team which is unfazed by any challenge.

Though the story told above is fictional, yet it exemplifies the importance of sensing opportunity in every challenge. Another example of great economist Mohammad Yunus Khan who took the challenge of financial inclusion of rural population of Bangladesh and taking this task by him as an opportunity for him to do something for the country and society created the famous 'Grameen Bank'. It is the result of his efforts that Bangladesh is now a country with a better financial inclusion status for its population.

It is clear from the above discussion that success and life both are linked by a thread which contains expectation, preparation and capitalisation. Expecting the best gives us energy required, preparation gives us the skills required and capitalisation provides us the fruit or the good result and together they form a partnership which transforms into an inspirational life.

This strategy of 'Expect the best, prepare for the worst and capitalize on what comes' needs to be applied in present day problems of global warming and climate change, terrorism tackling and bringing equality and justice to every strata of the society.

Climate change needs to be looked upon with hope that every country will understand this menace and come at a common platform. Nobody had thought that it would get so much attention when 'club of Rome' explained it first, yet the hope and efforts have taken the problem to be in a positive direction. Preparation in this case is building adaptation strategies and capitalisation is to take positives out of every engagement and make them happen in real world.

Similarly, these principles can bring the desired results in tackling terrorism and building equality and justice. Even the 'Disaster management' concept is almost entirely based on 'expecting the best and preparing for the worst' strategy.

Success and solution to every problem requires a strategy and initiating thinking on that strategy needs expecting positive results out of it, preparing for every outcome and capitalizing on every opportunity. These are the external principles to be followed in life. Cribbing and whining does not bring any good and only those who followed these principles rose to the top of the world.

Hence every human being with all patience and fortitude should keep making efforts, results are bound to come.

"KAMYABI CHOOMEGI KADAM EK DIN EK DIN"

□□

41 Role of Media in Elections

Pradeep Kumar Dwivedi, IAS (AIR 74 CSE 2018)

In 2005, the yearly World Press Freedom Day conference emphasized the role of media in transparencies, deepening democracy and ensuring accountability of election management body during the electoral process. The conference also emphasized the link between election management body and media and role of media as communicator and role of election management body as regulator.

This is one of several examples when media's importance has been highlighted and deliberated upon for a fair and transparent democratic process. This takes us to questioning, what constitutes media? How media plays a role in electoral process? How positively and negatively media can affect the results of an election and the process of election? What are the ethical issues of present time and what are the ideals that media should follow?

Media has been termed as 'fourth estate' of the democracy together with executive, legislature and judiciary. Being the fourth pillar, it plays multidimensional roles in this era of information technology. Media in twenty first century not merely means press and television, it has leaped beyond these boundaries and now social media has taken an equal importance in this area. Hence media can be defined as every medium that facilitates the flow of information to multiple audience.

Election commission understanding the role of media and legislature in Representation of People's Acts has provided for allotment of some time on national television to every political party. This itself explains that our legislators have understood the role of media for a transparent and fair electoral process.

The role of media in elections is not merely restricted to providing information about election dates and election commission guidelines. It goes beyond that. It provides for an informed citizenry. Media's duty and role is to make public aware about the credentials of candidates, provide a platform to debate on various issues which form the political agenda of parties, debating and analysing the manifestos and its repercussions without taking any partisan stances, and providing medium for the top leadership to convey their intentions to electorate.

Media's role is not restricted to pre-election campaign and debates only. After the elections, it is media's duty to ensure that the process is running transparently, exposing and making into public notice any irregularity, if running anywhere, noting down the concerns that arise in the process of election and making authorities aware about them so that next time these concerns can be rectified.

The 2012 elections of Bengal is an example before the world where media took active part by visiting every booth, talking to election officers, electorate and authorities and ensuring that transparency is maintained. This active role of media has helped in a big way in regaining the confidence of voters on electoral process there.

Roles are many and multidimensional. Examples also are many and multidimensional in a similar way. Constant concerns are being raised about the role of media in election process and in general. Ownership of media houses by political masters is one big concern. These channels instead of airing neutral and informed opinion based on rational evidences, try to take partisan sides and work for their political masters to help them in election.

Increasing race of TRP has led to sensationalization of news for gaining public attention and in the quest to sensationalise and serve 'masala' news to audience, relevant issues go deep down in the priority list. Another menace that is severely harming transparency is the growing instances of paid news; political parties and candidates hire media houses by throwing away hefty amounts and media houses become prone to selective reporting, and giving attention to the party of their interest. Since it is well known that media helps and influences the shaping of opinion, so paid news hampers the formation of a rational opinion.

Media trial by several journalists ends up in misrepresenting many people without even any proof of their guilt or even when the matter is sub judice. Many media houses repeatedly announce same person guilty and this affects that person's credibility and even if he may not be that corrupt or not involved in the crime, he ends up losing. Even Supreme Court of India has raised concerns about media trials and warned media houses not to try to establish anyone's guilt when the matter is sub judice.

The use of social media for defaming rivals and making political gains for electoral interest has been a matter of concern. In the recent exercise of demonetisation, many reports about relation of Urjit Patel (Governor RBI) and Mukesh Ambani has been regularly spread which are completely false and later found to have been related with influencing opinion for UP assembly elections. Similarly, social media has been negatively used during Muzaffarnagar riots to polarise the voters on communal lines, in a recent case some news report telecasted that Keshav Prasad Maurya's daughter is having ₹20 crore of new currency but later it turned out to be a false news as he has no girl child.

These instances of negative role of media in electoral process demand a self introspection by media houses as well as a tough and strict regulatory regime. One of the

7 sins described by Gandhiji is 'corporate without morality' in their functioning. Ethical journalism should be the guiding principle for journalists.

Ethical journalism demands that journalist or media houses should telecast everything with objective evidences. They should not engage in partisan interests and constantly seek excellence in ensuring transparency be it in electoral process or be it in day-to-day governance.

Another key to transparent and positive media is a strong regulatory regime. Election commission should play the part of regulator on media during the electoral process and a law should be enacted in this regard providing election commission sufficient powers.

Last but not the least is the need of better training schools for journalists and active role of media fraternity in this regard. Media should act as self regulator because "self regulation if achieved is the best regulation". Value chain and value system of media houses should be directed towards ethical journalism and hence a transparent media.

It is evident and a proven fact that for democracy to go deep and to ensure its functioning, a strong and transparent media is necessary, hence, media houses should realise their role in the process of nation building and deepening democracy and playing an active and healthy role in election process.

❑❑

42 Cooperative Federalism in the Era of Developmentalism

Rajarshi Shah, IAS (AIR 81 CSE 2016)

Cooperative federalism means different units of government – centre, state, local, etc. are equal partners and play important roles in the development of states and the nation as a whole. In the era of developmentalism i.e. moving on the path of faster, sustainable and more inclusive development, cooperative federalism has become much more important than before. This is because, development of local units can only ensure the development of states and it is only with the development of states that nation can develop as a whole. This requires that all these units are empowered with sufficient powers, funds and other resources to perform their respective functions without unnecessary encroaching upon each others' domain and functioning in an interdependent and collaborative manner to bring about empowerment of people and an integrated development of nation.

World over, different nations through their written or unwritten constitutions have prescribed the type of relationships between various units of government. In Britain, there is unitary form of government but yet we witness cooperative federalism between national government and local units. This particularly gained significance in the form of new localism in 1997 under Tony Blair Government with the devolution of managerial power to local units for an enhanced and speedy delivery of civic amenities and greater citizen participation in the process of development.

In the US, where there is strictly federal form of government, cooperation between the President and Senate is essential for various national and international matters.

Indian federation has been described by various scholars as quasi-federalism and has the provision of cooperative federalism in the constitution itself. This is present in legislative, administrative and financial areas. The provision of Rajya Sabha, inter-state council, resource distribution between states and the centre through constitutional body-finance commission are all in the direction of cooperative federalism.

With the 73rd and 74th constitutional amendments to bring government closer to people, a new federal unit – local self-government was introduced and thus the cooperation became more significant. Hence, cooperative federalism under current scenario can be viewed as:

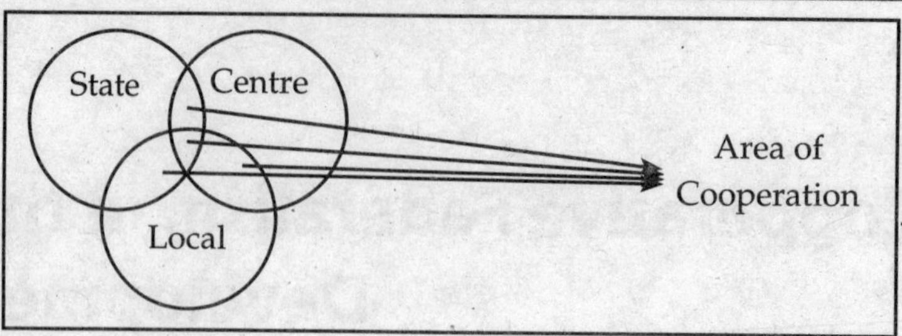

In the context of developmentalism which has evolved from welfare of citizens to empowerment of citizens with the addition of new contemporary trends and challenges like sustainable development, growing complex law and order problems, emphasis on good governance, to weed out corruption, cooperative federalism has became much more significant.

The achievement of goals under Millennium Development Goals, sustainable development goals, achievements of national priorities, poverty removal, unity and integrity of nation, etc. all require immense cooperation between centre and states.

Indian constitution has prescribed separation of powers between centre and states through Union and state lists respectively. Economic reforms on certain important issues like taxation reforms, land acquisition, labour reforms fall either in state list and concurrent list. These reforms are essential for the success of Make in India, ease of doing business, reducing inequalities and reverse the trend of jobless growth. As a result, meaningful cooperation between centre and states is required for the pursuit of national interest.

India currently witnesses the demographic dividend i.e. youngest population in the world. To reap the benefits of demographic dividend, we need a healthy, educated and skilled workforce. Again as these subjects are either in state list or concurrent list, centre has to handhold and guide the states and simultaneously allow flexibility to design schemes and programs according to their needs.

To ensure developmentalism, we also need peaceful environment in the states. The growing complexity of law and order and the growth of communism, regionalism, terrorism, extremism and naxalism hampers the developmental process. Again the centre needs to persuade the states to take positive reforms, help in modernization and bring better coordination between centre and states to ensure peace and stability which is a key driver of developmentalism.

It also needs to be noted that whenever there has been neglect and abuse of cooperation, developmental process has derailed. The era of 1970s and 80s when there was frequent imposition of President's rule, politicization of governor's post and centralized planning adopted by Planning commission brought about the so called Hindu rate of growth - 2.5%.

Under the current government, both cooperative and competitive federalism has been given push. NITI Aayog has been formed to replace the Planning Commission, zonal councils have been revived, and meaningful municipal reforms are being pursued through smart city project and swachch bharat ranking.

However, there is much to be done. Some experts say that NITI Aayog has been functionally directionless and is unable to bring about systematic reforms at the state level. The interstate council has become a defunct body. Though the government has accepted recommendations of 14th Finance commission, its own allocations towards state plans have fallen drastically.

Apart from that, there has been no meaningful devolution of funds, functions and functionaries by the states to the local governments. The absence of this devolution results in many problems like 21% population being below poverty line, 6 crore Indians without house and so on.

Thus, when India will be celebrating its 75th Independence Day we are aspiring for many universal goals like complete eradication of poverty, universal nutrition, housing for all, education, etc. But, all these will be possible if there is meaningful cooperation between all units of government. The need is to remove the differences and build upon achievements through multi-stakeholder, approach and rising above the party lines. It is then only India can realize her destiny and empower her citizens.

□□

43 Globalization is Making our Societies More Creative and Prosperous, but also More Vulnerable

Ravi Mittal, IAS (AIR 61 CSE 2015)

Globalization is akin to the Indian cultural value of 'Vasudhaiva Kutumbakam' which means world is one family. It involves movement of people, goods and ideas across nations transforming the world into a 'global village'. It has been facilitated by modern discoveries and inventions while acting like a double edged sword with its both positive as well as negative implications. Leveraging on its benefits and avoiding its negative fallouts can ensure faster, sustainable and inclusive growth for our nation.

The idea of globalization has been facilitated by many modern scientific inventions and discoveries, and also by the evolution of ideas about the nature of human existence by philosophers, thinkers and intellectuals. Modern means of transport like telephone, air travel, information metamorphosis which have brought all information at the distance of a click are some of the factors which catalyzed the transformation.

Globalization has had an impact on all spheres of life, affecting individuals of all age, gender, caste, religion without any discrimination. Its impact on culture, society, economy, and security of nations, environment and economy, field of science is especially notable.

Globalization has promoted the spread of ideas related to culture, customs, rituals, beliefs, traditions, arts, music, literature and so on at such a fast rate that is unparallel in the history of mankind. It has compelled the societies to introspect their nature and they are now inculcating the best practices from world over. At the same time, it has posed a challenge of sustaining their identities. As Thomas Friedman, a noted expert on globalization said, "The biggest challenge in the era of globalization is to maintain our identities while discoursing the ways to sustain ourselves". Due to this, various languages, cultures, have been struggling to sustain their survival, while also presenting them an opportunity to take it to the global level through vehicles of globalization promoting the principle of 'Anekantvada' i.e. plurality of ideas as propounded by Mahavira.

In the sphere of economy, it has brought prosperity through 'comparative advantage' where the various countries utilize their resources according to their best advantages and allow greater integration of world markets. Thus, it has allowed efficient allocation of resources, generated employment but at the same time, it poses unique challenges.

Failure of markets in one economy affects the entire world e.g. global recession of 2008-09, Asian crisis of 90's. It is against principle of 'self-determination' since bad decisions by one nation affects other nations also.

On the social front, globalization has been a boon. New, students in remote corners of world can take lessons from best of professors of the world through e-learning in the form of Massive Online Open Courses (MOOC). It has at the same time, allowed sharing best mutual practices in the field of healthcare and agriculture which has everlasting impact on the prosperity of nations and its people.

Moreover, globalization of NGO's i.e. social sector and social movements go a long way in alleviating issues as poverty, gender discrimination, and environment consensus and so on. A glaring example of how globalization impacted social and political movement is 'apartheid' movement in South Africa in which all the nations of the world virtually took part. A major area of focus in this regard in modern era is issues related to gender inequality and discrimination in few nations. Globalization has helped to solve the issue from multiple perspectives and gathered such a momentum, which is unprecedented.

Since capitalism has been one of the facilitator of globalization, economics based on efficiency has impacted the vulnerable sections of the society particularly the old and disabled, negatively and has reduced space for them, but ingenious solutions which globalization creates are a blessing in disguise for the vulnerable section.

Criminals & crime related activities like terrorism, money laundering, drug trafficking, piracy, cyber-attacks, organized crime syndicates have got a boost from globalization by leveraging on its products and services. It has facilitated their promotion and expansion as evidenced by recent rise of Islamic State of Iraq and Syria (ISIS), a terrorist group which is using the tools of globalization to inflict terror, violate rights of individuals, and causing massive damage. This is one of the grimmest negative fallout.

However, on the other hand, it has allowed the issues of 'disaster management' to be tackled jointly by the entire humanity in terms of preparedness, and response e.g. recent earthquake in Nepal drew attention of entire world with help coming in all possible forms, which was not possible before.

Thus, the experience vis-à-vis globalization has been diverse for India as well as for other countries. At one hand, it has made our societies more creative and prosperous, while on the other, it has made us vulnerable. We must remember the ideal of 'Ati Sarvatra Varjayet' i.e. excess of anything or extremes of anything are bad. Therefore, there is a need to maintain a judicious balance as far as our role in being an important element of the process of globalization is concerned. Balance involves absorbing and capitalizing on the advantages and at the same time avoiding and effectively tackling its disadvantages.

In the end, 'unity in diversity' is a source of envy for other countries and one of our strengths. In this respect, it is important to channelize the energy of globalization in making our society more creative and prosperous. In this way, globalization with its vulnerabilities will empower us to achieve growth and prosperity for all as stated in the following lines:

"Om Sarve Bhavantu Sukhinah Sarve Santu Niramaya"

❑❑

44 Vision of a Clean India: Prospects and Challenges

Ravi Mittal, IAS (AIR 61 CSE 2015)

"If you do not clean your backyard, your Swaraj shall be stinking" Gandhiji once said while addressing his disciples at the Sevagram Ashram while underscoring the importance of cleanliness. At that time, Gandhiji emphasized the importance of clean India in the backdrop of national struggle for freedom by linking it with the idea of 'Swaraj'.

The idea of 'Clean India' cannot hold more importance in any era than the present one. The vision encompasses multiple dimensions of our society, not just limited to social, economic, health, education, gender and environment. Although, it presents us with multiple challenges, but the opportunity it creates promises to transform India into prosperous nation in the truest of terms.

In terms of social aspect, 'Clean India' is intricately linked to the rights of scheduled castes and other backward classes. While it ensures cleanliness for all, at the same time, it promotes the ideal of 'social equity' by overcoming the inhumane practices of 'manual scavenging'. Abolition of such practices is an important part of the vision.

Also, it gives emphasis to 'preventive healthcare' where by ensuring cleanliness, large number of communicable diseases like dengue, chikungunya and others like typhoid, diarrhea can be prevented. It will reduce the unnecessary burden on the poor in terms of health expenditure, loss of employment, and at the same time, help to achieve goals of reducing Infant Mortality Rate (IMR) by ensuring better survival chances of the infants who are more susceptible to such diseases. It, thus, acts an important pillar in ensuring a holistic 'Health for All'.

Moreover, it has been seen in Annual Survey of Education Report (ASER) that in areas where schools have toilets, the attendance and enrollment ratios are much higher. This emphasizes the importance of clean environment on education outcome.

Not only are the social, health and education aspects intricately linked with cleanliness, but it has a strong association with gender issues, environmental impact, as well as tourism and overall economic development. In terms of gender inequality, toilets in rural areas ensure the dignity of women. One of our fundamental duties is to renounce practices derogatory to the dignity of women. 'In this respect, ensuring sanitation at homes is a duty of citizens. It also increases the levels of girls' education because it has been seen that girls are motivated to go to school which have toilets and are properly maintained.

Cleanliness has a deep impact on environment especially when we are facing the challenges of climate change. Moreover, innovative techniques turn compost into 'renewable energy', which can generate power in small industries and households. Thus, proper management of waste as part of 'Clean India' vision has enduring effects on environment and energy needs.

Tourism gets a major boost if cleanliness is ensured; adequate provision of toilets is made at sites. Thus, it indirectly impacts employment generation, brings in much crucial foreign exchange and promotes economic development. So, it is not only a consequential imperator but a matter of duty to ensure cleanliness. In this respect, vision of 'Clean India' serves this goal.

To achieve this success, various steps have been taken till now by the government, individuals as well as the social sector. Government came up with the 'Total Sanitation Campaign' renamed as 'Nirmal Bharat' and now re-launched as more comprehensive campaign called 'Swachh Bharat Abhiyan'. On the individual level, efforts such as 'Sulabh International' are commendable examples of social entrepreneurship to achieve social goals and objectives. The program of Swachh Bharat Abhiyan is linked to clean water, sanitation, waste disposal, behavioral change communication, construction of toilets and so on. Even judiciary has played proactive role towards the realization of goal by declaring 'Right to clean environment' as an implied right under Article 21 of the constitution.

However, overall efforts by all the stakeholders have not delivered desired results. Its impact on the social front is yet to be fully seen. At the same time, impact on health, education, economy, environment, tourism and gender issues is not as robust as had been visualized. The vision, in the light of its outcome, has presented with many challenges.

'Converting outlays into outcomes' is the major challenges that the government faces. Due to diversity of our nation, challenges also differ according to geography, society and people. While generating awareness about the importance is a challenge in UP, Bihar and other less literate states, at the same time reducing leakages to ensure delivery of requisite services is a challenge in other places. Moreover, budgetary outlays for the purpose have been lower than required due to fiscal constraints.

Any solution to overcome the challenge should involve all the stakeholders and be directed towards comprehensive targeting of the issue. Both the Central and State governments with local governments i.e. Panchayati Raj shall have to act according to 'cooperative federalism'. NGOs, which act as eyes and ears of the government, have a big role to play at all levels. Furthermore, private enterprises should be encouraged to spend a part of their CSR (Corporate Social Responsibility) towards this objective. Towards the development of newer technologies, scientific fraternity in the national institutions can help in developing 'ingenious and indigenous solutions'.

To ensure full public participation, public awareness campaigns should be promoted along with enacting bye-laws to punish those who fail to follow the principles. Moreover, international cooperation such as from Singapore and Germany can bring in expertise in human resources and technology along with best practices. The campaign can be dovetailed with other initiatives such as 'Smart City', 'Make in India', 'Skill India' as well as 'Digital India' due to its comprehensive nature.

In the end, since India is the 'world's oldest civilization with youngest population' in order to leverage its strengths of 3Ds i.e. Demand, Democracy and Demography, vision of a clean India is sine qua non for ensuring sustainable and inclusive growth. 'Toilet seat' is as important for us as the 'UN seat' and only sustained commitment, proactive approach, single minded focus and strong administrative action can ensure the achievement of this goal. Although the vision poses multiple and diverse challenges, but at the same time it presents us with great opportunities which has eternal prospects for our development. As Victor Hugo said, "Nobody can stop the idea whose time has come', the idea of clean India will fructify in all its aspects and it's time has come. Vision of clean India will ensure a prosperous nation with happy future for its children while ensuring Gandhiji's dream of 'wiping tears from every eye' and India will achieve 'Swaraj' in the truest of sense.

□□

45 Management of Indian Border Disputes – A Complex Task

Rishab Jain, IAS (AIR 23 CSE 2018)

India is bordered by 7 countries in the Northern and Eastern part. It shares long borders with Pakistan and China in the North and East, Nepal, Bhutan, Myanmar and Bangladesh in East and a small portion with Afghanistan in the North. We also have a 7,000 km of coastline. Our border management is complex because of the varied terrain and topography, multiple nations, languages and cultures, historical reasons and global geopolitics. Recent Doklam standoff between India and China, redrawing of map by Nepal, regular terrorist incursions from Pakistani Soil, issues in Galvan valley shows the complexity of India's border disputes.

To understand why management of border disputes is complex, we must understand the history of such disputes.

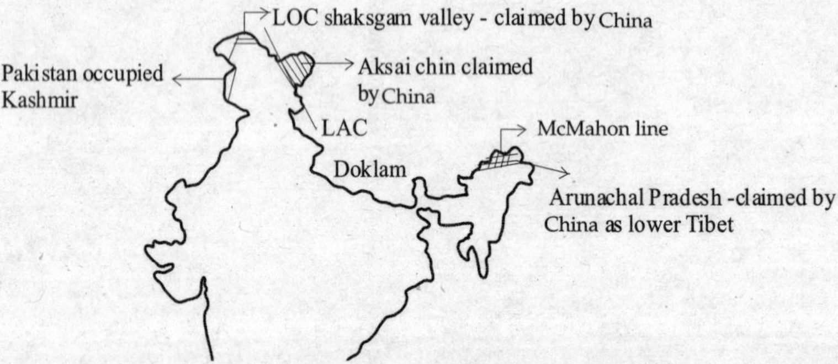

Fig 1: India and its border disputes

In the Western part, the border was delineated by Redcliff before independence. Though much was settled, in the Indo-Pak war of 1998, Pakistani tribes had occupied certain portions of Kashmir which is now known as line of control demarcated Pakistan occupied Kashmir. Border dispute management is complex here because the Pakistani establishment trains terrorists form Al-Qaeda and Taliban and arms them to create troubles, e.g. Uri attack and Pathankot attack. Though India has always tried to maintain peace through establishing Rail and Bus connectivity, providing medical visas, giving Most Favoured Nation status to Pakistan, these were not reciprocated from that side. Apart from these, the challenges of manning the borders in harsh weather and varied terrain, religions radicalization in Kashmir, sleeper cells etc. have made solutions to border disputes with Pakistan complex. The military control over the government in Pakistan, near absence of democracy, non-independent judiciary have also made the dispute much complex to manage.

In the Northern and Eastern sector we share a long boundary with China. Though during our Independence, we didn't share any border, the sub segment annexation of Tibet by China brought two large countries much closer. Though India-Tibet border talks have solved many issues, Chinese government hasn't accepted those talks, hence, border dispute remains with Aksain Chin and Arunachal Pradesh being showed in China's map as their territory which is strongly opposed by India. Also, most of the points marked on map haven't been demarcated on the actual point which is causing disputes with China claiming a larger territory than one that's settled e.g. Pangong Tso Lake. Also, the China-Pakistan Economic corridor under the Belt and Road Initiative has escalated further tensions as these infrastructure projects violate the sovereignty of India. With China's growing economy, one-party controlled government and aggressive stance along the South China Sea as well as other border countries, the issue will grow even more complex in future.

In the Eastern sector, Nepal and Bhutan and all friendly neighbours are there, and they act as buffers to China's border issues. But in recent days we could see the Nepal's communist government's growing bonhomie with China. This could be seen by China's railway connectivity with Kathmandu, teaching Mandarin in Nepal schools, supply of Petroleum, changes in Nepal's map etc. Growing Chinese influence is making border disputes more complex.

As from the above discussion we could see that our major border dispute is with Pakistan and China. With countries like Bhutan, Bangladesh and Myanmar, border areas all well-settled. In fact, with Bangladesh, through the 100th constitution Amendment Act, we have exchanged various enclaves. With Pakistan, the dispute has become complex due to historical reasons such as Pakistan's non-cooperative attitude, continuous terror activities, radicalization etc. "Terror and talks cannot happen together" is the stand taken by India after Pakistan's terrorists supportive acts.

Steps taken by India

India has solved several border disputes in the past through continuous negotiations and diplomacy. An account of such solved disputes is as follows:

(1) **India** – Pakistan border dispute at Rann of Kutch has been solved successfully through peace talks.

(2) **Sikkim** – which was claimed by China as its own territory was also solved.

(3) **Katchatheevu** – a small island was given to Sri Lanka.

(4) **Transfer of Enclaves** – between India and Bangladesh was also carried out through a constitution amendment act.

Thus India is a peace-loving nation which always goes for peace talks first to solve any dispute. Even for the current border disputes, India has put on several mechanism and institutions in place.

Regular confidence Building Measure exercises and talks happen at border areas to ensure peace and tranquility. Track II diplomacy works behind the screen before any major meeting with China. India is a part of several international organizations such as BRICS, Shanghai cooperation organization etc. through these organizations we are able to speak and negotiate at the highest level. India is also actively utilizing the international forums such as UN Security Council as a non-permanent member, UNGA etc. to bring international attention to cross-border terrorism perpetrated by Pakistan.

With the recent constitutional amendments, Article 370 has been made as irrelevant and the status quo in Kashmir has been changed.

The economic and military powers are very important for any nation to solve major disputes in today's world. India is moving towards a $5 trillion economy while militarily we are growing stronger every day. Having the 2nd largest standing army in the world, our military expenditure and indigenization of technology has also been consistently rising. Examples are the indigenization of LAC Tejas and 2nd Aircraft carrier INS Vikranth.

Apart from these measures border areas are getting strengthened on a regular basis. Supported by advanced technologies, Comprehensive Integrated Border Management System is being implemented. Also, through Hill area development program and Border area development program, basic infrastructures are getting created in those areas. Certain strategic projects like rail connectivity to Leh, Tawang, and Kashmir etc. would bring economic development in those areas and also enable the armed forces to ensure better control.

Due to the varied history, geography and culture, border management is a complex task. But with a strong economy, dynamic diplomacy and leadership, these disputes would be solved through discussions and will ensure a peaceful and resourceful neighbourhood.

❑❑

46 Risk of Artificial Intelligence Outweigh Benefit

Abhisek Oswal, (AIR 154 CSE 2019)

"$20 Trillion is what could be added to world economy in the next decade, with the adoption of Artificial intelligence," read the newspaper headline as I was about to gulp my coffee. This made me curious to dig deeper into the article.

Change is the only constant and nothing could be stopped whose time has come. This is the era of globalisation soon to be transformed to digital villages. Artificial intelligence has the fire power to lead the evolution in multiple spheres.

Imagine you wake up in the morning, switching down your alarm. You move to kitchen and find that your favourite coffee is already brewed .Your car is on its mark to self-drive you to the office. That kind of easy life could be with a world of Artificial Intelligence.

But mind you that's the only beginning of this technology and its application and potential limit is equivalent to sky. Artificial intelligences will transform the way we work. The technology will provide equal opportunity, overcoming the biological limits. Female and male will be at par in terms of sphere and domain of employment because it is individuals who will be regarded and mind you 'Mind Has No Gender'.

Vulnerable could preserve their dignity, while robots take over inhuman work of manual scavenging. Disabled could use their brain power to excel and overcome the physical limit. People will move a step above in their carrier with new skills and opportunities like the big data and internet of things.

Mouse will replace tools, hands would be replaced by autonomous arms. Thus, output efficiency will improve astronomically. New budding entrepreneurs will find a wave of opportunity to invest and innovate. World will be a more secure place. Robots could guard our borders, safeguard the citizens and nation from state and non-state political actors. Life of soldiers due to frequent 'incidents' could be saved.

Good governance and informed decision this could be best possible outcome of artificial intelligence. Government could identify the needy target. Vulnerables will uplift them from poverty. Blackboards are already being replaced by digital boards, doctors are reaching the remote areas via telemedicine thus overcoming the geographical limits.

Lessening of human interference will make the process transparent, smooth and corruption free. Timely decision could be rewarding for business where 'Time is money'. Manufacturing process could be made more efficient; ten men could be replaced by a single robotic arm, thus drastically cutting down the cost. Driverless metros, cars will be the new norm. Seamless, pollution free travel will ease the living style. But mind you risks outweighs the benefits, 'Think over it'.

With this the article concluded. The immense potential of artificial intelligence are truly limitless. But I thought is it panacea for all evolution taking place? Won't it have an ethical, societal economic repercussion? Will benefits weigh over the risk? Should one adopt the technology in all spheres and walk of life? With this I began questioning myself with a hope to find an answer.

An equal, gender less society? Yes at first instant artificial intelligence will provide equal opportunity to men and women. But will it reduce gender biasness or skewed sex ratio? With help of technology the child sex ratio has come down to alarming 917, thanks to sex selective abortion. Will it not further put the life of female in womb in danger?

New opportunities but far few? True that Artificial intelligence will create new skills, job market, improve efficiency and productivity. But the question is – Is it going to be universal or selected, will it not create another class of have or have nots?

One with low skills is surely going to miss the train; he will be left stranded and unemployed. This risk of structural shift in way we work surely will outweigh the benefit of artificial intelligence.

Fourth domain of warfare! Yes this is what I think that artificial intelligence will open new fronts of confrontation. True soldiers precious life would be saved, boundaries will be better safeguarded, but won't it have an ethical ramification? How can you accept a 'bot' to differentiate between an innocent and terrorist, child and enemy soldier. AI will overlook war – dharma' with sole motto to indiscriminately annihilate the opposition. The aforesaid benefits will put the humanity at risk.

And what about the privacy? The whole technology of AI would be based on data – the new oil. Won't it give an unfettered privilege to state surveillance on food, communication and activities. A free state would be turned into a police state, putting liberty at risk!

Making life easy or making life inactive? This is the next question I ponded upon. Yes to an extent artificial intelligence would help to overcome physical disabilities. But at the same time, it is making the human physically inactive. Football, cricket, tennis which were traditionally played on fields today took up the place on screens. This has ramification on health, making youth obese, reducing the cognitive and physical skills. Thus this is indirectly putting health at risk.

Good governance is only one side of the coin! I recollect reading, how a UK based Artificial intelligence company was able to access the data of online users and manipulated their decision during the national elections. AI, which shows the prospects of informed decision, also shows the other side of dictated decision. The technology is putting the ethos of democracy at risk.

Frankenstein Monster? The way and the pace AI is taking our space and workplace it is practically substituting humans. The intelligence implanted on the machine by human will make it capable enough to learn by experience. What if one day the machine intelligence overtakes human intelligence and reduce use of slaves. At the dangerous end it may even develop capability to refuse its master and at large eliminate him. This will put the entire human survival at risk.

With all such risks and danger should we stop the evolutionary technology and maintain status quo? To me this is not possible, since change is the only constant. But we also know that every change and evolution had a knee-jerk reaction and ramification but it gradually stabilised and acclimatised for good.

Historically, we are aware that when Henry Ford brought out his favourite four wheeler cars, it threatened the livelihood of cart pullers and carvans. But later this gave birth to new industries like wheels, gears, opened up new garages and today it is providing jobs to millions across globe.

I also believe that we are already amidst web of using Artificial Intelligence. Driverless cars to google navigation, Robot Waiters to stock market algorithm, AI has adapted and co-existed. It made our life easy and also created new innovative opportunities.

The future with AI is unavoidable but we could be future ready. Skilling the population to ensure technologically inclusive world evolving with limitations will make AI beneficial and outweigh the risks.

'Any futuristic technology will be dangerous when it leaves behind a part of achieving the benefits and not the whole'.

□□

Start by Doing What is Necessary, Then Do What's Possible and Suddenly You will be Doing What's Impossible

Shreyans Kumat, IAS (AIR 4 CSE 2018)

"Kaun kehta hai asman me surakh nahi ho sakta, ek patthar to tabiyat se ucchal k dekho yaro"

(It is possible to create a hole even in the sky, just try throwing a stone with all your willpower)

Is it possible to reach impossible? Why was it called impossible if it was possible? If it has been done by stalwarts, how can I do it? Here a Japanese proverb comes to rescue- 'If one can do it, anyone can do it and if one can do it, you must do it.' But how?

The topic of the essay provides us with the path. 'A job started is a job half done'- so it is important to start by doing whatever is necessary. At this level of experience we would easily phantom the extent or possibility in front of us. So the next step would be to do what's possible. Now, every next step from us would be beyond possible. Viola! We are now doing what's impossible.

But such things are easier said than done. Agree. But one has to start somewhere; something from nothing will or should lead to everything or not? Let us look at some examples.

One girl, belonging to small village wanted to study. But the surroundings didn't allow. Somehow, she reached school after fighting with her parents. Then she saw possibility of motivating other children to be students with her. She worked hard for it. Soon she faced problems from the terror group and even she had to take a bullet for her cause. Soon, she was inspiring millions of girls to attend school. Yes! Malala Yousafzai.

She showed that quality like perseverance and fortitude helped her in her journey. But can this apply at the level of an organization?

Ever heard about Grameen Bank? It is a world renowned microfinance institution which pioneered and perfected micro-lending. Mohammad Yusuf was an economics teacher in a university. He was distressed by the situation of the women in nearby areas. They lacked money but were very good artists. He didn't want to give charity.

Why give fish when you can teach how to fish? Mr. Yusuf loaned a women money at almost zero interest rate. It was much less than the moneylender rates. This allowed the women to benefit from loans by selling their art and also their self dignity was intact.

This start led to many possibilities and now, lakhs of institutions are working all over the world to help people come out of poverty.

But such an endeavour is possible at the level of society or nation? Just take a look at the Indian National Movement.

Revolts at different parts of the country especially of 1857 gave it the required start. First Moderates and then Extremists were exploring the possibility of Dominion status and soon, we demanded 'Poorna Swaraj' and no less. Finally, we achieved it on 15th August 1947.

In all the above examples it was necessity of education, of money and of autonomy which led to the start respectively. 'Necessity is the mother of all inventions.'

When we resolve and start doing what's necessary, it leads to invention and innovation. Early man can only dream of flying, but today we are sending astronauts to space. He could only use fire with flint stone and now we can't live without electricity.

But what is the use of all this if world would end because of global warming and sixth mass extinction and other such possible phenomenon. In this case too, we have started with what is necessary and exploring what is possible and surely with International cooperation in treaties of Paris, protocols like Montreal, CITES and conservation efforts by various organizations, we will achieve the impossible.

It's time that our country too starts doing what's necessary in every field. In a recent SBI report, experts warned India to achieve developed country status in next 10 years or we will miss the bus. This would mean a perpetual developing country status. NO!

Former President Late Shri APJ Abdul Kalam in many of his works has devised plans to use the demographic dividend, developing smart villages with PURA approach and has inspired youth to devote themselves to the cause of the nation.

Every citizen, in whatever field, way, state or region should start with doing what is necessary. We should start by being empathetic, tolerant, liberal, democratic and inclusive. Then we can look at the possibility of collaboration with people nearby to improve education, health, basic amenities etc. This will open more possibilities.

Indian constitution makers already gave us the necessary start as an ideal nation. It's time for citizens to imbibe those values and walk forward. When people will be in sync with those values and strive for sustainable development, miracles are bound to happen.

Taking inspiration from the words of Swami Vivekananda, 'Arise, awake and stop not until the goal is reached', we need to inspire our dear ones with the path provided- start with necessary, do possible and see the magic happen.

Because impossible itself says 'I M POSSIBLE'.

□□

48 The Greatest Threat to Our Planet is the Belief That Someone Else Will Save it

Shreyans Kumat, IAS (AIR 4 CSE 2018)

One fine morning, Mr. Mehta was enjoying his breakfast with the news on. News anchor was discussing how India is hosting the 'World Environment Day' by United Nations Environment Programme this year. The Theme was – 'Beating Plastic Pollution'. Mr. Mehta was delighted to hear the programme. He told his wife about the efforts of UNEP and also appreciated the steps taken by our country. Later that day, Mr. Mehta went to market and bought vegetables and fruits in various polybags. Due to the scorching heat, he also bought a coconut and threw it away with the straw after drinking.

Here, Mr. Mehta is an aware citizen but he is not putting those awareness points into action. He is just relying on the nation and UN to save the planet. But does such belief serve any purpose?

What is at Stake?

Literally our existence is at stake. According to a recent Living Planet report, we exhaust the yearly carrying capacity of earth by August 2 or 3. This means that it would take almost "two Earths" to fulfil human demands. Our habitat and practices at each level is causing harm to our planet.

Individually, we are drifting towards consumerism and materialism. Everyone is looking for more that what one can consume. Cosmetics, exotic items, leather wearable, fur etc. are new normal. We do not see the violence which went behind their production and just enjoy the fruits.

As a society, we are drifting away from values that cherished nature and were grateful for its fruits. In the run for becoming more prosperous, instances like 'Bellandur Lake' of Bangalore is becoming increasingly common.

As a nation too, we are running away from the responsibility of our actions. The Act of US leaving Paris Climate Agreement is condemnable. In the name of development, we are also destroying nature indiscriminately. We are suffering from ironic situations- wastage of food and food security; malnutrition and obesity.

Globally, despite many talks of a peaceful and sustainable world, horrors like Hiroshima and Nagasaki continuously reminds us of the impending third world war possibility. Rather than reducing consumption, we are relying on scientific advancement possibility to avert climate change.

Not just few people, but almost everyone is waiting for others to take the lead, solve problems and do some miracles so that our cherished planet could be saved.

Before It's Too Late

This impending threat could be averted with everyone's efforts – however big or small.

At individual level, we can start with 3R – Reduce, Reuse, Recycle to contribute towards saving the environment. Participation in events like 'Earth-Hour' where one switches off electricity for an hour could lead to a multiple effect. One can follow rules; take our jute or cloth bags to market for shopping instead of using polybags like Mr. Mehta.

As a family, we can have different dustbins for segregating wastes. This will also imbibe such values in the children. One can practice vertical gardening, roof gardening to get organic produce. Here one can use waste compost as a fertilizer as well.

As a society, awareness about various programmes could be the first step. This would make more 'environmentally responsible citizens'. Civil society initiatives like use of solar lamps under SOULs programme, using biodegradable appliances like Mitti Coll etc. would be steps in the right direction. Such efforts would also complement governmental efforts.

Governmental efforts are crucial in bringing about uniform and widespread reformation. In different aspects such as Mitigation, Adaptation and Funding, many steps are needed.

Legislations like Environment Protection Act, various pollution acts, rules and regulations like plastic management, e-waste management etc. and above all constitutional directive and duty to save environment should be the guiding light.

Using it, efforts to achieve the target of 33% forest cover in the country would ensure achievement of INDCs (Nationally determined contributions). This would also help India in getting better international status and easier technological access.

In the quest to use renewable energy, International Solar Alliance (ISA) by India reiterates that we are not waiting for someone else to save the planet. Use of renewable energy would solve both energy security and environmental problem, if pursued properly in the future.

Saving the ecosystem using traditional methods could be a positive step. Taking help of tribals in Joint forest management, sacred graves protection would ensure dense forests are safe. Improving under sea water agriculture practice of Kerala (included under globally important agriculture heritage) on modern lines could be called an action with a foresight.

Learning from International best practices could save us from 're-inventing the wheel'. Collaborations with countries like Netherlands for waste management, Israel for water efficiency etc. would open many possibilities of better resource utilization.

Globally, being part of successful protocols and conventions like Montreal Protocol, Vienna convention, Kyoto Protocol has shown us that averting the threat is possible.

Not just through technology transfer and technology groupings, one can learn from noble acts. Recently, Senegal fans repeated the feat done by Japanese fans in the FIFA WC 2018. They cleaned plastic and other waste segregating them for easier disposal after the match was over. Everyone, an individual, society, nation and global grouping can learn from it.

Learning from present as well as past can help us bring a better future. Ancient Indian practices at every step ensured that environment is in harmony with human existence and vice-versa. Whenever resources were exploited, enough time was given to it to regenerate and rejuvenate e.g. shifting agriculture in earlier times.

Nobody then relied only on the king to do all the environment-friendly work and no one was deep under the material pleasures. Similarly, it is time that we learn and start taking action to save the planet. There are many ways to do it but one has to start somewhere.

If not for the ancestors who left this beautiful mother earth to us, we should do it for our next generations from whom we have borrowed it. In line with the ethos of humanity, environmentalism progress, we should strive for sustainable development. Aiming to achieve sustainable development goals (SDGs) in time in mission mode could be the way forward.

Unlike Mr. Mehta we should shed the belief that someone else would save the planet. We must be guided by the words of Gautama Buddha- 'Atma Deepo Bhavah' (Be your own light). While in our efforts to live a comfortable life, we must remember a very important thought given by Gandhiji and should swear to act as the trustee to the great resources provided by mother earth.

"The world has enough for everyone's needs but not for anyone's greed".

Live and Let Live

49 Consumption, Consumerism & Environment

Somesh Upadhyay, IAS (AIR 34 CSE 2016)

Little girl Sunita watches her richer counterpart shop bright new clothes for the upcoming festive season. She cravingly stares at them while breathing in the smokes off cars running by her shabby tent on the footpath. Sunita is a victim of consumerism.

Our modern economic systems hinge on mass-consumption. The measure of a country's 'growth' is defined by the amount of consumption. The industry, capitalists and governments push for higher growth by driving consumption. In such situation, we ignore the limit of our needs, breeding the culture of consumerism. And as Gandhiji pointed out much before Rio '92 conference, there is not enough for everyone's greed.

In our blind chase for consumerism-driven economic growth, we have failed to factor in the environmental cost. It is a capital that is not accounted for. The result is that we are exceeding earth's carrying capacity even as millions go hungry. The externalities are affecting the world's poor disproportionately by vitiating the environment.

Vandan Shiva in 'Stolen Harvest' has exposed the precarious environmental situation created by fast food chains like KFC. Water guzzling animal breeding farms is run on cleared Amazon forest land to feed the consumerism. At the same time the world is staring at water wars and global warming.

This unsustainable lifestyle promoted by consumerism has created glaring inequalities. For example, the Times Square, NY consumes as much electricity in one night as the entire Zimbabwe in one year. Such massive inequality further forces the poor to adopt unsustainable methods like log burning to meet their energy needs. Thus, the cycle of environmental degradation continues.

Closer home, we have seen the negative effects of unsustainable methods of agriculture in Punjab. In our focus on meeting consumption demands, the environmental costs were ignored. The result is salinated soil, depleted ground water and higher incidence of cancer.

Consumerism has promoted 'Climate Injustice'. The colonial countries and developed nations consume disproportionately larger amount of resources. However, their demands are met by vitiating the environment in poorer nations. The 5th IPCC Report points out how the developed nations have exported their production factories and thus externalities to the developing nations.

Thus, while the cocoa farmer in Cameroon does not know what chocolate is, his farm could be hit most by the global warming. And while Sunita's parents cannot afford a house or a car, they will take in the dirty air from others' vehicles.

Consumption driven economy is also behind the food shortage and its fallout has been on the environment. About 70% of the cereals grown in the USA are fed to the animals in the meat industry. The extensive monocultures, mechanization, use of chemical fertilizers, extension of agriculture in forest areas and overuse of water have affected the environment. It has caused habitat destruction, loss of biodiversity, and global warming due to methane and food scarcity.

The biggest beneficiaries of consumerism, at least in the short run, are the corporate. A section of the big corporates has also promoted climate change denial to keep accumulating wealth uninterrupted. Oil companies like Shell have allegedly funded a section of scientists and politicians to deny the effects of climate change so that there is no moderation in consumption levels. Such activities have further harmed the cause of environmentalism.

The global community, however, has built a consensus around the idea of sustainable living and development. Right from the Club of Rome to the UNFCCC summit in Paris, the efforts have been to contain climate change by promoting sustainability. Remarkable success of the Montreal Protocol and modest achievements of the Kyoto Protocol are testimonies to that effort. Unfortunately, the global community has skirted the question of consumerism even at this point.

The Nationally Determined Contributions (NDC) of different nations talks about reducing emissions, increasing emission efficiency, peaking emission targets. However, moderation in consumerism, an essential component of sustainability, has been ignored. Similarly, the sustainable development goals (SDGs) have multiple targets to achieve equality, reduce poverty, etc. There has been a consensus on the minimum standards of living but no talk of the ceiling on the standards.

In India, the culture of consumerism entered with the opening of economy in 1991. While still at its infancy, the effects of unsustainable living are already showing up. The Uttarakhand floods were largely driven by 'developmental' activities in the flood plains and fragile Himalayan ecosystem. Even the Chennai flood of 2015 was apparently caused by the greed of builders and promoters, driven by consumerism.

For a developing nation like India, the challenge is even greater. On the one hand she has to sustain the culture of frugal living amidst the onslaught of consumerism, on the other hand she has to ensure that there is social and economic justice through economic progress. This, however, is definitely achievable.

To contain the gluttony of consumerism without compromising the need for development, the world has to firstly define the upper limits of standard of living. While we have tools like Multidimensional Poverty Index, Poverty Line, Depth of Poverty, etc. there is no definition of a sustainable lifestyle. All the nations have to promote the acceptance of such a lifestyle to achieve environmental sustainability.

Additionally, a cultural shift is needed in the global community. The fashion of wealth display has to make way for the fashion of ecological consciousness. A society where green living is promoted will naturally avoid the clutches of consumerism.

The industry and big corporates have a big role to play. They are the ones who promote blatant consumerism through advertisements, rapid churning of new models and glorifying the culture of flaunting. In the longer run, they have to realize that the ever-expanding consumption is not sustainable. A responsible corporate community must tone down the promotion of consumerism.

A living example of how Capitalism can be blended with Socialism and create sustainable living with high standards comes from the Nordic countries. The Nordic Socialism, as it is called, has had higher taxes, cradle-to-grave welfare programs, environmentally sustainable energy programs etc. Denmark is a wind energy surplus country while Sweden imports garbage to run its waste-to-energy programs. Another example is Bhutan which ranks high on Gross National Happiness Index and is a carbon negative country. The global community can follow these models and protect itself from the dangers of rampant consumerism. This will ensure that the cocoa farmers of Cameroon tastes the fruit of his own labour and Sunita's parents can afford a home and her education in a safe and healthy environment.

□□

50 Information is the Ultimate Power in the Digital Universe of 21st Century

Swapnil Hanmane, IAS (2019)

A young, graduate farmer named Balwant from Marathawada of Maharashtra, one of the water scarce regions knows how to use internet, mobile. He gets daily weather updates, agricultural know how, market prices, information about government schemes, subsidies, etc. on his phone. With this he is cultivating crops scientifically and is known as progressive farmer. He knows the benefits of education and knowledge. Therefore, he sent his daughter and son to nearby city for better education.

On the other hand Hanumant, a young farmer from same Marathawada, who is illiterate and don't know about internet and mobile phone. His crops failed due to lack of inputs. He doesn't know about market, which crop to grow, what are government schemes etc. Because of his rising debts due to continuous droughts, he decided to end his life. His son, daughter and wife are now struggling to survive.

What these two incidents tell us? How the life of an ordinary person is getting affected by different kinds of information? It is not just individual, all societies, governments, nations today are on the cusp of digital revolution. The creators, holders of this digital information are changing the power equation of the world. Let us analyze, what this information is all about? How this information is shaping strength or power in the digital universe of 21st century?

Starting with, we must have quick look about information. Information is nothing but things which we know or can be known. During old Roman period, the geographical information about far off places was considered most essential. During medieval period, information about resources, people, states, military strategy resulted into shaping the world order.

Moreover, when we look back, we all can agree that, it was economic, military, politically strong nations or individuals who were said to be ultimate powerful. European countries ruled the world because of their strong powerful military and strong capital economy.

However, today with rise of digital technology, these aspects are overshadowed by information. Let us first examine, what information can be called as the ultimate power?

Today, with evolution of knowledge economy, older concepts of means of production are changing. For instance, Uber, the longest taxi aggregator does not own a single taxi. Alibaba, largest trading platform does not own single inventory. But these groups are worth of billion dollars within a single decade. What is the reason for this?

The reason for this is, Uber knows who is in the need of taxi, who is ready to provide the taxi service. It is with this information it just connects the two segments of economy. It is similar with Alibaba.

Further, today inventor or creator gets Intellectual property rights. With this the individuals or companies are dominating the world today. For instance, Apple, Microsoft could dominate today only because of creating technical knowhow.

Going further, this IPR, is creating divide between haves and have nots. For example, the Pharmaceutical companies which know about the drugs formula, charges heavy prices for medicines. The companies, countries which own them are becoming powerful at the cost of people who lack this information.

Moreover, the data/information generated has become very fast. The data generated in last two decades is equal to total data generated in life of human (World Bank). With rise of Big Data analysis, artificial intelligence is changing not only economic aspects but political and military aspects also.

Recent incidents of Cambridge Analytica, where information about votes, is used to change the voting behaviour. This can change political power. Today various political parties are using such digital technologies, big data analysis to influence voter. This can change the demographic balance.

Further, the concept of war has also changed. With countries like USA, China inverting in Artificial Intelligence to upgrade military application of AI. With rise of AI, we don't need humans anymore to fight wars. Information about military bases, strategies, technological knowhow can decide today's war results.

Moreover, this information power is not limited to politics and military. Today definitions of resources have changed. Superior brain power is finding new resources. We can site various examples. Information/knowledge about shell oil/gas has changed the geopolitics of the world.

Further today, the countries like India, having realized the power of information, started to invest in education and human resource development. The digital India program is addressed mainly to take the benefits of information. Aadhar, the largest biometric information platform in the world, is making impact in the public service delivery.

Further digital India program is hoping to reach out to the remotest corners. The farmers like Hunumanta who could not get the information about technological knowhow in agriculture, now can get access. This information is not just property of one individual today. With growth of digital technology, every individual can access large pool of information from anywhere in the world.

Having discussed how the information has become ultimate power today. Let us also look at the negative fallouts of such information power.

Firstly, the people who don't have access to information can lag behind the race. The people like Hanumanta will not be able to adapt to this world. It can create divide between people. According to various reports, In India, 20% of rural people have access to digital world, while 50% of urban people have digital access. This gap can further enhance inequality in income and opportunities.

Further, the rise of cyber threats, hacking, and frauds can cripple the digital economy. Recent incidence in Tamatara village in Jharkhand, where most of the wealth of village people is snatched away by cyber frauds makes us worry.

Moreover, the attacks on digital infrastructure like Critical Information Infrastructure, Power grids, banking infrastructure can cripple countries. Information about nuclear weapons, their proliferation can lead to massive disasters. Use of digital technology in growth of ISIS, a terrorist organization, has further made challenge.

Thus, information has affected every aspect of human life. Right from the revolutions like Right to information in India which helped to improve the governance, to the revolutions like Aadhar where big data base has created individual identities.

This information or data has become new oil today, like in previous decades; the country which had oil became powerful and wealthy. Today countries that are creating information are getting powerful.

Similarly, we have also challenge to address the gap of haves and have nots. To fill the gap like Balwant and Hanumanta, we need to ensure the digital literacy is improved. Till the time every individual is on board, the combination of physical and digital information access can solve the challenge of this gap. For Hanumanta, we need to provide physical vikas centers at his village.

Further, the data protection rules will ensure the individual's data or information is safeguarded. The draft Data Protection Bill 2018 drafted by B.N.Srikrishna Committee on the lines of European Union's General Data Protection Rules will strengthen the governance of information infrastructure.

Thus, information is essential for survival in 21st century. We need to empower the individuals like Hanumanta, so that they can live life like Balwant.

❑❑

51 There is No Education Like Adversity

Swapnil Hanmane, IAS (2019)

In 1945, world learnt the lesson that without strong international organization bringing peace and avoiding wars like World war I and II is not possible. This led to formation of United Nations. Similarly, lessons learnt from black side of imperialism, colonialism and world wars, the countries like India, Egypt and others founded Non Alignment Movement.

Seventy years later, after learning from effects of global warming and climate change, world came together and signed historic Paris climate deal in 2015.

Above examples shows that, adversity like wars, global warming and its effects have taught us the lessons. They educated us. Then we took steps to avoid such adversities in future.

Let us examine how adversities educate us. Why it can be said that there is no education like adversity? Can we also learn without facing adversity? Then finally we will conclude by identifying certain challenges with their solutions.

Starting with, we can sight many examples for arguing how adversity is the best form of education.

Human after facing disasters like tsunami, earthquake, cyclone learnt how to overcome it. What are the causes of such disasters? This enquiry led to creation of early warning systems. India after facing 2004 Tsunami formed Indian early warning system in the Indian Ocean.

Further, after realization of challenges of water scarcity due to micuse, unmindful utilization, pollution of water bodies, we started advocating the better water management practices like watershed management, micro irrigation etc. Weather this is new knowledge or existing one?

The answer for this question is – No. It is old traditional knowledge about better utilization. It is just we have re-learned it.

Further, in India, when we realized farmers are facing crisis due to various issues like crop failure, price fluctuation etc. we came out with various programs and schemes like Pradhan Mantri Fasal Bima Yojana to help them.

Adversity of corruption, poor governance became the obstacle in the eradication of poverty. Having learned the lesson we came up with Right to Information Act 2015, Lokpal Act 2013 and others to reduce corruption.

Similarly, our experience with ration card which helped the growth of fake beneficiaries, exclusion and inclusion of beneficiaries has made us think for better solution. Hence, came the solution of JAM trinity (Jan-dhan, Aadhar, Mobile).

Having discussed how adversity is the better form of education. However, why it can be said as better form of education, what about education without adversity?

To address this question, we must understand what is education? Education is nothing but getting knowledge about different things and applying this knowledge in day- to-day life. The knowledge achieved without adversity may or may not be applied. The part of ignorance overshadows when one is not faced with the adversity.

To cite the example for the mentioned argument, take example of terrorism. World before attack on WTC in USA, never realized the menace of terrorism. Having faced the brunt of it, in 2001, USA launched all out war against terrorism. This means having awarded about black side of terrorism, people don't apply it in real life unless the adversity is faced by own people, family and society.

Further, some people don't learn from adversaries. What happens to them? Take again same example of terrorism, some countries despite knowing the worst side of it, don't take any action against it. They selectively apply such knowledge.

Selective application like 'your adversity is not my adversity', creates a barrier in the learning. When industries pollute the rivers, they fail to recognize the challenges faced by people downstream.

Moreover, such selective application is also leading to moral crisis in the society. It has also created 'crisis of credibility', for instance, we forgot the lessons of partition in India. The rising intolerance, lynching of minorities has raised the questions over our learning from past incidents and ethos of Indian cultures.

Hence, it is important to learn from such adversity. We have learnt what happens when the institution of governance faces crisis, the light of justice becomes dim. We need to take steps to make our learning to apply to solve such issues.

Having discussed how education out of adversity has helped us to become more learned. Going further to address the barrier into application, we must ensure we don't make any differentiation of adversity.

According to Gandhiji, there is no better education than conscience. When we learn from adversity of others, we can apply same to our personal life.

Society having learnt from menace of terrorism, wars, environmental crisis, poor governance need to take steps collectively to overcome the challenges.

We are optimistic people. Despite USA's walkout of the Paris deal, other countries stood firm to take it forward. Collectively everyone can ensure learning from adversity is not ignored for sake of few.

Finally, the steps like sustainable development goals, which have taken to address the adversity faced by human life right from poverty, hunger to crisis of environment and peace, are the biggest lessons of mankind.

To conclude, we need help of conscience of individuals to implement such lessons without making any differentiation on the basis of individual, society or nation.

□□

52 Democracy and Socialism are Means to an End, Not the End in Itself

Vaibhav Jain, IRS [(IT) CSE 2017]

On the eve of passage of our constitution, the father of constitution Babasaheb Bhim Rao Ambedkar observed:

"On 26th Jan, 1950, our nation is going to enter into the life of contradictions, where the people will have political equality but would lack social and economic equality."

What was the relevance of this statement? 26th Jan 1950 was the day when our nation India became the world's largest democracy. Still Babasaheb appeared to be apprehensive about the inequality present in our society.

This simply suggests that our constitutional forefathers by adopting democratic form of government with socialist characteristics provided political equality to the citizens. This was envisaged as a tool/means to achieve our real socialistic ends of social and economic equality.

But some unanswered questions still remain. What is the true essence of democracy and socialism? What all ends do we really want to achieve? How democracy and socialism can have the way for those ends? Is it limited to India only? What can be done to ensure that utopian and ideal world?

Democracy in the words of Abraham Lincoln means – for the people, of the people and by the people. It is a philosophy which is people centric, participatory and has a bottom-up approach.

Similarly socialism too is a philosophy which calls for the "ways and means" to achieve "welfare of the masses".

Both of these values are enshrined in our Preamble which on behalf of the people of India solemnly resolves to make the country a democratic and socialist country. However it never considers it as an end in itself and envisages to provide social, economic and political justice, equality of status and opportunity, liberty of thought, faith and action and fraternity to the people of India.

However our ends are not limited to this. They are multidimensional and capture the hopes and aspirations of the 1.3 billion people in socio-economic, political, cultural and technological domains.

Since its inception, India has been an electoral democracy with first past the poll system. However, this political structure entails various political ends of robust local participation in the form of Panchayat Raj Institutions and Urban Local Bodies. Similarly, as citizens of India, people longs for a well balanced structure of fundamental rights and entitlements.

These political ends had social implications in form of attaining social harmony and social justice. It calls for an end of caste distinction and class divides, curbing of communalism and racial discrimination.

The social imprints are also quite apparent in maximizing the capabilities of people. For this health and education are the basis which one desires to be the best. 100% literacy with inculcation of right values and intentions is an end that one seeks. However, this can't be possible without the healthy mind, body and soul. Both these parameters can act as a great lever to make our nation the DEMOGRAPHIC CAPITAL of the world.

Similarly, the economic aspects like removal of poverty, building of infrastructure, attaining inclusive growth and development and having robust macroeconomic fundamentals are some ends that one desires and aspires for. However, these economic ends can't be attained in SILOS.

The technological ends of building scientific temper in our society, boosting R&D in fields of science and technology, bringing new innovations are equally important and vital for other ends.

These ends might seem too much but DEMOCRACY and SOCIALISM can act as a right means to achieve these ends. Let us see how it can lead to this.

Our democracy empowers people with right to vote i. e. right to choose his/her representative. This has led to his political empowerment. The 73rd and 74th constitutional amendment Act on 24th April 1993 was passed which made PRIs and ULBs a reality.

Further the democratic setup has given space to the 3 organs of the state i.e. legislature, executive and judiciary to empower citizens with fundamental rights and entitlements form time to time. Keshvananda Bharti Case, Maneka Gandhi Case etc. are examples where Judiciary played its part. Similarly by passing Right to Education Act, 2009, Right to Information Act 2005, our legislature ensured various rights to people of India.

In the social domain, the idea of SOCIALISM AND DEMOCRACY has worked in tandem to bring social equality. These two philosophies led to the origin of concept of reservations which are positive affirmations given to the weaker class to reinforce social justice. The idea of secularism is the origin of communal harmony in our diverse nation.

In health and education too, building right infrastructure like Mid Day Meals, Anganwadi centers, Primary health care centres, free drugs and diagnostics etc. have been possible due to this democratic-socialist regime. The creation of AIIMS, IITs, various government schools with various schemes and policies has led us to achieve near 100% primary school enrollment and 75% literacy rate.

Similarly, the transition from a colonial economy to a robust economy has been the outcome of people led democratic setup of the country. The socialist aspect led to Right to livelihood under MNREGA scheme ensuring economic security.

The technology and science has not been left behind. The development of ISRO and institutes like DRDO, IISc and watershed revolutions like Green revolution under M.S.Swaminathan and white revolution under Verghese Kurien are an outcome of the democratic model of government.

However, the major contention is that the benefits of democracy and socialism are not limited to India only. But it is a scalable concept which can be applicable globally.

USA the oldest democracy is today the world's largest economy. Similarly, China and Russia both socialist countries have attained milestones in other economical and technological fields.

The institutions like UNGA, WTO, IMF, G-20 all follow the democratic model to attain socialist ends of welfare of all.

However, democracy can sometime turn ugly due to its weakness of majoritarianism. Similarly socialism has seen its failure in countries like Vietnam, Cuba and North Korea etc.

But this fact is undisputable that "Democracy is the worst form of Government, except for all the others that have been tried" – Winston Churchill

The need of the hour is to direct the principles of democracy and socialism with values and visions of great leaders. Gandhiji's idea of Trusteeship, Lincoln's idea of equality, Tagore's idea of humanism, Socrates' idea of Rationality, Mandela's idea of non-violence and Teresa's idea of love and peace must be infused in the democratic principles and socialistic philosophy.

The inclusions of all these ideas will not only lead to individual developments of each nation but will also ensure peace, plurality and prosperity for Earth as a whole. It will lead to realization of the philosophy of Vasudhaiva Kutumbakam (world as a single family), Sarvdharm Sambhav (equality of all religions) and Sabka Sath, Sabka Vikas (welfare of all) all at once to achieve our UTOPIAN ENDS.

❑❑

53 A Good Life is One Inspired By Love and Guided By Knowledge

Vaibhav Jain, IRS [(IT) CSE 2017]

How to live a good life? As simple as the question looks, the answer seems to be more complex and complicated. Many scholars, philosophers, saints, gurus, intellectuals have tried to come up with the answer since the dawn of the mankind but were unable to reach a consensus over it. Having said that there are some underlying principles and values that are considered as indispensable ingredients to live a GOOD LIFE.

From the ancient times to the modern age, New Delhi to New York, Alaska to Australia, age of cognitive revolution to that of Artificial intelligence, Gautam Buddha to Dalai Lama, and what not, we have seen and observed numerous examples of Good Life and Bad life. And, what was found in it was the value of True Love and True Knowledge which has been the True Essence of a Good Life.

	Love (Yes)	Love (No)
Knowledge (Yes)	Good Life	Hateful Life
Knowledge (No)	Insignificant Life	Bad Life

But before venturing into the necessities of True Love and True Knowledge to lead a Good Life, one needs to get an idea of what Good Life is?

Good Life: Ultimate Desired End of Every Being

Though on the surface, Good life as an end looks subjective because everyone has their own explanation and idea of what all components make one's life good. But if we still want to bring some objectivity in it, then one can point towards Happiness which is true, ever-lasting, long-term and satisfying as a basic parameter for Good Life.

Looking ahead, there has been a healthy discussion on measuring happiness or quality of well-being as parameters of Good Life. As a result, many internationally recognized pioneer organizations like World Bank, World Economic Forum etc. have come up with the concept of Human Development Index and Social well being Index at National levels. Further certain countries like Bhutan has come up with Gross National Happiness to ensure Good Life.

Now analyzing it at more individual level, one can say that if one's basic needs are fulfilled then one is said to have achieved a Good Life. In this scenario, I firmly believe that true knowledge as a guide and true love as an inspiration can do the job.

True Love: An All Pervasive Inspiration to Lead A Good Life

Love as a value and a concept has numerous meaning similar to life. But one needs to look with deeper and broader perspective. True love resonates with the idea of respect, empathy, tolerance, non-violence, peace, companion, non-discrimination, humanism and fraternity. From individual to international levels the meaning of it changes.

Internationally, the idea of humanism, common brotherhood, the principle of Vasudhaiva Kutumbakam, empathy towards weaker section etc. are components of true love. From the likes of countries like Canada, Germany, Scandinavian countries, India, we have seen translation of love into Good life. Canada by asking apology for Komagata Maru incident has won the hearts of Sikhs population who have witnessed the progress of the country.

Similarly, India by promoting its ethos of non-violence and non-cooperation (at time of cold war) has made a deep impact on the global community enhancing its own soft power and global footprint.

At National Level, value and ethos of fraternity, social justice, national consciousness and belongingness can be said as true components of true love. Taking example of Bhutan, Norway, Sweden, and Israel, one can justify that these values have led to Good Life of their residents. Bhutan by ensuring not just socio-economic well being of people, but giving healthy environment (75% of forests) and rejuvenating its cultural heritage has shown people the meaning of true happiness. As a result, it has become a pioneer in providing Good quality of life to its people. Gender parity and social equality norms of Norway have made it a shining star which is evident in its top ranks in Human development Index and Social wellbeing Index. Israel on the other hand, has been really successful in promoting the true National consciousness amongst its citizen. Evidentially it has done wonders in technological and defense field.

Filtering it to more familial and individual level, the idea of true love means the idea of respect for all, helpfulness, and gender equality. Taking the example of Mahaveer Phogat who showed true love for her daughters Geeta Phogat and Babita Phogat by being non-discriminating against them. As a result, they converted this love and brought success in their own life and national honour by winning gold at prestigious common wealth games. At more individual level, love for self i.e. self respect makes a person more confident and caring leading to good life.

But the unanswered question remains whether the notion of true love is an inspiration enough to guide a good life or it should be complemented with true knowledge?

True Knowledge: An All Pertinent Guide for a Good Life

Knowledge as the name suggests refers to the idea of accurate and well directed information about various spheres of life. Here also, true knowledge reflects various ideas i.e. knowledge about self (Know THYSELF), knowledge about ethical conduct (What I ought to do?), knowledge to live healthy life, knowledge to satisfy one's need (differentiating between needs and greed, necessities and wants), knowledge about social, economic and psychological well-being and so on and so forth.

Reflecting upon the life of great visionaries, leaders and reformers, we can get sufficient idea about how true knowledge has led to good life. Gautam Buddha after getting true knowledge of pain and desires led to path of salvation for self. Similarly, Nelson Mandela with true knowledge about non-reciprocity won the hearts of not only white population but also natives of his country.

Mother Teresa, Nobel peace prize winner after guided by true knowledge of service towards mankind elevated many from cruel curse of Leprosy and attained the self-actualization. Similarly, Mahatma Gandhi after gaining true knowledge of non-violence and Satyagraha guided millions to the idea of good life.

Having established the positive correlation between true love and knowledge and good life, the question remains how to cultivate these components in oneself?

Cultivating Love and Attaining Knowledge: Path to Good Life

Cultivating love requires constant effort of looking things from broader perspective. It involves getting inspired by great readers, thinkers and reformers. Learning compassion from Mother Teresa, vasudev Kutumbkam from Indian Vedas, Fearlessness from Malala Yousafzai, Humanity from Dalai Lama, non-violence from Mahatma Gandhi.

Similarly, attaining true knowledge requires persistent efforts too. It involves guidance from teachers, parents and mentors. It includes self-introspection and reflection, learning and re-learning via application of ideas, cultivating creativity in self etc.

Thus, this idea of true love and true knowledge can be a guide to lead a Good Life. Once, these are indicated, one can expect to live a peaceful and satisfying life which resonates with the idea of Mask Karen:

"Only as high as I reach,
Can I grow
Only as far as I seek,
Can I go
Only as deep as I look,
Can I see
Only As much as I dream,
Can I be."

❑❑

54 Water Water Everywhere, Not A Drop To Drink

Swapnil Hanmane, IAS (2019)

The city of Chennai faced one of the worst droughts in the country such that water had to be transported by rail: virtually bringing the city to a standstill, despite being a coastal city situated close to the sea. The same city was devastated by floods about 3 years ago. At the same time, parts of Maharashtra like Sangli, Satara and parts of Vidarbha are battling with serious flooding. These are the same regions where more than 95000 farmers have committed suicides in the last 10 years due to drought.

Isn't it a paradox that the same places are facing both the problems simultaneously? Water water everywhere, not a drop to drink. The island archipelago of Maldives was brought to its knees in 2015, when its desalination plants stopped working, virtually cutting off its supply of even drinking water. Indian Navy intervened with Operation Cactus supplying water in ships.

Earth's surface is 70% water covered in various forms like oceans, snow cover, polar ice, glaciers etc. giving it the name 'blue planet'. Rising sea levels have been the cause of worry for smaller islands nations and even countries like Bangladesh, India etc. Excess of rains have been creating havoc very frequently as witnessed in Kerala, Uttrakhand and Nepal floods. Thus, no doubt exists that there is abundance of water on our planet, perhaps much more than our needs and requirements.

Ironically at the same time, we are in the mid of the worst ever water crisis in the history.

NITI Aayog's composite water management Index indicates more than 21 major cities of India will run out of ground water by 2020. A recent report of ICIMOD on Himalayan glaciers warns of serious glacier retreat and threat to Perennial River flooding whole of South and South East Asia. A glacier in Norway recently had its funeral done officially. WHO Report indicates more than 58% of water consumed in Asia and Africa exceeds the permissible levels of toxic metals.

We are sure heading towards a man-made disaster, and knowingly or unknowingly are a part of it.

A very obvious inference from the above facts is that the problem does not limit to water availability rather than distribution (both spatial and temporal) and the quality of it. It is important to understand the underlying causes behind the skewed supply as well as the quality degradation.

A part of the reason for the non-availability is natural variation of rainfall, and river distribution. Historically, great civilizations prospered around river valleys like Nile, Ganges etc. owing to easy availability of water. Climate change has indeed taken a toll on the natural patterns severely increasing the frequency of extreme climatic conditions like cyclones, droughts and floods. But the major blame lies to the anthropogenic causes.

The rampant pollution of both the surface and ground water resources has rendered them unusable. Lakes, rivers and oceans have become the global garbage bin with more than 70% waste ending in them. The efficient discharge from industries, runoff from agricultural fields and untreated sewage from urban areas have led to contamination of not just fresh water but also the surroundings.

The unplanned urban development and growth of slums has led to encroachment of water bodies and lakes, wetlands in urban areas. Bangalore, once called the city of lakes with more than 130 water bodies has hardly less than 20 left. The Varthur and Bellandur Lake often catch fire in the foams.

Further, the modern metropolitan centers like Mumbai, Chennai, New York etc. have unusually high demand for water, owing both to the huge population and the modern urban lifestyle. The industrial centers like textile, power plant etc. need huge water supplies and often end up consuming precious drinking water. Agriculture, though important for food security of the globe, depends on ground water for 70% of its needs and is being heavily exploited thanks to free electricity and subsidies.

Livestock sector, consumes more than half of total water supply of the world, as per a WEF report of 2016, thus having serious repercussions and domino effect on the entire world.

The foremost and most visible effect is in the form of poverty, in the sub-Saharan Africa, Asian countries and Latin America. Low incomes due to heavy dependence on Agriculture, coupled with diseases due to contaminated water further aggravate the dreadful situation as indicated by the Lancet Report.

Women bear a large brunt of this, having to walk long distance to fetch water, along with children who face stunted and wasted growth, various social tensions and conflicts arise between haves and have not's in the society.

In the economic sphere, all the sectors- primary, secondary as well as tertiary heavily rely on water and effects on GDP of country are evident. The political scenario has taken new turns with water assuming new roles in both domestic and international affairs. India's relations with Pakistan, China and Bangladesh heavily focus on river water sharing agreements. In the domestic arena, federalism has been effected due to interstate conflicts very often as recently seen in Cauvery issue of Karnataka and Tamil Nadu.

The environment and biodiversity has been negatively impacted both due to water shortage and contamination. While water shortage leads to deforestation, loss of natural river flow pattern desertification etc. Contamination leads to death of animals and often ends up with bio-accumulation and bio-magnification in the food chain.

Before the situation worsens and impacts become further serious, there is an urgent need to address the issue holistically with a two pronged approach, firstly looking at ways to ensure 'water for all' and secondly to mitigate pollution and focus on conservation measures.

At an individual level, we follow the principle of 4R's- Refuse, Reduce, Reuse and Recycle to ensure judicious use of water in our homes and offices. Water harvesting techniques must be installed in homes and used for landscaping and toilet water.

At the level of society, civil organizations, NGO'S and other youth groups must come forward to launch cleaning campaigns for rivers and lakes. 'Run for rivers' launched by 'Isha foundation' is an appreciable step. Role of schools in teaching children the value of water conservation will take us a long way.

At a local level, decentralized water conservation ponds, check dams must be created, rivers must be desilted and lakes deepened. Such activities may be undertaken under MGNREGA. Use of traditional methods like Baori in Rajasthan, Ahar-Pyne in Bihar, Kyre in Karnataka, Bhandares in Maharashtra must be promoted. Laporiya village of Rajasthan with chukkas created by waterman of India – Rajendra Singh presents a good example.

At national level, there is a need for both strict laws as well as behavioural change campaigns to address the issue. Sewage treatment plant under Swach Bharat Abhiyan, Jal Shakti Abhiyan and Namami Gange Mission etc. are all welcome steps. Pricing of water on a partial basis may be tested as suggested by NITI Aayog. Water efficient methods in agriculture like micro-irrigation, zero budget natural farming need to be promoted.

Improved international collaboration and treaties like Stockholm Convention and Rotterdam convention for waste disposal in sea, needs implementation. Use of technology like desalination plants, OTEC plant in Lakshadweep, etc. will further supplement the efforts.

Water has been accorded the status of 'Varuna' God and mother Goddess Ganga in India. The best of civilizations cannot survive without water and as was the case with Harappans. We must all come together and work towards water management.

'Jal hi Jeevan Hai and Jal Hai to Kal Hai'

❑❑

Tourism: Can This be the Next Big Thing For India?

Nav Goel, IRAS (2014)

"If there is a heaven on earth, it's here, it's here"

Amir Khusrau

Though these words of Amir Khusrau captures the sheer beauty of Kashmir in particular but this famous line is applicable to the whole of India as well. India is endowed with diverse cultures, religions, physical features, climates etc. and that makes a unique blend which positions India as one of sought-after tourist destination.

Tourism roughly contributes around 7% of GDP of India. And still there is a lot of potential which is left untapped. Our exotic beaches of Goa, snow-capped mountains of Himachal, tiger reserves of Madhya Pradesh have the potential to be transformed to Miami, Switzerland and Jungles of Maasai Mara respectively. Besides this, religious, medical and wellness tourism gives a further boost to India's tourism. Though there are some challenges in our tourism sector but we can overcome them. So now, we will see how Tourism can be the next big thing for India!

Tourism Potential: What India is endowed with?

Religious Tourism: India has been a home to almost all major religions of the world. Buddhism and Jainism originated in India while Christianity, Judaism and Islam came very early to India. In fact, as per the oral legend St Thomas the Apostle landed in Kerala around 52 CE and he was welcomed on shore by a flute-playing Jewish girl. So technically Christianity came to India before it reached Europe. This places India in a very unique position. No other country has such a vast religious heritage.

Bodhgaya in Bihar and Sarnath in Uttar Pradesh receives a huge number of tourists every year from around the world. Further for most of the Indians, tourism is synonymous to pilgrimage. Many domestic tourists travel around the year based on their faiths. 'Char-Dham Yatra, 12 Jyotirlingas and 51 Shakti-Peeths' have their own importance in Hinduism and moves many devotees across the continent. Further Urs Festival held in places of major Sufi Orders also attracts many domestic as well as international tourists. Like Urs of Khwaja Moin-ud-Din Chishti attracts more than 5 lakh people every year and there are many Urs like that in India. Further Varanasi, the city of Lord Shiva, also receives many international tourists owing to its cultural heritage.

Leisure and Adventure Tourism: Backwaters of Kerala, Beaches of Goa, Sand Dunes of Jaisalmer, Palaces of Jodhpur, Ruins of Hampi, Architectural heritage of Agra and Delhi, Treks of Himachal, adventures of Uttarakhand etc. lures tourists from all over the world. The unique thing about the International Tourists is that they visit for a longer period like 1-2 months. This results in boosting our economy by multiplicative factor.

Medical and Wellness Tourism: India receives a lot of International tourists owing to its economical treatment facilities, expert surgeons and one of the most caring nursing culture in the world. The fluency of doctors in English, the cheaper treatment which is approximately 75% less costly as compared to USA, experience of doctors in executing complex surgeries outside India makes it a most sought after destination for medical treatment.

Further wellness therapies of Yoga, Ayurveda, Siddha, Reiki, Meditation along with the Spiritual philosophy has been a way of life in India for so many years and westerners have been looking upto India for salvation and alternative healing. Even late Apple Inc. Co-founder Steve Jobs came to India seeking to find his inner self and longing to be enlightened. The cities of Kovalam, Haridwar, Rishikesh, Varanasi thus have a lot of untapped potential.

Wild-life Tourism: India is a land of various wild-life habitats and also has diversity in terms of species. One-Horned Rhino of Kaziranga, Asiatic Lions of Gir, Tiger Reserves of Madhya Pradesh, the Valley of Flowers and unique diversity of Nilgiris have brought many footfalls of wildlife enthusiasts. Now wild-life tourism has emerged into a separate field of tourism. These places of natural diversity also have a lot of unlocked potential to lure tourists of all ages, which needs to be showcased.

What is locking down this potential: How Tourism can become a next big thing in India?

In the last few paragraphs we have seen that there is lot of potential in Tourism Sector of India. But still it is not as big as it should be. What are the reasons behind that? Let's have a look at that.

Lack of Infrastructure and a perception battle is a major challenge for Indian Tourism. Hotels connectivity, human resources, hygiene, health facilities, etc. are largely under-developed in India.

The major international tourist destinations like Bodhgaya, Sarnath, Varanasi, Tiger Reserves of Madhya Pradesh and many other places still don't have proper connectivity via roads or airports. Nowadays people want to enjoy the journey as much as they want to relish the destination. But the scarcity and quality of Indian Roads is a roadblock in unlocking the potential of these tourism destinations. Many tourists eliminate the not so well connected places out of their itinerary, thus harming their economic prospects.

Further local transport in and around tourist places is also a problem area as taxi drivers also sometimes play mischievous and there is no prompt grievance redressal.

Further there is not much standardisation in services at the tourist places. For example Foreign Tourists either take a personal guide or want an audio system guide to visit an architectural heritage for example, Mysore Palace or Taj Mahal. Guides often quote very high prices to foreign tourists and audio guides are often not working. This carries a bad image through word of mouth. In addition to this, there is a general perception about lack of hygiene in food and drinking water which is because of uncontrolled mushrooming of food joints near the tourist places.

The famous temples of North-India can often be seen poorly managed due to the lack of crowd control mechanisms and incompetent coordination on the part of management. Further they are surrounded by beggars. Many fraudulent Pandits can be seen who promise the tourists to take them to temple in half an hour in exchange of money. These issues cause trouble to all the visitors and harms India's image.

Also it is often seen that, foreigners, owing to their white skin, height and different clothes, stand out and attract attention. This is particularly a problem for women travellers. And Indian men often stare at them and make unwanted advances, often including groping and photographing. The problem here is lack of prompt grievance redressal mechanism for foreigners.

Besides that, unfortunately some of the most beautiful places in India like scenic beauty of Kashmir, diverse North-Eastern Part of India, and wildlife areas of Chhattisgarh have been struggling with their violent past and present instability, the perception and uncertainty about violence.

In addition to above issues, India has also not been very successful to portray itself as a desirable tourist destination because of lack of marketing. Self-Image correction exercise is required to tackle all the negative publicity it gets because of exaggeration by tourists from abroad.

How to unlock this inherent potential: Indian Tourism can be a big thing!

Both Central and respective State Governments need to make conscious efforts in improving the connectivity to major tourist destinations. Many steps have been taken in this direction, for example, Central Government has gone ahead with recognising major Tourist Circuits like Buddhist Circuit, Desert Circuit etc. Some years ago, there was no direct train to Vaishno Devi, a major tourist destination. Now a dedicated and special train is launched which has facilitated many tourists. Steps like these are sine qua non for our emerging tourism sector.

Further all the Architectural Heritage destinations should be standardised in terms of facilities and price. Foreigners come with a lot of expectations and unless we meet them, word of mouth publicity won't work in our favour. There should be grievance redressal

Booths and Apps in all the major tourism cities and it should be given wide publicity in social media as well as locally. This will work as a two prong strategy, firstly in making tourists aware and secondly creating a fear factor in local residents.

Places like Wildlife Reserves need to upgrade their facilities. For example, some modern adventure sports can be organised in safe area but in the near vicinity, small restaurants and stay points can be established, so as to give an altogether different experience. Initiatives of Kruger National Park of South Africa can be emulated in this field.

In comparison to domestic tourists, foreigners usually want to spend more time at a particular place. Cultural events like dances, songs, shows can be organised so that they can be motivated to stay for one extra day and create a virtuous economic cycle.

Intensive marketing campaign like "Incredible India" should be organised on all social media platforms about the unique things of a particular place along with bringing all the bookings online will help increase the reach.

Conclusion

India with its belief of "Atithi Devo Bhavah" and all its diversity is very well positioned to catapult its tourism to next level. With increasing middle class incomes and an upward trend of travelling in India and foreigners increasing focus on wellness amidst all the chaos, it's high time that India develops its tourism infrastructure. This along with innovative offerings and concerted campaign can definitely make it a market leader in Tourism.

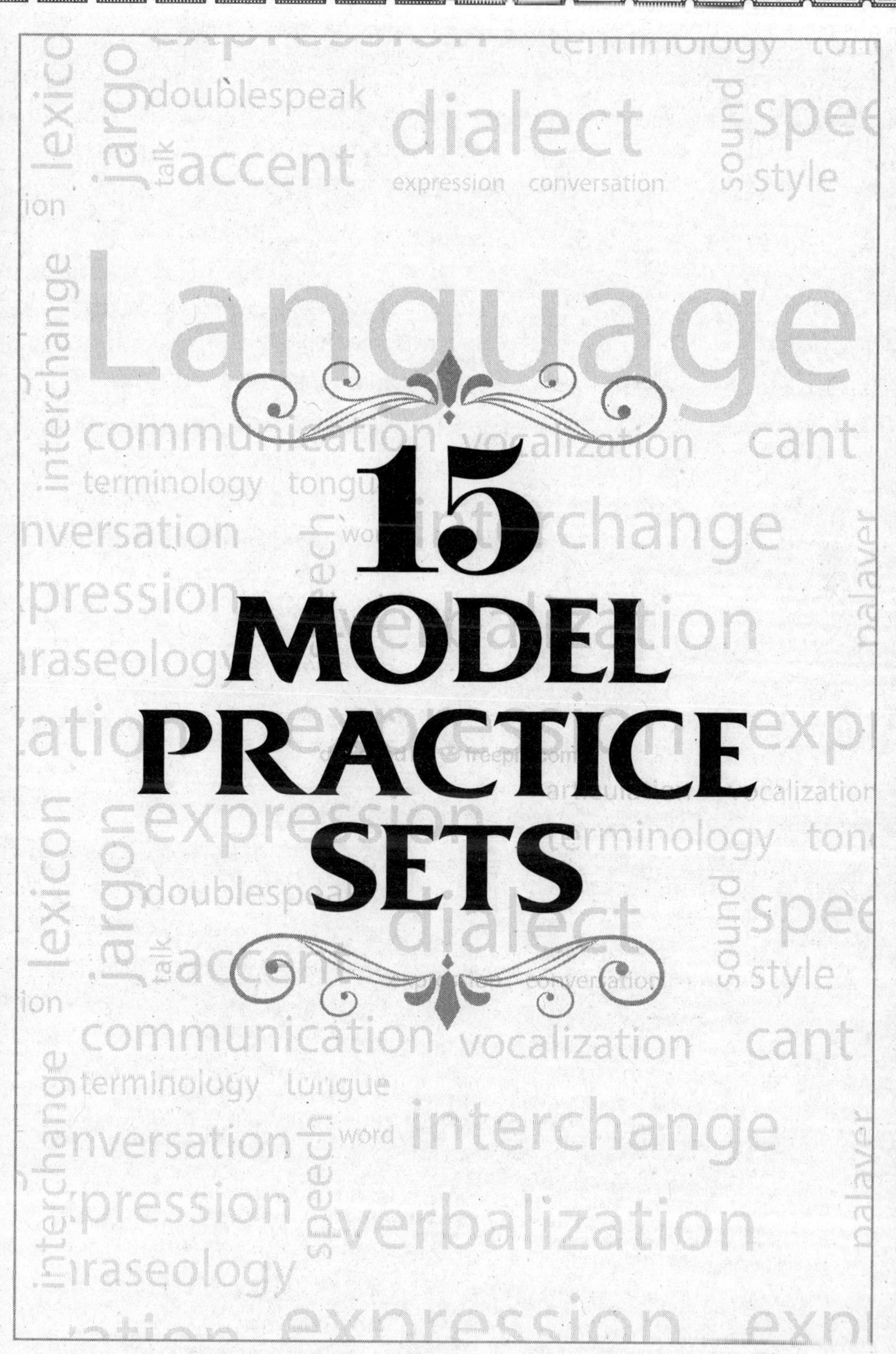

15 MODEL PRACTICE SETS

Practice Set-1

Write two essays, choosing one topic from each of the Sections A and B, in about 1000–1200 words each:

SECTION – A

1. As you Start to walk on the way, the Way appears
2. How do we gain initial knowledge: an experience or constant processing of information?
3. All that we are is the result of what we have thought.
4. Values are not what humanity is, but what humanity ought to be.

SECTION – B

1. In order to understand the world one has to turn away from it on occasion.
2. Uncertainty should ignite creativity, not depravity.
3. It is hard to free fools from the chains they revere.
4. Time is all we have and don't.

Practice Set-2

Write two essays, choosing one topic from each of the Sections A and B, in about 1000–1200 words each:

SECTION – A

1. Knowledge will give you power, but character will give you respect.
2. To ease another's heartache is to forget one's own.
3. Never Let a Good Crisis Go to Waste.
4. The whole problem with the world is that fools and fanatics are so certain of themselves, while wiser people are so full of doubts.

SECTION – B

1. History repeats itself first as a tragedy second as a farce.
2. A clear conscience fears no accusation.
3. Our world has achieved brilliance without conscience.
4. Not what we have But what we enjoy, constitutes our abundance.

Practice Set-3

Write two essays, choosing one topic from each of the Sections A and B, in about 1000–1200 words each:

SECTION – A

1. Innovation distinguishes between a leader and a follower.
2. A good life is one inspired by love and guided by knowledge.
3. Never interrupt your enemy when he is making a mistake.
4. Lending hands to someone is better than giving a doll.

SECTION – B

1. The role of the family in the modern marriage and philosophy of heritage.
2. Indecisiveness is the rival of Progression.
3. Our common humanity demands that we make the impossible possible.
4. Mind – a beautiful servant? Or a dangerous master?

Practice Set-4

Write two essays, choosing one topic from each of the Sections A and B, in about 1000–1200 words each:

SECTION – A

1. All differences in this world are of degree, and not of kind, because oneness is the secret of everything.
2. Pandemics such as COVID-19, though Catastrophic, are in the end Meant to Reset Humanity and its Priorities.
3. The fool doth think he is wise but the wise man knows himself to be a fool.
4. Virtue is Knowledge.

SECTION – B

1. Freedom is not worth having if it does not include the freedom to make mistakes.
2. When the power of love overcomes the love of power, the world will know peace.
3. The definition of happiness is the full use of your powers, along the lines of excellence.
4. Those who have wisdom have all: Fools with all have nothing.

Practice Set-5

Write two essays, choosing one topic from each of the Sections A and B, in about 1000–1200 words each:

SECTION – A

1. Knowledge speaks, but wisdom listens.
2. Not everything that can be counted counts, and not everything that counts can be counted.
3. No one can make you feel inferior without your consent.
4. "He who has never learned to obey cannot be a good commander." Aristotle.

SECTION – B

1. A bad conscience is easier to cope with than a bad reputation- Friedrich Nietzsche.
2. The journey is a reward as well as destination.
3. Culture of entitlement comes with unreasonable expectations and insecurities.
4. Nothing in the world is more dangerous than sincere ignorance and conscientious stupidity.

Practice Set-6

Write two essays, choosing one topic from each of the Sections A and B, in about 1000–1200 words each:

SECTION – A

1. The true measure of a man is how he treats someone who can do him absolutely no good.
2. Happiness is not an ideal of reason, but of imagination.
3. First they ignore you, then they laugh at you, then they fight you, then you win.
4. Before criticizing a man, walk a mile in his shoes.

SECTION – B

1. Prejudice is a burden that confuses the past, threatens the future and renders the present inaccessible.
2. The price of our vitality is the sum of all our fears.
3. Time changes everything except something within us which is always surprised by change.
4. Power of vested interests is vastly exaggerated compared with the gradual encroachment of ideas.

Practice Set-7

Write two essays, choosing one topic from each of the Sections A and B, in about 1000–1200 words each:

SECTION – A

1. Reason has always existed, but not always in a reasonable form.
2. Don't let what you cannot do interfere with what you can do.
3. The mind is everything. What you think you become.
4. Sometimes it takes a natural disaster to reveal a social disaster.

SECTION – B

1. True knowledge exists in knowing that you know nothing.
2. Glory is fleeting, but obscurity is forever.
3. Nearly all men can stand adversity, but if you want to test a man's character, give him power.
4. Ability will get you success, Character will keep you successful.

Practice Set-8

Write two essays, choosing one topic from each of the Sections A and B, in about 1000–1200 words each:

SECTION – A

1. Parable of the Cave as the reflection of modern-day life.
2. Contentment is natural wealth, luxury is artificial poverty.
3. The curious paradox is, only if we accept things as they are, things can change.
4. Knowing oneself is the beginning of all wisdom.

SECTION – B

1. Development must lead to dismantle all kinds of human unfreedom.
2. To live is the rarest thing in the world. Most people exist, that is all.
3. Science is organized knowledge. Wisdom is organized life.
4. Gratitude is not only the greatest of virtues, but the parent of all the others.

Practice Set-9

Write two essays, choosing one topic from each of the Sections A and B, in about 1000–1200 words each:

SECTION – A

1. Problems worthy of attack prove their worth by fighting back.
2. Morality is subservient to materialistic values in present times.
3. Dogma is the sacrifice of wisdom to consistency.
4. Quick but steady wins the race.

SECTION – B

1. The grass is always greener on the other side of the fence.
2. Trust take years to Build, Seconds to Break.
3. Happiness equals reality minus expectations.
4. You can avoid reality, but you cannot avoid the consequences of avoiding reality.

Practice Set-10

Write two essays, choosing one topic from each of the Sections A and B, in about 1000–1200 words each:

SECTION – A

1. A friend to everybody is a friend to nobody.
2. Imagination is more important than intelligence.
3. All war is a symptom of man's failure as a thinking animal.
4. The whole is more than a sum of its parts.

SECTION – B

1. Any fool can know. The point is to understand." Albert Einstein.
2. It is our choices, that show what we truly are, far more than our abilities.
3. Crisis Faced in India – Moral or Economic?
4. The marks humans leave are too often scars.

Practice Set-11

Write two essays, choosing one topic from each of the Sections A and B, in about 1000–1200 words each:

SECTION – A

1. The Best Things in Life are Free.
2. The past' is a permanent dimension of human consciousness and values.
3. Tradition becomes our security, and when the mind is secure it is in decay.
4. Life fritters away when distractions become your lifestyle.

SECTION – B

1. Modern Society and its digital addiction.
2. Learning is more precious than grades.
3. When the going gets tough, the tough get going.
4. Forgiveness is the final form of love.

Practice Set-12

Write two essays, choosing one topic from each of the Sections A and B, in about 1000–1200 words each:

SECTION – A

1. A great leader is never angry.
2. Courage is resistance to fear, mastery of fear, not absence of fear.
3. The enemy of stability is complacency.
4. Strength comes from an indomitable Will.

SECTION – B

1. Feminism isn't about making women stronger. Women are already strong; it's about changing the way the world perceives that strength. - G.D. Anderson.
2. Indian Agriculture: Towards Evergreen Revolution.
3. Biased Media: A threat to Democracy.
4. Artificial Intelligence: Jobless future vs tool for modern society.

Practice Set-13

Write two essays, choosing one topic from each of the Sections A and B, in about 1000–1200 words each:

SECTION – A

1. We Need not a social conscience, but a social consciousness.
2. Facts do not cease to exist because they are ignored.
3. Solutions emerge if situations are not forced.
4. Subtlety may deceive you; Integrity never will.

SECTION – B

1. Talent wins games, but teamwork and intelligence win championships.
2. Do I not destroy my enemies when I make them friends? Abraham Lincoln.
3. Is Secularism in India on Shaky Grounds?
4. A low carbon future is the only choice we have.

Practice Set-14

Write two essays, choosing one topic from each of the Sections A and B, in about 1000–1200 words each:

SECTION – A

1. The only thing necessary for the triumph of evil is for good men to do nothing.
2. Life is long journey between human being and being humane.
3. A house divided against itself cannot stand.
4. Fortune favors the bold.

SECTION – B

1. Cool people do not deserve a warm planet.
2. The World is full enough of hurts and mischances without wars to multiply them.
3. One has to win his internal battle to light his consciousness.
4. Morality is the basis of things and truth is the substance of all morality.

Practice Set-15

Write two essays, choosing one topic from each of the Sections A and B, in about 1000–1200 words each:

SECTION – A

1. Fire is a good servant but a bad master.
2. Ability is nothing without opportunity.
3. War is the ultimate Price we pay for lasting Peace.
4. Everything we hear is an opinion; not a fact.

SECTION – B

1. We are in danger of destroying ourselves by our greed and stupidity.
2. What you do makes a difference, and you have to decide what kind of difference you want to make.
3. The climate is changing, and so should we!
4. Democracy depends on a web of institutions.

PREVIOUS
7 YEARS
ESSAY
PAPERS

Essay Question Paper – UPSC Civil Services IAS Mains – 2018

[125 × 2 =250 Marks]

Write two essays, choosing one topic from each of the Sections A and B, in about 1000–1200 words each:

SECTION – A

1. Alternative technologies for a climate change resilient India.
2. A good life is one inspired by love and guided by knowledge.
3. Poverty anywhere is a threat to prosperity everywhere.
4. Management of Indian border disputes – a complex task.

SECTION – B

1. Customary morality cannot be a guide to modern life.
2. "The past' is a permanent dimension of human consciousness and values.
3. A people that values its privileges above its principles loses both.
4. Reality does not conform to the ideal, but confirms it.

Essay Question Paper – UPSC Civil Services IAS Mains – 2019

[125 × 2 =250 Marks]

Write two essays, Choosing one topic from each of the Sections A and B, in about 1000–1200 words each:

SECTION A

1. Wisdom finds truth.
2. Values are not what humanity is, but what humanity ought to be.
3. Best for an individual is not necessarily best for the society.
4. Courage to accept and dedication to improve are two keys to success.

SECTION B

1. South Asian societies are woven not around the state, but around their plural cultures and plural identities.
2. Neglect of primary health care and education in India are reasons for its backwardness.
3. Biased media is a real threat to Indian democracy.
4. Rise of Artificial Intelligence: the threat of jobless future or better job opportunities through reskilling and upskilling.

Essay Question Paper – UPSC Civil Services IAS Mains – 2020

[125 × 2 =250 Marks]

Write two essays, choosing one topic from each of the Sections A and B, in about 1000– 1200 words each:

Section A

1. Life is long journey between human being and being humane.
2. Mindful manifesto is the catalyst to a tranquil self.
3. Ships do not sink because of water around them, ships sink because of water that gets into them.
4. Simplicity is the ultimate sophistication.

Section B

1. Culture is what we are, civilization is what we have.
2. There can be no social justice without economic prosperity but economic prosperity without social justice is meaningless.
3. Patriarchy is the least noticed yet the most significant structure of social inequality.
4. Technology as the silent factor in international relations.

Essay Question Paper – UPSC Civil Services IAS Mains – 2021

[125 × 2 =250 Marks]

Write two essays, choosing one topic from each of the Sections A and B, in about 1000–1200 words each:

Section A

1. The process of self-discovery has now been technologically outsourced.
2. Your perception of me is a reflection of you; my reaction to you is an awareness of me.
3. Philosophy of wantlessness is Utopian, while materialism is a chimera.
4. The real is rational and the rational is real.

Section B

1. Hand that rocks the cradle rules the world.
2. What is research, but a blind date with knowledge!
3. History repeats itself, first as a tragedy, second as a farce.
4. There are better practices to "best practices".

Essay Question Paper – UPSC Civil Services IAS Mains – 2022

[125 × 2 =250 Marks]

Write two essays, choosing one topic from each of the Sections A and B, in about 1000–1200 words each:

Section A

1. Forests are the best case studies for economic excellence.
2. Poets are the unacknowledged legislators of the world.
3. History is a series of victories won by the scientific man over the romantic man.
4. A ship in harbour is safe, but that is not what ship is for.

Section B

1. The time to repair the roof is when the sun is shining.
2. You cannot step twice in the same river.
3. A smile is the chosen vehicle for all ambiguities.
4. Just because you have a choice, it does not mean that any of them has to be right.

❑❑

Essay Question Paper – UPSC Civil Services IAS Mains – 2023

[125 × 2 =250 Marks]

Write two essays, choosing one topic from each of the Sections A and B, in about 1000–1200 words each:

Section A

1. Thinking is like a game, it does not begin unless there is an opposite team.
2. Visionary decision-making happens at the intersection of intuition and logic.
3. Not all who wander are lost.
4. Inspiration for creativity springs from the effort to look for the magical in the mundane.

Section B

1. Girls are weighed down by restrictions, boys with demands – two equally harmful disciplines.
2. Mathematics is the music of reason.
3. A society that has more justice is a society that needs less charity.
4. Education is what remains after one has forgotten what one has learned in schools.

❑❑

Essay Question Paper – UPSC Civil Services IAS Mains – 2024

[125 × 2 =250 Marks]

Write two essays, choosing one topic from each of the Sections A and B, in about 1000–1200 words each:

Section A

1. Forests precede civilizations and deserts follow them.
2. The empires of the future will be the empires of the mind.
3. There is no path to happiness; Happiness is the path.
4. The doubter is a true man of science.

Section B

1. Social media is triggering 'Fear of Missing Out' amongst the youth, precipitating depression and loneliness.
2. Nearly all men can stand adversity, but to test the character, give him power.
3. All ideas having large consequences are always simple.
4. The cost of being wrong is less than the cost of doing nothing.

❑❑